HOW TO GET INTO

The Right

LAW
SCHOOL

Paul Lermack, Ph.D.

Printed on recyclable paper

VGM Career Horizons
a division of *NTC Publishing Group*
Lincolnwood, Illinois USA

Library of Congress Cataloging-in Publication Data

Lermack, Paul.
     How to get into the right law school / Paul Lermack.
          p.   cm.
     Includes Bibliographical references and index.
     ISBN 0-8442-4127-X (alk. paper)
          1. Law schools—United States—Admission.   I. Title.
KF285.L47   1996
340'.071'173—dc20   96-26638
                                                              CIP

Published by VGM Career Horizons, a division of NTC Publishing Group
4255 West Touhy Avenue
Lincolnwood (Chicago), Illinois 60646-1975, U.S.A.
©1997 by NTC Publishing Group. All rights reserved.
No part of this book may be reproduced, stored in a retrieval
system, or transmitted in any form or by any means,
electronic, mechanical, photocopying, recording or otherwise,
without the prior permission of NTC Publishing Group.
Manufactured in the United States of America.
67890 VP 987654321

Contents

1

The Task Ahead of You

These are exciting times to be a law student. Law schools are upgrading their facilities by building new buildings or renovating and modernizing old ones. They're embracing the electronic age by computerizing their libraries, wiring their offices and classrooms for computer networks, and setting up home pages on the World Wide Web. They're expanding their educational offerings with innovative courses in legal writing, ethics, and clinical work, and whole new programs of study in emerging legal specialties. And many are expanding geographically, forging closer working relationships with foreign lawyers and law schools, developing study-abroad options, and bringing foreign students and professors to their American campuses.

Because of all this activity, law schools are creative and dynamic places to spend your days. And they offer good career prospects to their graduates: according to the U.S. Department of Labor's *Occupational Outlook Quarterly*, "[e]mployment of lawyers . . . is expected to continue to grow much faster than the average for all occupations through the year 2000." These young lawyers can look forward to interesting work that is socially beneficial. They can expect to enjoy solid middle-class incomes. Many will do well financially, and a few will make fortunes.

So if you want to become a lawyer, you've made a good career choice. But before you can join the roughly 35,000 men and women who enroll each year in the freshman classes of the law schools accredited by the American Bar Association, you will have to get yourself admitted to study. This is no sure thing. Of the people who apply to these 178 law schools, about half are accepted to at least one. Half, that is, are rejected, and have to try again a year or more later, or else find other careers.

And if you are going to have a good law school experience, you'll have to do more than simply find a school that will accept you. Law schools vary in living conditions, stress levels, and "lifestyle orientation," so you will have to find one that you will be comfortable attending. Because law schools are beginning to offer more and more specialized programs, to introduce you to a profession that is becoming increasingly diverse and specialized, you will have to find one that offers the subjects that you want to study. If you are an idealistic urban sophisticate, for example, with an interest in environmental or consumer protection, you may feel out of place at a law school in a college town that orients its students toward the world of corporate practice. Since there are so many law schools to choose from, finding the right law school for you may not be an easy task.

You are likely to do best if you regard the choice of law school, and the campaign for admission, as a task that you will work at—a task, that is, like working at your studies, learning to play the piano, or saving up the money to buy a car. You should work at getting into law school over a period of time. Like piano playing or basketball, you're likely to do best if you start early, keep your eye on the goal, and work steadily and consistently. And as with any important task, you'll do best if you "work smart" as well as "work hard."

"Working smart" means that you have to know what you must do. You must break the overall task down into manageable parts, and work at them in the right order. You will need a strategy for collecting the necessary information, organizing the work, and managing your time.

In this book, I will guide you through the long and tedious application process. At each stage, I will explain what you must do, help you develop strategies for doing it, and give you some tips on presenting yourself in the most attractive way possible. I will lead you, line by line, through the various forms you will have to fill out, and warn you about traps and pitfalls that have harmed previous applicants.

Why You Need a Strategy

All law schools require that you have completed at least three years at an accredited undergraduate college or university, and most require you to have actually received your bachelor's degree before they will allow you to begin your legal studies. If you are applying to law school while you are still in college—if, in the phrase used by admissions officials, you are a "traditional candidate"—you should begin the formal application process during your junior year of college. You will have to

- register for, prepare for, and take the Law School Admission Test—the dreaded LSAT;

- decide how many law schools you want to apply to;

- choose *appropriate* law schools from among the 178 on the American Bar Association's "Approved List" that accept freshman law students;

- secure the necessary application forms;

- pay each school's application fee;

- register for and submit college transcripts and certain other pieces of information to an information management outfit called the Law School Data Assembly Service, or LSDAS;

- select, collect, and submit other material (samples of written work, proof of attendance at non degree-granting institutions) that will make you attractive to law schools;

- find professors, employers, or others to write letters of recommendation, provide these references with the necessary forms, and make sure that the letters are actually sent; and

- write, proofread, and submit one or more brief essays or "personal statements," sometimes on subjects that the law school dictates, but sometimes on topics you choose yourself (an optional step, but one of critical importance for certain applicants).

(I'll provide a somewhat more complete listing, arranged as a timetable for you to follow, in Appendix A.) You must complete all of these steps before each law school's formal deadline, usually before February 15 of your senior year if you plan to begin law school the following autumn.

If you are a "nontraditional" student—if, that is, you graduated from college some time ago and are seeking law school admission after having been in the labor force—you will have to complete the same steps and provide the same material. You will be able to work at a somewhat more leisurely pace. But because you are not attending college, you may find it more difficult to obtain information and make the necessary arrangements.

At each stage of the process, you will have to make important decisions. Each decision will require information and strategy. To do your best on the LSAT, you will have to know something about the test before you take it. To choose law schools that you have a good chance of getting into, you will need to know something about each law school's admission standards and evaluation procedures. In order to fill out the applications in such a way as to emphasize your strengths and minimize your weaknesses, you will have to know what your strengths and weaknesses are.

If you ask around, you'll find many people who are willing to help you collect the necessary information and make the critical choices. Relatives, lawyers, law students, and undergraduate professors are often quick to give advice. There are reference books you can buy and specialized courses you can take. There's even a private company, Legal Education Analysts, Inc., that promises to "expedite the art of law school admissions" by providing a full service program of data collection, LSAT preparation, and expert advising, all for a single flat fee. (You can contact LEA Inc. at 1-800-909-4899, at info@lsatprep.com; or at http://www.lsatprep.com).

You can rely heavily on others. In my opinion, however, you are best advised to organize your application campaign on your own. You will learn a lot, and you will be better prepared for law school and for a legal career, if you conduct your own research and rely on others only for specific services.

Sometimes it is hard to make sure that the information you collect is accurate and up-to-date. There's a lot of error out there. At each stage of the admissions process, there are pitfalls that you must avoid. Many applicants make common errors: they don't begin the process early enough, or they don't choose law schools properly, or they don't apply to enough law schools, or—perhaps most critically—they don't observe the necessary rules or deadlines when they file their applications. Other candidates, though they get accepted somewhere, make poor choices and wind up in law schools unsuited to their needs.

In many cases, applicants who were universally rejected are indistinguishable from more successful candidates—except that they were heartbreakingly poorly advised. They've relied on outdated reference books or listened to hearsay, rumor, and gossip. I'm still mad at the uncle, himself a lawyer, who told his nephew that it didn't matter if he waited until after the formal deadline to apply to a certain law school because that school never filled its freshman class and had empty seats available to latecomers who could afford the tuition. His advice was based on his own experience at that school—in 1965!

Some candidates neglect submitting some piece of information that they've been told was "unimportant" or "never even looked at," and had their applications rejected as incomplete. Others chose law schools based on the experience of fraternity brothers or other friends, not realizing that these law schools were too selective for them. Still others committed the common error of applying to too few law schools, omitting their "insurance schools," and were universally rejected because they applied in a poor placement year, when there were more applicants than expected and law schools raised their standards.

In all these cases, the applicants had information—but it was faulty, outdated, or incomplete. You will have to evaluate, as well as collect, the information you will need. In the following chapters, I'll identify reliable and up-to-date sources of information, and give you some tips on how to use each one. I will devote a chapter or so to each part of the application process, explaining how to get the necessary materials, how to evaluate your options, and how to develop simple strategies for presenting yourself in the best possible way. I will show you how to avoid clerical errors and incompleteness by using simple checklists. With these guidelines you should be able to avoid the classic blunders of the poorly informed.

How to Make Law Schools Want You

At most law schools, the ultimate power to set admission standards and to accept or reject any applicant is vested in a committee of law professors. (At a few schools, including Lewis and Clark College's Northwestern School of Law, students, as well as professors, sit on the admissions committee.) Because these professors have only limited amounts of time for this task, they are assisted by full-time admissions officials. The Dean (or Assistant Dean, or Director) of Admissions and a staff of counselors, recruiters, financial aid officers, and "staff professionals"

- publicize the law school and encourage you to apply;
- attend law school forums and fairs (of which, more below in chapter 5) to meet prospective students;
- maintain Web sites and other information sources;
- answer your questions (on the telephone and in writing);
- mail out catalogs, application forms, and other publications; and
- perform a wide variety of other admissions-related chores.

When you apply, these staffers will assemble all the data you submit—all those forms, essays, transcripts, and letters of recommendation—into a file. They may compare the files with one another, rank the candidates, and make recommendations about which should be admitted. In clearcut cases, they may make the actual admit/reject decisions. The law professors supervise the work of the full-time staffers and make the admit/reject decisions in marginal cases. They deal with any unusual events that arise. And since they make rules and set standards, they must consent to any requests for waivers or exemptions.

All this standard-setting, recruiting, and evaluating is directed toward one overriding goal: to identify and enroll students who will be able to do law school work, survive, and graduate. The law school doesn't want to flunk out any students. Nor does it wish to admit people who will drop out. Poor retention rates are wasteful. If a law school has room for, say, 150 freshmen, it wants to recruit 150 people who will work successfully for three years (paying tuition all the while) and then graduate.

Admissions committees have other goals as well. For example, they want to put together a diverse freshman class, and they often have affirmative action goals. Being lawyers themselves, the committee members naturally try to identify candidates who will become capable and ethical lawyers. They'd also like to turn out graduates who will become successful, who will support the alma mater, and who will contribute generously to the school's fundraising efforts. These other goals are important, and you need to know about them to present yourself properly. (I'll show you how to take advantage of some of these objectives in the chapters that follow.) Nevertheless, these concerns are clearly and explicitly secondary. Everything else pales before the need to find 150 freshmen who will be able to do the work, survive, and graduate.

It's not as easy as you may think to identify people who have the potential to be successful law students. Law school work is intense and demanding. We know that the people most likely to succeed are physically healthy, disciplined, hardworking, intelligent, good at speaking and writing, and possessed of large vocabularies and good reading skills. How can a law school tell if any one applicant possesses these qualities? How can a law school look at a person it doesn't know—at *you*, for example— and determine whether you have the necessary combination of talents, skills, and work habits? The professors can't look inside your head (and wouldn't know what to look for if they could). They can, however, subject you to various tests and make you produce information about your past career. A test or bit of information that correlates with success in law school is called a "predictor" of success. The admission test, the LSAT, is one such predictor. Experience has demonstrated that applicants who do well on the LSAT are more likely to survive law school.

Some tests or criteria are better predictors than others. Because no single predictor is perfect, law schools use a variety. That's why you have to provide so much information when you apply. Yet of all the predictors that have been tried through the years, the one that consistently works best is the undergraduate grade point average, or GPA. Put simply, the better you did in college the more likely you are to make it through law school. Therefore the one predictor that every law school will look at most closely will be the GPA. It is usually expressed on a four-point scale, according to which a straight-A record converts to a 4.0; a transcript that contains only Bs becomes a 3.0; and a college record of all Cs becomes a 2.0. At present, even some little-regarded law schools are reporting that their incoming freshman classes have median GPAs of 3.2 or 3.3.

Knowing this, the most valuable thing you can do to maximize your chances of getting into law school is to

GET GOOD GRADES!

Good grades will never hurt you. If your grades are good, you may be able to attend one of the most prestigious law schools, you'll have many more career options than applicants with poorer grades, and you'll get a better start toward accomplishing your career goals, whatever they are.

If you have poor grades, your options will be relatively limited. Poor grades will hold you back. You will always be trying to explain them away, or compensating for them. (I'll give you some tips on doing this in later chapters.) You'll have to attend a less prestigious law school, and graduate with fewer career options. If your grades are *extremely* poor, you won't be able to go to law school at all, at least not right after you graduate from college.

How to Obtain Guidance

If you are a high school student, or if you are just beginning your college years, you have time to make your grades as good as possible. If not, you are pretty much stuck with the record you have. In either case, you will have to choose law schools most likely to admit you, and then make your applications as attractive as possible. To do this, as I said above, you will need to collect information, develop strategies, and make some critical decisions.

You will certainly need help. The most knowledgeable individuals available to you are the prelaw advisers who are found on all college campuses. They are most often professors of subjects related to law— political science, history, business—who advise students about applying to law school on a part-time basis. On many campuses, a committee of professors shares this chore. On large campuses, prelaw advisers may be full-time professionals with degrees in counseling or experience in law school admissions.

According to their national organization, prelaw advisers should be "facilitators;" they "bring . . . together in an appropriate mix knowledge of the advisee's needs and ambitions with information on various law schools and legally related careers." Among other things, they often

- run prelaw clubs and similar voluntary organizations;

- publicize and make available application materials for the LSAT, law camps, and similar programs;

- make available application materials for the private proprietary schools that offer cram courses to prepare applicants to take the LSAT (or, in some cases, run such courses themselves);

- maintain libraries of law school catalogs and other useful materials;

- maintain Web sites (like the University of Richmond's at http://www.urich.edu/~polisci/prelaw.htm, or Skidmore College's at http://Don.Skidmore.edu/~tschmeli/prelaw.html); and

- sponsor programs that bring lawyers, legal educators and law students to campus.

They may also review and critique completed applications, write letters of recommendation or arrange for other professors to write them, and help candidates interpret the often cryptic messages they receive from law schools about the status of their applications.

From your point of view, their most important function is that they answer questions and give advice on a one-on-one basis. They're good people to know. Prelaw advisers regularly speak to law school admissions officials, and receive and distribute posters, leaflets, catalogs, videotapes, and reference books describing law schools, prelaw programs, scholarships, and other things that you should know about. They speak to students and alumni, to people who are trying to get into law school and to people who have succeeded in the past. They may belong to one of the regional associations of prelaw advisers, organizations that distribute additional information. And finally, they communicate with Law Services, the organization that administers the LSAT and compiles statistics on the admissions process. Law Services passes along to them the information it has accumulated, including some that is not generally released to the public.

As a result of this constant exchange of information, prelaw advisers know a great deal about how selective various law schools are, and what kinds of applicants are likely to succeed at which schools. They know what works in the applications process. More than anyone else, they can provide detailed, practical, and up-to-date answers to your questions. They can critique your application strategies, review the list of law schools you intend to apply to and advise you which of them are within your reach, and in general give you accurate and useful advice and assistance.

Everything I know about the application process I've learned in my 25 years of service as prelaw adviser at Bradley University, a medium-sized school with a good reputation for preprofessional placement. I know that the tips I will give you will be helpful, because successful applicants have used them in the recent past. My experience qualifies me to write this book. But no book can be as specific or as up-to-date as a conversation with a knowledgeable and concerned individual. If you have trouble applying my general advice to your specific situation, or if you have unique problems that I don't address in the chapters that follow, your prelaw adviser is the person to ask for help. As a rule,

WHEN YOU HAVE SPECIFIC QUESTIONS THAT THIS BOOK DOESN'T ANSWER, CONSULT YOUR PRELAW ADVISER

If you are still an undergraduate, don't wait until the last minute to make the acquaintance of your prelaw adviser. Your adviser will be best able to help you if he or she knows you well. You can take one of your adviser's courses, become acquainted at meetings of the prelaw club, or—if nothing else—stop in once a year for a chat.

The danger is that on today's overcrowded and underfunded campuses your prelaw adviser may simply not have the time to work closely with you. You may have to compete with other students for attention. You'll have to make do with occasional fifteen- or twenty- minute meetings, for which you may have to make appointments well in advance. Therefore it is important for you to know how to make the best use of the limited time you'll be allotted. Because prelaw advisers are most helpful when they can give precise answers to specific questions, you should prepare a list of questions before each appointment and bring it with you to the adviser's office. At various points in the following chapters I'll indicate the kinds of specific information that you should seek from your prelaw adviser.

A Word of Encouragement for Nontraditional Applicants

I'll refer to you as a "nontraditional" if you are applying to law school at any other time in your life than right at the end of your undergraduate days. If you've been out of school for a while, you are probably wondering whether you can compete with traditional applicants. There's a simple answer: you can. In fact, you'll probably find that you are in demand. Law schools know that the qualities they seek—drive, self-discipline, and motivation—tend to improve as you get older; conversely, the ability to learn doesn't decline (at least not until you get very old). Unless you have an employment history of frequent firings, undependableness, dishonesty, or substance abuse, your work experience is likely to be an asset. You've certainly learned something since you left school and, since law is a diverse field, whatever you've learned is probably law-related. As a law student, you will add valuable diversity to a freshman class that is otherwise made up of 22-year-olds who have all had similar educations.

Consequently, most law schools now enroll large numbers of nontraditionals. In some freshman classes, as many as 40 percent of the students have had some time elapse between college and law school. Some law schools, like the new District of Columbia Law School, give priority to nontraditionals. Others run night and part-time divisions to make it easier for people who cannot attend full-time.

Like traditional applicants, you must have attended an accredited undergraduate college or university for at least three years. If you made good grades, you have an advantage. Your GPA remains an important admission criterion. But if your undergraduate grades were poor, law schools will look for some other predictor of law school success—some other evidence, that is, that you can do the rigorous intellectual work that law schools require. If you present it properly, your work experience may partly compensate for poor grades. Indeed, the more distinguished your career has been, the less important your undergraduate record will be. Like traditional applicants, you'll have to take the Law School Admission Test and do well on it, and you'll have to submit various other pieces of evidence for the admission committee to evaluate.

If you aren't sure how law schools will view your record, if you're over forty years old, or if there's anything else in your background that you think law schools will question, you should call the admissions offices of the law schools you intend to apply to and request informational interviews. I'll have something to say about these interviews in Chapter 12. For now, you should know that you can always discuss your record with a law school official. This way you can get some idea of how your application will be received.

If you are not currently a college student you won't be able to work closely with a prelaw adviser. This will place you at a disadvantage when it comes to collecting information. You'll probably find that the prelaw adviser at your alma mater will be willing to answer your questions if you call or visit. Most schools try to provide this service to alumni on a time-available basis. If you can't contact your alma mater, or if you live far away, investigate any nearby campus. Many prelaw advisers will answer questions from neighbors—again, on a time-available basis. At a minimum, they'll usually provide registration materials for the Law School Admission Test. You should also be able to use the law school catalogs and other relevant publications in the college library.

You may find, however, that you'll have to contact law schools, Law Services, and the various other organizations on your own. Later I give directions for doing so; now that we have 800 numbers, the Internet, and frequent forums, this is less difficult than it used to be.

The important thing is to get your questions answered, even if it requires considerable persistence to do so. (Energy and persistence are good qualities to have if you are going to be a law student.) Don't rely on what you remember from your undergraduate days. Law schools and the application process have both changed dramatically in recent years. They've changed considerably since the first edition of this book in 1992. They're evolving. That's why law schools are such exciting places.

2
Your College Education

The path to law school begins at an accredited college or university. In this chapter I will give you some tips on using your undergraduate years to your best advantage. Because law schools will judge you on your grades and academic accomplishments, you will have to create a solid record of achievement. You can also use this time to learn things that will make law school work easier and help you do well once you get there. If you are still in high school, or if you're just beginning your college career, you will be able to use most of this information. If you are a college senior or a non-traditional applicant, you will need to live with the undergraduate record you already have. But read this chapter anyway to get some perspective on how law schools will evaluate your education.

Choosing a College

There are more than 3,000 accredited colleges and universities in the United States. They vary in quality and reputation, ranging from world-famous schools like Harvard and Swarthmore to local schools unknown outside of a small region. There are many advantages in being the graduate of a distinguished school. But if there ever was a time when it was necessary to graduate from Harvard to go to the Harvard Law School, that time is long over. *For the purpose of getting into law school*, where you went to college is much less important than what you studied and how well you did.

All accredited colleges are now much more alike than they are different. Most now offer the standard liberal arts and business subjects that law schools want to see on your transcript. They hire their full-time teachers from the same few graduate schools, and these teachers organize their subjects in the same ways and use the same textbooks. Compare the descriptions of, say, a political science major in various college catalogs. All the colleges— Hometown State as well as Harvard—require thirty or so semester hours of work in courses with titles like American government, international relations, political philosophy, and public law. Bigger schools may offer a larger variety of specialized courses. Better schools have more well-known scholars on the payroll. But all of the programs are similar in outline.

Being from an unusual background may actually help you. Law schools have learned that the most fertile educational climate exists when the students come from diverse backgrounds and bring diverse experiences to their studies. Top law schools have long sought "a diversified student body" as an important secondary recruiting goal. Regional schools that are trying to improve their reputations stress diversity even more. Ethnic and racial diversity are important, and the best law schools all have dynamic affirmative action programs. But geographic diversity is even more important. Admissions committees fear winding up overloaded with students from their immediate localities. They try to avoid what they call "inbred" or "incestuous" freshman classes.

Regional diversity is now considered an important sign of quality in a law school. In 1991 Drake University proudly advertised that its freshman class "is drawn from nearly half the states." The roughly 500 students enrolled at the University of Dayton in 1995 were drawn from more than 200 undergraduate institutions. The University of Connecticut has drawn its present student body from 188 American and 10 foreign universities. And the University of Pennsylvania, a very distinguished law school, has drawn its present students from more than 150 colleges, 40 states, and 9 foreign countries.

That's not to say that all undergraduate colleges are equal. Some are known to be especially good at preprofessional preparation, while others excel at placement. You've probably heard rumors that some law schools have equivalency formulas: a B earned at prestigious college X is worth as much as an A if that A came from second-rate college Y.

It doesn't quite work that way. It's true that law school administrators tend to view more favorably graduates of colleges from which the law school has gotten good students in the past, or of colleges with reputations for solid prelaw preparation. Here is how Rennard Strickland, himself a law school admissions committee member, put it in his 1974 book:

> In truth, I think the quality-of-school question is more a "burden-of-proof" question. Students from a lower prestige school or one with a poor performance record must have higher grades and LSAT test scores than students from an institution regarded as higher in quality. This is especially important in cases of borderline applicants and individuals with almost identical scores. This is just one of the facts of life. . . . At the undergraduate level, quality of the school can be important but not necessarily determinative.

In my experience, however, the direct benefits of a prestigious school are not as great, and certainly not as systematic, as Strickland suggests. Grades, converted to a four-point scale, are usually equated as though all schools are the same. At most, there's a slight tendency to give the candidate from the better-regarded school the benefit of the doubt if he or she is near the borderline between acceptance and rejection, or to take the applicant from the better-regarded school when a choice must be made between two candidates with similar records.

The advantage of the better schools is chiefly indirect. Because they provide smaller classes, more knowledgeable and concerned faculty members, and like-minded and well-motivated fellow students, they make it easier for you to work hard and get the good grades that law schools require. Good fellow-students are especially important, because similarly ambitious colleagues stimulate each other with friendly competition and help each other along the way. If you attend a large state university, with crowded classes, long lines in front of each professor's office door, and students who begin the competitive beer drinking the day after the semester starts, you'll need to be more motivated, more self-disciplined, and more of a self-starter in order to do well.

For all these reasons, you're well advised to go to the best undergraduate college that you can. But you're not banned from law school forever because you didn't attend a distinguished institution. Law schools know that most undergraduates don't have much choice about where they will go to school. They know that there are good students everywhere, even at poor schools. Even if you attended old Hometown State, law school recruiters will notice you—if your grades are good enough. "I don't care if a kid comes from a nowhere school," a law school dean once told me. "If a professor writes a letter that says, 'This is the best such-and-such major I've seen in twenty years of teaching,' then I want to at least take a look at that kid."

Choosing a Major

Law schools do not require any particular course of study. Some give no clue to their preferences. "Studies show that there is no correlation between undergraduate major and success in law school," asserts the University of Nebraska. The University of Michigan, one of the country's most selective law schools, says only that

> . . . one could receive satisfactory preparation in most undergraduate majors, depending on the strengths and weaknesses of the particular college, department or instructors involved.

Some law schools discuss prelaw courses of study in terms of the skills that should be developed. Here, for example, is the University of Utah:

> Most undergraduate majors can provide the preparation needed for law study. Whatever your chosen major, the program should equip you with the intellectual tools needed for the study and practice of law. These tools include the ability to express concepts clearly; the capacity to read concentrated materials with precise understanding and attention to detail; and the power to reason, weigh facts and solve problems. You should emphasize studies that develop powers of comprehension and that cultivate creative and logical thinking. . . .

In other words, any major is OK as long as it teaches you to read, write, and think clearly and well. Here is how The University of Michigan Law School judges the value of a major:

> Preparatory instruction is effective to the extent that it makes demands on students to enlarge their capacities to read, write, speak, think and see the relationships among ideas and their human contexts.

If you're a college freshman trying to choose a major, statements like these probably make you frustrated and impatient. They offer little guidance behind platitudes. You're probably wondering if they conceal some hidden agenda. Do law schools secretly favor some majors over others?

There has been little systematic research on this question. I know of only one study, published in September 1995 in the newsletter of the *Academy of Criminal Justice Sciences*. William J. Chambliss and Aida Yassa sent questionnaires to law school deans, 107 of whom responded; 20.6 percent said that an applicant's choice of major played no role in the law school's admit/reject decision; 17.8 percent said that it had very little influence. Although about 60 percent admitted that it played some role, most said it counted for very little. Only 6.5 percent said that the choice of major had "a great deal of influence" on the law school's decision.

When they were asked to name favorably viewed majors, the deans who said that choice of major played some role most commonly listed English. Philosophy, economics, and political science were also frequently viewed favorably. Criminal justice, sociology, and business were viewed unfavorably enough for the authors to suggest that undergraduates in these majors who hoped to go to law school should consider a double major, or at least a minor, in a more favorably viewed subject.

Overall the choice of major makes such a little difference, and the diversity of views among deans about what majors are desirable is so great, that the study offers little practical guidance. The authors certainly haven't found anything resembling a nightmarish plot among law schools to give great advantage to applicants with major X.

I think that the reason for the great difference of opinion among all these deans is that law school administrators don't think about majors very much when they think about undergraduate preparation. Instead, they talk about a "broad general background" or a "good, solid general education" in the humanities and social sciences. They suggest some coursework in English literature, political science, philosophy, psychology, sociology, American history, communications (including forensics and speech), economics, business administration, and accounting. I'll refer to these broad general education subjects as BGEs. (My students used to call them beegies.) They are all subjects that will help you do law school work. Law schools want you to study them broadly. By the time you graduate, you should have coursework in each on your transcript.

With that as your goal, the rule of thumb is that you can major in any intellectually challenging subject as long as your grades are good and you have time to work in all these varied BGEs.

But what should it be? Some statistics may help. At Bradley, we find that prelaws are scattered over a wide variety of majors. Political science is most common, followed by English, accounting, and business administration. Valparaiso University Law School found that the 168 students in the class of 1994 represented 48 different majors. Political science was most common, followed in descending order by history, English, business, finance and psychology. Four years ago, Columbia found that about 20 percent of recently enrolled students had backgrounds in political science, 15 percent in history, 15 percent in economics, 10 percent in English and 5 percent in philosophy.

Even if you confine yourself to these common majors, you will still have to choose from a long list. Each one has something to recommend it. One Chicago lawyer who started as a teacher of English literature believes that the best preparation for the study of law is the study of poetry, because poetry teaches you to pay close attention to a written text. He is quite correct. Accountants remind us that almost all law is business law, and that accounting is the way that you learn to understand the world of business. They are also correct. Political scientists note the close linkage between law and politics, and they are correct, too. Even journalism and public relations link the forensic skills that they teach with success in the legal world, and even they are correct. There seem to be few bad choices.

One strategy is to major in something that you like and enjoy, so you will be motivated to study hard and get good grades. Never lose sight of the main point: the BGEs should be on your record, and they will help you do well in law school once you are there, but undergraduate grades are what you need to get in. They are more important than the choice of major. If you choose this route, make a list of your interests. You may want to wait until the end of your freshman year in college before declaring a major, so that you have time to see which college subjects stimulate your curiosity.

A second option is to pick from among the BGE subjects whichever one is the favored concentration among the serious prelaws on your campus. Some colleges encourage prelaws to major in one field, so you can be advised by professors who are familiar with law school admissions. If you take this route, you will have a better opportunity to work closely with the faculty members and students with whom you have the most in common. As I said above, undergraduates are stimulated by like-minded people; they tend to achieve higher grades in such circumstances. But remember that fitting in with other prelaws is a means to an end, not an end in itself. Don't major in any such field if you absolutely hate the subject.

A third option, available on some campuses, is to design your own major. If your college catalog describes a "non-major major" or a "general liberal arts program" you may want to consult one of the program's advisers. He or she will ask you if there's a subject you are particularly interested in. Perhaps you are fascinated by ancient Egypt. It may be possible to design a do-it-yourself major that would include history courses in Egypt, art appreciation courses in Egyptian antiquities, political science courses in international trade that deal with the problems of regulating the traffic in stolen or forged art objects, business courses dealing with the art business, foreign language courses in Arabic, and so on.

Do-it-yourself majors can be very valuable. Simply by creating the major you are signaling that you have unique personal intellectual interests. You should be able to make good grades, because you will be working largely in your strength. And if the program is a rigorous one, you will be doing a lot of writing, which is impressive in its own right for reasons I will return to. However, there are some pitfalls you must beware of. Advisers in such programs may not be familiar with law school admissions. You will have to make sure that any program you design has enough room for a good selection of BGEs.

For most people, these are the best strategies because they maximize the likelihood that you will be able to accomplish your main goal, which is to get good grades in a program that the law schools will perceive to be good preparation for legal study. But students with unusual majors also go to law school. Bradley has an engineering school, and at least once each year an engineering senior comes into my office and says, "Professor Lermack, you're going to think I'm crazy but I want to go to law school." I'm no psychiatrist, but I feel confident when I tell these students that they're sane. The Columbia University Law School study that I quoted above found that about 5 percent of the law students had backgrounds in engineering or pure sciences. My engineering students go to law school if their grades are good enough.

If you're a nontraditional applicant and your college major doesn't fit into one of the three best categories listed above, don't despair. Through the years I've counseled a chemistry professor, a laid-off librarian, several fine arts majors (one of them a painter), and numerous others whose backgrounds were best described as unconventional. All went to law school. Among N.Y.U. Law School's 1994 freshmen were a former classics professor, a former executive in the fashion industry, a Hispanic journalist, and a Ph.D. in chemistry.

OK, you may ask, but are there ever circumstances when a college freshman who knows that he wants to go to law school should deliberately choose one of these unusual majors? The best rule to follow is that you should do so only if you have some career goal for which such a major is appropriate—that is, if you want to practice some form of law for which one of these subjects is useful. Some of my engineers, for example, wind up practicing patent law. Their engineering background is very valuable. One, who was trained in highway construction, now writes and reviews contracts in the legal department of a major highway construction company. Similarly, if you want to imitate the present head of the Food and Drug Administration, David Kessler, who is both a lawyer and a physician, then you are best advised to pursue an undergraduate premed program.

If you are interested in environmental protection law, a rapidly growing field, you should investigate a major, double major, or minor in some appropriate scientific or technical field. If you are going to protect, say, rivers and streams from pollution, it is helpful to understand the chemical processes by which water is threatened and the common industrial processes that use polluting chemicals. Washington University (St. Louis) Law School, a leader in environmental protection law, is so sure that the future belongs to technically educated lawyers that it offers three joint-degree programs. Each combines a law degree with an MS or MA degree in some field of environmental engineering or technology. To study science or engineering on the graduate level, you will need to understand the undergraduate levels of these fields.

Legal specialties are evolving rapidly, and more and more of them are requiring specialized undergraduate educations. If you want to practice international law, foreign languages are helpful; for Native American or civil rights law, some knowledge of minority cultures is essential. If you know that your goal is some such specialized area of the law, discuss your plans with your prelaw adviser. He or she can help you choose the appropriate major, double major, or minor.

As you read this long list of good choices, you may be wondering if there is such a thing as a *bad* major. Well, there aren't many. But there are a few pitfalls. First, beware the easy major. Here is the advice of the Law School Admission Council:

> High academic standards are important when selecting your undergraduate courses. The range of acceptable majors is broad; the quality of the education you receive is most important. Undergraduate programs should reveal your capacity to perform well at an academically rigorous level. An undergraduate career that is narrow, unchallenging or vocationally oriented is not the best preparation for law school.

The University of Michigan Law School makes an even stronger statement: ". . . students who have devoted their undergraduate careers to the avoidance of challenges, or who have sought rewards for rote learning, are poorly prepared for law school. . ." Since law school admission decisions are known to rely heavily on grades, the integrity of the process is threatened by students who inflate their averages by taking only the easiest courses. Law schools are extremely sensitive to this danger and are quick to reject applicants whose averages appear padded in this way. You can't avoid an easy course or two along the way, but you should shun anything resembling an easy major. Ask around. If everyone on your campus seems to know that all the lazy boneheads are doing well in, say, elliptics, then you should assume that the law schools also know it.

Did you notice the phrase "vocationally oriented" in the Law School Admission Council's statement? You should think carefully before choosing a major that is heavily specialized in career-related subjects far removed from legal relevance. You need to find room in your schedule for the BGEs; if you major in one of them, your scheduling will be easier. But if your program is filled with career-related subjects, you'll find it difficult to schedule the BGEs. In my experience, most fine and performing arts majors expose you to this danger, as do physical education programs. Music majors, for example, typically emphasize vocal or instrumental prowess. In addition to classes, students must spend long hours practicing and rehearsing. The musical skills must come first, and there's a temptation to let the academic subjects slide. These programs are intense and demanding. They certainly can't be described as easy. But they are designed to prepare you for a specialized profession. They shouldn't be faulted, because they leave time for nothing else, but they're poor choices if you want to go to law school.

Some of these programs have a second disadvantage: they grade on a pass/fail basis. You should avoid taking too many pass/fail courses. Because law schools don't know how to evaluate your performance, they tend to ignore pass/fail grades. They must therefore place more reliance on your other grades and your LSAT.

Though it's unlikely, you may still come across something called a "pre-law major" that involves studying a lot of business and real estate law. Years ago, many colleges had such majors. Most, if not all, have discontinued them because law schools frown on an immersion in law on the undergraduate level. Undergraduate law courses can't be taught with the same rigor and sophistication as law school courses, because undergraduates do not yet have the necessary background in the BGEs to understand law on that level. So law schools prefer that you concentrate on the BGEs in college. You can take an undergraduate law course or two for familiarization, but you should leave the immersion in law for law school.

Finally, to complete the circle, you should avoid choosing any course of study just because it is known to be hard. True, law schools want applicants to demonstrate intellectual ability and they are impressed when they see good grades in, say, nuclear physics. But you shouldn't spend four years on a subject far removed from legal relevance if you have no interest in it and see no career utility for it. Without motivation, you'll find it hard to make good grades.

Whatever you decide to major in, consult with your academic adviser regularly, even if you have to stand in a long line to do it. *Be sure that your adviser knows that you intend to go to law school.* Work the information into your first conversation with your adviser, and ask that it be written down in your file. Each semester, when you review your program and choose your courses, make a point of reminding your adviser of your interest in law school. It is his or her responsibility to make sure that you are making progress toward your career goals.

Choosing Courses

About one-fourth of your undergraduate coursework will be in your major subject. If you major in a field related to law, your adviser should be able to help you select courses in your major that will be useful in law school. At Bradley, for example, business majors can profit from a course titled "Legal Environment of Business," and political science majors can study constitutional law. You will probably have to take a group of courses required of all students, often called the "core curriculum" or the "distribution requirements." And whatever your major, you should take at least the introductory courses in each of the BGEs.

Beyond that, you're on your own. Depending on your major, you'll have free choice of as many as half of the courses you'll take before graduation. How do you pick specific courses?

Your four-year transcript will ultimately become a kind of résumé, and law school admission officers will read it for insight into what kind of person you are. You'll want that résumé to proclaim that you have broad interests, that you aren't afraid of a challenge, that you are interested in (and good at) subjects that are related to law —but also that you don't hesitate to pursue some unique personal interests. To shape the résumé in this way, you can choose courses for their subject matter. The BGE subjects all include coursework relevant to legal study; not only business majors can profit from that course in the legal environment of business.

Sociology offers courses in family structure, which are of value to people pursuing careers in family law, and area studies programs offer courses in foreign legal and business institutions. Your academic adviser can help you identify these courses, as can your prelaw adviser. In fact, your pre-law adviser may keep a list. One of the values of mentoring programs, prelaw clubs, and talking to alumni who are now law students is that all these contacts can steer you toward useful undergraduate coursework.

You may have to do some digging to find out what is useful, and the answers may surprise you. When I was in college, older students often advised prelaws to take mammalian anatomy, a biology course then required for medical school. The course required students to dissect a cat and memorize the names and locations of bones, muscles, and other body parts. I don't know if any law student has ever had a use for these details. I rather doubt it. But the course was useful because it taught students how to memorize lists of unfamiliar words and how to organize memorized information for easy recall. Law students have to memorize large quantities of detail, and they have to be able to recall the names of all of the cases that bear on a particular point of law. If your memory is poor, you're well advised to take steps to strengthen it, and mammalian anatomy is one way to do so. (Poetry courses, constitutional law, and many other subjects also require extensive memorization. If you can't bear the thought of dissecting a creature, there *are* other options.)

A second strategy is to choose advanced courses by teacher. You can either take more courses by BGE professors whose introductory courses you have enjoyed and profited from, or you can gather information from the student grapevine. I don't suggest that you choose only courses given by popular professors, but some teachers will challenge your intellect more than others. Some will teach by more congenial methods, or hold you to a higher standard. And some simply have more knowledge to pass on than others. You'll learn more, and polish your intellectual skills more fully, if you study with these teachers. As long as you've completed all the university requirements and put the BGEs on your transcript, it doesn't matter much what subjects these teachers teach.

Working on Your Skills

As the example of mammalian anatomy shows, there is value in choosing courses best suited to developing the skills you will use in law school. The most basic of these are reading, writing, and speaking. Developing them won't help you get into law school, except to the extent that they help you improve your undergraduate grades. But these basic skills will be of incalculable value once you become a law student.

Reading

This is what law students do each day: they wake up, they have their coffee, and then they read and write. Sometimes they communicate with each other about what they have been reading. Sometimes they apply what they have learned in classrooms, moot courts, or clinics. And sometimes they are tested on their ability to recall and apply what they have read. That's it—that's what a legal education is. Practicing lawyers may spend proportionately more time communicating orally. But they still read. Since you're going to be spending most of your time doing it, reading should be easy and enjoyable. If it isn't, then your working life as a lawyer will be a living hell.

Blunt words, but necessary ones. I know that many of you read only if you are forced to, and that you certainly don't enjoy it. You need to make some effort to improve your skill, or else look for some other line of work.

Reading skills improve with practice, and one strategy is to choose courses with especially heavy reading loads. Something like an English literature course in the novel, in which you read a novel a week for 14 weeks, is good practice. Courses in constitutional and administrative law, in political philosophy, and in social science theory, offer similar opportunities. Ease in gradually and don't take more than one or two heavy reading courses each semester.

Coursework can be valuable if it gets you into the habit of reading. But beyond that, reading in your spare time is more efficient. It doesn't much matter *what* you read. Some law schools hand out prelaw reading lists, typically indexes of commonly available books about law school and legal practice. Some suggest novels that describe legal procedures; these can include such diverse books as Charles Dickens's *Bleak House* and Scott Turow's *Presumed Innocent*. If you're interested in law-related reading, you can consult Marke and Bender's *Deans' List of Recommended Readings for Prelaw and Law Students*. The books on such lists tend to be rather heavy going, perhaps best suited to filling up that eleven-hour airplane ride between New York and Frankfurt. But if you work through such a list systematically, you'll gain valuable discipline, improve your reading, and put some of the legal classics in your head, where they may come in handy in law school.

It isn't necessary to read only the heaviest material. The point is to improve your reading skills. You do that by reading . . . anything. It's much better to devour popular novels than it is to carry around a copy of Holmes's *The Common Law* that you never get around to opening. And you're more likely to get a broad general education if you read various kinds of materials.

One value of reading for pleasure is that the habit will increase your recognition vocabulary. The larger vocabulary will make it possible to read more difficult texts in the future. Although I can't prove it, my experience suggests that students with large vocabularies tend to do better on standardized tests like the LSAT. If you feel that your vocabulary is deficient you may want to investigate courses in vocabulary building. These are offered as electives by English departments on many campuses. Essentially, they are courses in memorizing lists of big words. They prepare you for reading on your own. But they won't replace the reading habit. The big words will only stick in your head if you use them over and over.

I've found little value in speed reading courses. They seem like a good idea, since you're entering a field in which there is so much to read. Studies indicate that at least some speed reading courses can improve your reading speed. In my experience, however, they don't improve the aspect of reading comprehension that enables you to grasp the important points in a complicated text. They seem to produce a kind of rapid skimming. As a result, speed reading techniques aren't useful in handling legal texts. I know several lawyers who took such courses as students in the 1960s; none of them now use speed techniques in their legal work.

Writing

Strong writing skills are important for law students, who must take required courses in legal writing and turn out seminar papers, outlines, course summaries, and essay exams. Writing skills are, if possible, even more important for practicing attorneys, who spend much of their time drafting letters, memos, briefs, contracts, and even legislation.

Most law professors believe that the writing skills of law students have deteriorated. As I travel around the country and talk to law professors and admissions officials, I hear the same complaint over and over: These kids can't write anymore! To some extent, this is the usual griping of older people who are unhappy with the younger generation: In my day, we walked six miles through the snow (uphill both ways), and we didn't talk back to the teachers, and we learned to write! But these young whipper-snappers, with their MTV and Nintendo, they can't write anymore.

I don't know whether this is true. But the perception is useful. If you can prove that you write well, you will look much more impressive to these cranky old law professors than if you can't. Evidence of good writing skills won't replace good grades, but it may actually improve your chances of getting into law school. That evidence can come in the form of publications, literary prizes, or evaluations by undergraduate teachers. In Chapter 9, when I explain how to fill out law school application forms, I will show you how to submit this evidence.

For now you need to create the evidence by finding ways of showing off your skill. Creative writing courses, poetry contests, publication in school or "little" literary magazines, working for the school newspaper, writing position papers or pamphlets for political candidates—all are good opportunities. Or you can take a seminar that requires a long research paper. Applicants often send particularly good seminar papers along with their law school applications.

If you don't write well, you should consider taking courses in which you can learn such basic techniques as organization. English departments offer expository writing courses; at some large schools, there are courses at various skill levels. Since writing is a skill that improves with practice, you should seek out opportunities to write. Don't shirk courses that require term papers and essay exams. (Remember, the University of Michigan Law School frowns on students who devote their undergraduate careers to the "avoidance of challenges"!) The most valuable courses are those in which you have the opportunity to rewrite the same story or essay several times, under a teacher's close supervision. Some creative writing courses fit this description; look for small class size and a teacher who is also a writer.

Sometimes opportunities to write can be found in extracurricular activities or even on the job. One recent Bradley graduate edited the little newsletter that our faculty development office puts out to advise professors of opportunities for research grants and fellowships. She described it as an extremely useful experience. Another alumnus told me that his boss sent back an expense account report three times. Only on the fourth try did he write clearly enough to convince his boss that there was a good reason why he took a cab from the airport to the convention hotel rather than a bus.

Speaking

If you watch a lot of television you probably believe that lawyers must possess the gift of public speaking because they produce dramatic, and spontaneous courtroom orations. In real life, few lawyers make a lot of speeches in court. (Most lawyers rarely go into court.) Even when they must speak, lawyers have the opportunity to prepare their remarks. They rehearse, and they are allowed to bring their notes into the courtroom. You can have a rewarding legal career even if you don't possess the oratorical skills of a Ronald Reagan or a Jesse Jackson.

However, all lawyers have to express themselves clearly. Even if they don't go into court, they have to confer with clients and negotiate with other lawyers. Law students have to answer questions in class and speak in public in mock trials and moot courts. If you speak reasonably clearly and performed reasonably well in your required college course in public speaking, you won't need any special training in forensics. But if you're painfully shy or have trouble expressing yourself in classroom discussion, you should schedule some remedial work. Speaking skills are skills, like reading and writing, and are improved—surprise, surprise!— by practice.

Some colleges offer advanced courses in speech. In addition to making you more comfortable before an audience, these courses often deal with the organization and structure of communications. Students who are painfully shy are advised to consider dramatics, at least on the laboratory level. Many people who find it difficult to speak in public nevertheless find it possible to play a role before an audience. Perhaps there's something about pretending to be someone else: if you embody a character like, say, Macbeth, you put on his good characteristics like a costume. While you are playing Macbeth, you are not your usually shy self. Dramatics courses may also help you to strengthen a frail voice or improve an undesirable accent. Finally, some poetry courses include oral performance. Ask around.

Many colleges offer forensics programs or teams as extracurricular activities. On a performance team, students with good forensic skills can develop themselves, with practice and coaching, into polished orators. Forensics teams are therefore of value to prelaws who want to go into trial law or politics. But they are also useful for very shy or inarticulate people. With supportive coaches and colleagues, shy people can often develop into capable speakers, even if they don't have the talent to become great orators.

Fewer schools now offer programs in debating. That is a pity. Unlike forensics, which emphasizes speaking only, debate combines persuasive speaking with research and writing. In debating, points are awarded for the strength of the argument as well as for the skill of the presentation. In the nineteenth century, college debate teams were the training grounds for future politicians. If you feel the need to work on your speaking skills and have access to a debate program, debate is an excellent choice for an extracurricular activity.

Other Useful Skills
Foreign Languages

Americans rarely study languages the way Europeans do, beginning in childhood and continuing as a routine and required part of all formal education. Overwhelmingly, the few Americans who study foreign languages beyond the elementary level are people who need to do so because they are pursuing some career goal that requires languages.

Prelaw students rarely perceive any career value in foreign language study. That is unfortunate. Many attractive legal careers are open only to bilingual lawyers. Traditionally, criminal law and government practice in many parts of the country require some knowledge of Spanish. Languages open doors to careers in the private sector as well. As American companies increasingly establish themselves in other parts of the world, they need executives and lawyers who can do business in more than one language. International law, a specialty now largely concerned with the legal environment of multinational companies, is expanding rapidly. American lawyers live and do business in Europe, Latin America, and the Pacific Rim countries. Even more lawyers keep an eye on international business operations from corporate headquarters in American cities.

In recent years, many American law schools have pursued an eager policy of internationalization. They offer courses in foreign law, bring foreign lawyers to campus as students and visiting teachers, offer study-abroad programs, and even operate foreign branches or research centers. As a priority, many are trying to make their students think of law as an international subject. They are impressed by students who are comfortable in a foreign culture.

But to be impressive, and to qualify for one of these good jobs, you must be bilingual. This requires more than simply completing a few college courses. If you are lucky enough to have learned a foreign language as a child, you should by all means keep up your competence. If you are starting from scratch you should begin language study as a college fresh-man. In either case, you should plan on doing something in your language each semester. In addition to coursework, language study can include reading, viewing foreign films, or simply belonging to a foreign-speaking social group and attending multilingual Sunday dinners. And you should invest in whatever travel, exchange, and junior-year-abroad programs you can afford. Try to make friends in your foreign country, subscribe to a newspaper or foreign-language cable TV outlet, and get into the routine of living a regular part of your life in your foreign language.

Computer Skills

If you are below the age of 30 you probably can't imagine a world without computers and Nintendos. If you haven't already done so, you will prob-ably be required to pass a course in computer literacy. But you may not be aware of the extensive use of computers in the legal world. The old oak-paneled law library, with its heavy matched books and sturdy reading tables, is now a museum piece. Most legal research is done on computer-ized systems like LEXIS and WESTLAW, and most law library materials are now routinely available on networks or CD-ROMs. Law firms use computers for billing, time management, fee calculation, checkwriting, scheduling, inventory control (including the management of trial exhibits), word processing and editing, and electronic mail. And many of the legal issues that business lawyers must deal with involve disputes over the use of computers.

Law schools won't expect you to know how computers work and they certainly won't teach you programming. You'll never have to be more than an end-user. But law firms depend on computer experts, and if you are a whiz with computers you should consider becoming such an expert. There are good jobs out there for lawyers who really understand this technology.

For such a career, you should investigate a major or double major in a technical subject. But high tech is like a foreign language: you don't become an expert simply by taking a few college courses. You have to spend part of your time working at it regularly. In this case, internships or work-study opportunities that take you into the world of computer busi-ness are very valuable. Needless to say, you shouldn't pursue this kind of career unless you really enjoy it.

Learn to Type!

The only computer skill that you absolutely must possess is typing. You don't need to be a hundred-word-per-minute speed demon, but you should be able to clack away without looking at the keyboard and without making so many mistakes that the text you produce is unreadable. Even a mediocre typist can type faster than the average person can write in longhand. Once you get into the habit of typing, you'll find numerous timesaving uses for the skill. Many law students now bring their laptops to class and type their lecture notes directly onto their hard disks. (Some law schools are rewiring lecture rooms to make this easier.) Some law professors will allow you to type essay exams. (They usually provide a separate room.) In the near future, many law schools will require written assignments to be turned in in some electronic form, rather than on paper. The widespread use of computers has made the old professional typist an endangered species. If you can't type yourself, you may have trouble finding someone to type your homework.

Shorthand

Lawyers are always taking notes: in the classroom, in the law library, and especially in the courtroom. (Television lawyers are rarely shown taking notes, but that's why they call it fiction.) Shorthand is a useful skill. But unlike typing, shorthand is difficult to learn. If you are good at note taking you have probably found that you have developed your own system of abbreviations and symbols. It isn't worthwhile for you to invest the large amount of time you will need to develop a good facility at some commercial shorthand system.

3

Education Outside the Classroom

For traditional students, good grades are the chief requirement for law school admission. Your work inside the classroom is much more important than your work outside of it. Don't expect your extracurricular activities to compensate for a poor GPA.

In this respect, law schools are different from MBA programs, large corporations, and, indeed, most of the things that non-prelaws will do after they graduate from college. People who want to work for large corporations, especially, are often advised to become members of fraternities or sororities, to hold elected office in these social clubs, to participate in team sports, and in general to show evidence of being group-minded people.

These large businesses (and the graduate programs that support them) are looking for evidence that the people they hire will be team players. The quarterback of a football team has provided such evidence, as have the members of the offensive line. Presumably, they will bring their team-orientation with them to the sales meeting, the committee, and the corporate working group.

But law schools are looking for a different kind of person. They want people who are self-starters, who can work alone, and who have the discipline to work by themselves for a long time on some long-term project. Good grades, which indicate individual achievement, are much better predictors of your ability to do law school work than anything you can do outside the classroom.

Some law schools ignore the extracurricular activities of traditional applicants, judging them entirely on their grades and LSAT scores. But most law schools pay some attention to the outside activities. They say that they want their students to be "well-rounded" and to have diverse backgrounds, and they can judge these secondary characteristics from the organizations that their applicants join. In addition, applicants who have extracurricular activities in addition to good numbers must necessarily have a lot of energy, good self- discipline, and good organizing and scheduling skills. Undergraduates who join organizations will fit in well with lawyers, who tend to be gregarious and great joiners. Finally, law schools know that some extracurricular activities provide useful experience and teach law-related skills.

For all these reasons, extracurricular activities "count." For students on the border between acceptance and rejection at a particular school, they can count a great deal. If your extracurricular record is strong, and especially if your activities demonstrate leadership, you should apply to law schools that promise in their catalogs to "go behind the numbers" and "judge the whole person," and you should be sure that all your activities are fully described on your applications.

But extracurricular activities don't count that much. Don't let your classroom work go on the assumption that your outside activities will make up for your lapses. *Whenever you have to choose between making good grades and spending time on a club or sport, you should work on your grades.*

(If you are an older nontraditional applicant with a long employment record, your accomplishments after college may partly compensate for poor undergraduate grades. I'll have more to say about how you should handle your applications in the section on "Work Experience," and again in Chapter 9.)

Choosing Extracurricular Activities

For application purposes, it really doesn't matter what college clubs or teams you join. Each of the traditional school activities—Greek-letter organizations, affinity clubs, student government, even athletics—has something to recommend it. Law as a profession is so diverse that it would be hard to find an activity that would not be useful to some lawyers or law students somewhere. If you are a good tennis player, for example, you probably don't think of your skill as being particularly useful to your legal career. But the late United States Supreme Court Justice Hugo Black was a tennis fanatic and played almost every day well into old age. Like all Supreme Court justices, Black hired one or two law clerks each year from among the many honors graduates of top law schools who eagerly sought those prestigious positions. He could choose whomever he wanted, and he made sure that he always had a suitable tennis opponent working in his office.

The moral of this story is that you never can tell what will come in handy. If you are trying to decide what activities to participate in, consider continuing whatever you did in high school. Or join whatever your friends join. Or go to the organizational meetings that clubs hold at the beginning of each school year and talk to the members. Look for congenial people and don't try to guess which things will most impress law school admissions committees.

Once you've found activities you enjoy, stick with them. It's marginally better to have a record of continuous participation in a few things than a record that lists numerous activities with only one or two semesters in each. A student who is continually dashing from group to group leaves himself open to the criticism that he isn't really interested in the activities but is merely fattening his résumé. Either that or he can't get along with anyone.

Law-Related Social Activities

Since you are interested in law, it's natural for you to be interested in activities related to law. Your campus will offer a wide variety of such activities—so many, in fact, that you may have difficulty choosing among them. You can concentrate on activities that will help you to develop skills that you will use in law school, or that will give you the opportunity to show off law-related talents. In the previous chapter, I mentioned the value of forensics teams and dramatics for polishing your oral expression, and of literary magazines and school newspapers for polishing your prose. Newspaper jobs offer the possibility of publication, and clips can be sent along with law school applications. In addition, many newspaper jobs pay salaries.

Students interested in political careers often participate in student government. I hesitate to recommend this for everyone, because on many campuses "school politics" has become an ineffectual joke. Too often, student government attracts the windy, the self-serving, and the self-important. Or it becomes an arena in which disputes between self-aggrandizing social organizations are played out. You'll have to judge your own campus for yourself. At its best, student government can be an excellent teacher of group "deliberation"—that is, of making decisions by discussing, compromising and voting. It may also be the best way to meet the other students on your campus who are interested in legal careers. At its worst . . . well, let's just say that at its worst it's not worth your time.

Most campuses offer other government-related activities. Model United Nations programs and their close relatives, model legislative and model state government programs, offer good practice in deliberation and may be free of the posturing and cynicism that affects traditional student government. Some schools also sponsor law day programs or essay competitions on legal themes.

The best choice for students interested in political careers is to bypass student activities entirely and get involved in real-world political campaigns, or to schedule internships in state or local government. The best way to learn about politics is to go out and *do* politics. Campaigns recruit numerous volunteers. Since they are perennially short-handed, they are usually willing to let young people take on important and responsible work. In fact, the traditional path to becoming a paid political campaign professional begins with volunteer work on a local campaign. However, campaigns will make severe demands on your time, especially in September and October. You shouldn't let this work interfere with getting good grades. Presidential primary campaigns, which usually occur in January, February, and March of a presidential election year, may be a better choice than traditional general election campaigns. And although some campaigns pay part-time workers, most do not—at least not at first. If you need to earn money during the school year, you may not be able to schedule this valuable experience.

Prelaw Clubs

Campus prelaw clubs are designed to acquaint undergraduates with law school, law school application procedures, and legal careers. At their best these are small organizations with a strong social component; they bring like-minded students together to exchange information, tutor the laggards, and, in whatever ways are required, support each other's efforts to make good grades and present themselves well to law schools. Prelaw clubs often bring law students, young lawyers, and other knowledgeable people to speak on campus, and they may arrange trips to nearby law schools. Sometimes they publish newsletters and keep track of alumni who have gone on to law schools. And they usually are in close contact with the campus prelaw adviser, so they serve as a dissemination channel for the information that he or she collects. Prelaw clubs can help you learn about the options that are available in legal careers and collect the information that you will need when you have to choose which law schools to apply to.

You may still find some prelaw clubs that run cram courses for the LSAT, although private proprietary schools have taken on the lion's share of this work. Some prelaw clubs, especially on large campuses, field teams that participate in local or national mock trial competitions, or in "moot courts," a kind of simulated appellate legal procedure. These competitions are a specialized kind of debating; they combine the attention to presentation that forensics teams specialize in with research on legal topics. (At Bradley, the mock trial team is separate from the prelaw club but has overlapping membership. As mock trial competitions become more popular, more schools will probably organize their programs in this way.)

Phi Alpha Delta

As I write this, Phi Alpha Delta national legal fraternity has about 140 coed chapters on undergraduate campuses and is expanding at the rate of 10 to 15 new chapters a year. These prelaw chapters offer the same social activities, programs, and tours that local prelaw clubs do. They provide the same opportunities to meet and work with like-minded students. But because they are members of a national organization, they have more informational resources and they can communicate and share information across campus borders. (The most visible sign of this is their flourishing electronic bulletin board and discussion group. There are often notes from students planning to visit other campuses for some special program, to collect information, or just to hang out.) Phi Alpha Delta also offers at least one national conference each year. Because national officers assist them, local chapters have more continuity from year to year than other prelaw clubs. Finally, because Phi Alpha Delta has more than 135,000 members, organized into 172 chapters at ABA-accredited law schools and about 90 alumni chapters, their prelaw members have unparalleled opportunities for networking and mentoring. Members delight in listing the dignitaries—governors, state supreme court justices, law professors— who are among their fellow-members.

The best way to obtain information about Phi Alpha Delta is to send an e-mail query to PADPRELAW@AOL.com, or to call (818) 360-1941. Their executive offices are at 10722 White Oaks Ave., P.O. Box 3217, Grenada Hills, CA, 91394.

Subject-Related Organizations

Your campus may have "affinity clubs" for other fields. At Bradley, a medium-sized school, there are active clubs in accounting, advertising, marketing, financial management, international business, criminal justice administration, political science, psychology, journalism, and sociology. There are also several clubs whose name begins "Women in—." Most of the members are students majoring in the subject, and the main objective of the club is to provide the members with career-related information, networking, and mutual support. So they are good places to meet like-minded students.

In many professional fields, notably accounting and journalism, there is a tradition that working professionals will take an interest in the education of the next generation. As a result, accountants and journalists often contribute both time and money to the work of student clubs. The clubs are thus good places to begin your professional networking.

Honorary Societies

If you are eligible, you should certainly join an honorary society or two. These organizations resemble social fraternities and sororities in being national bodies with relatively autonomous local chapters and lifetime membership. They resemble affinity groups in collecting young people with similar interests. Most honorary societies are open to students in particular majors (or groups of majors in "social science" or "education") who maintain good grades. For example, the Pi Sigma Alpha political science honorary society is open to all political science majors who maintain an overall 2.5 grade-point average and a 3.0 GPA in their political science courses. The Order of Omega is open to students with good grades who are also members of social fraternities. Some larger honorary societies, like Mortar Board, are open to all seniors with good academic records.

Typically, if you are eligible for an honorary society, you will be asked to join during your junior year. You should do so. The cost is small and the work involved is nominal. You may be asked to help organize programs, publish a newsletter, run a tutoring program, or raise money for charity. Some honorary societies also do social work for the community. But most are largely social. In exchange for minimal participation, you get the opportunity to socialize with like-minded students and network with alumni. And you can list the name of a prestigious organization on your law school applications under the heading "Awards and Honors." It will be one more opportunity to call attention to your consistently excellent grades.

Law Camps

Summer prelaw camps have been designed in imitation of the computer, basketball, and music camps that have proliferated in recent years. They offer from one to seven weeks of summer programs designed to provide information about law school, legal practice, or both. Some are residential and provide living accommodations, usually on a college campus. Others resemble day camps; their activities may be held mostly in the evening and they do not provide living accommodations. Typical activities at prelaw camps include moot court competitions, computer training (in the handling of WESTLAW and similar legal research software), field trips to courts and law firms, programs of speakers, preparation training for the LSAT, and the like. Law camps do what prelaw clubs do, and therefore may be valuable for students whose campuses lack those important organizations. They present the information systematically, and without the need for the students to do the organizational work, in a short period of time during which you are surrounded by similarly oriented students with no distractions. But some law camps also do what no prelaw club does: they offer real or simulated legal coursework, to provide a realistic taste of law school and to prepare people for the challenges they will face there. Some prelaw camps are run by individual law schools. McGeorge Law School of the University of the Pacific, for example, offers a five-week program on its campus in Sacramento. Your prelaw adviser should have information about programs near your campus. (The McGeorge admissions office can be contacted at 3200 Fifth Ave., Sacramento, CA, 95817.) Some special camps are run by private foundations for the benefit of minority prelaws. You will learn more about these special camps in chapter 13.

The National Institute for Legal Education (NILE), a private organization, offers two- week intensive camps for college students at Stanford University or American University. Its activities are in many respects a model of what should be provided. NILE camps are designed to teach skills useful in law school, or, in the words of executive director Chris M. Salamone, to "adapt students to the law school process." To this end, NILE offers 70 hours of classroom instruction in law school subjects such as civil procedure, contracts, and property, taught by distinguished law school faculty. The courses are taught up to law school standards, and include realistic exams. There is also a separate program in legal writing. Salamone says that of the 1000 or so students who attended NILE camps during their first six years of operation, not one has flunked out of law school or dropped out. NILE is expanding and expects to have about 1000 people attend its 1996 summer camps.

In addition to college-level offerings, NILE has programs aimed at high school students. The organizational headquarters is at 4800 North Federal Highway, Suite 106D, Boca Raton, FL, 33431; (800) FYI-NILE or (407) 392-2220.

Prelaw camps may help you to make up your mind if you aren't sure whether or not a legal career is for you. Because they provide a realistic taste of legal education, they may also help you identify deficiencies in your vocabulary, reading ability, or other law-related needs. And Salamone's statistics indicate that at least some camps succeed in helping to prepare students for the challenges of law school. (The camps are also designed to familiarize people in other careers, like journalists and educators, with the peculiarities of law schools.)

The main drawback to prelaw camps is the cost. This year NILE will charge students $1095 tuition and an additional $500 if they need accommodations. Some financial aid is available; about 20 percent of the students have scholarships, and there is a separate assistance program for minorities. So if you are close to the financial margin, you should ask about help. But if you need to earn money in the summer, prelaw camps are probably out of reach. You certainly shouldn't plan on holding a job while you attend an intensive summer program.

I know of only one undergraduate school, Cheyney State, which presently offers academic credit for attendance at a prelaw camp. Although it may be possible on some campuses to finagle credit for a camp under the heading of "independent study," and although other campuses may offer more explicit credit in the future, you should plan on the assumption that you cannot earn academic credit for attendance. The value of prelaw camps lies elsewhere. And although attendance shows an interest in a legal career and should be listed on your law school applications (either along with your other extracurricular activities or under the heading of continuing education), it will probably be of little interest to law school admissions officials.

A Word about Volunteerism

Law schools, ever sensitive to the popular image of law as a profession, try as a secondary goal to recruit students of good moral character. One way to demonstrate that you are the right kind of a person is to begin in your college years to make the charitable contributions to the community that adults are expected to provide. The charitable work won't compensate for poor grades, and you should never put in so many volunteer hours that your grades suffer. But volunteering won't hurt your application status. Besides, it's good for your soul.

Many of you have been doing this all along . High school service clubs are presently enjoying a boom. For most of you, volunteer efforts are available in your church or synagogue. Helping out with a hot lunch program, a meals-on-wheels program, or a tutoring program for disadvantaged children won't teach you law-related skills. But you will learn something about people, and you may actually enjoy the effort.

At present, the fastest-growing charitable program on many campuses is Habitat for Humanity, which builds houses for low-income families. Habitat workers work hard; they may learn useful skills like household carpentry and painting, and they have a chance to network with similarly minded people. Environmental activism is also popular on campuses.

As a rule, you will learn more if you become involved in the ongoing work of the charity—like tutoring or construction—than if your involvement is limited to fundraising. But don't sneeze at fundraising efforts. Door-to-door soliciting, telephone canvassing, and organizing fundraising events are all essential; without volunteer fundraisers, most charities couldn't continue to exist.

Work Experience

For traditional applicants, work experience won't "count" enough to outweigh grades as the chief variable in determining law school admission. For nontraditionals, however, it may. If you have a long work career, or a distinguished one, or both, your grades will become less important. If you are over thirty and moving from one career to another, you should seek personal interviews at the law schools you are going to apply to. (See Chapter 12 on informational interviews.) Because you bring another kind of diversity to the law school's student body, you may find that you are a very attractive candidate.

If you are a traditional student, you probably have to work at least some of the time. If you are like most students, you don't have much choice about what you will do. There are part-time jobs on campus, often provided as part of your financial aid package, or there's the minimum-wage ghetto. Consider yourself lucky if you can find a job that pays above the minimum wage, gives you some flexibility in scheduling your hours, and teaches you something.

You will have to describe your work experience on your law school applications. If you can distinguish yourself by rising to a responsible position or winning a job-related award or competition, or if you can persuade an employer to write a letter of recommendation that identifies you as a superior employee and describes something noteworthy that you have done, then your work experience may marginally improve your chances of getting into law school.

If you have a history of being fired for incompetence, insubordination, or dishonesty, your work experience will hurt your chances of law school admission. You probably won't be able to conceal a poor employment record: some law school applications ask if you have ever been fired from a job and, if so, why.

Law Firm Employment

It is extremely valuable to find a part-time or summer job in a law firm or in some business or profession closely related to law. At one time, such jobs were rare and they were usually obtained through an old-boy network. Favored students would find employment in law firms run by their parents, relatives, or family friends. The old-boy network is still there and it remains the only way to get such jobs in some firms. I advise Bradley students to use all their political capital to find a law firm job. This means asking parents to contact business associates, distant relatives, and political contacts.

But many firms are making conscious efforts to broaden the base from which they draw their part-timers. They ask professors for recommendations, participate in co-op programs and other campus employment services, and—perhaps most important—make affirmative action efforts. Some even advertise in local newspapers. If you are trying to obtain a part-time job and aren't able to invoke some family favoritism, your first stop should be your campus prelaw adviser or your academic adviser. You should also check the bulletin boards, electronic postings, and newsletters of your campus placement center. Look also for openings in the legal departments of large corporations; office jobs for such legal-service professionals as court reporters, videotapers, publishers and detectives; and jobs for regulated industries.

And you should persevere. Getting a job in any small business—and all law firms are small businesses, by corporate standards—is always largely a matter of being in the right place at the right time. Each year, it seems, one or two of my advisees obtain jobs in the Peoria-area legal community simply by knocking on doors and filling out unsolicited job applications. One young woman drew up a résumé, with the assistance of one of Bradley's job placement counselors, and sent copies to every law firm in the county.

If nothing else, working in a law firm for a few semesters will allow you to say that your ideas about what a lawyer does each day were not formed solely by television programs. Even though your job as a part-timer will largely be spent doing office busywork, you should also learn something about legal language and procedure. Perhaps more important, you'll begin to make the acquaintance of lawyers. Networking will occupy a large part of your professional life. Finally, you'll begin to learn about the unwritten codes of dress, manners, and customs that lawyers are expected to follow.

Law firm work may marginally improve your ability to get into law school in two ways. You may have the chance to do something responsible, and then you can write on your law school applications that you did research for appellate briefs, or helped lawyers conduct interviews, or—as one of my students did a few years ago—improved the computer program that the law firm used for account management. You will be able to write an interesting application essay about such an accomplishment, and your essay will demonstrate the possession of skills useful in law school.

Second, if you are a conscientious and impressive employee, one or more of your firm's lawyers will write useful letters of recommendation for you. This is a tangible end-product of mentoring, and can marginally improve your chances of admission. I'll have more to say about the value of such letters in Chapter 11.

One danger of law firm employment is that you may be left doing nothing but busywork. I know of some students who spent tedious hours dusting the books in the law library. You can expect to spend some of your time making coffee and photocopying documents. Law firms need to have these things done. But if, after you have been there a semester, you conclude that your job isn't teaching you anything, you should consider looking for another one. Don't quit in a hurry if the job pays well and the alternative is flipping burgers for minimum wage. But look around and see if you can do better.

A second and even greater danger is that the reverse will happen: your job will become so enjoyable, and teach you so much, that you neglect your studies. The lawyers you are working for, who want you to put your time into helping them, may be especially seductive. They'll promise to help you get into law school, they'll brag about their influence back at the old alma mater, and they'll tell you how well their previous proteges have done. Remember, lawyers are especially persuasive people; they may be able to make you believe that your part- time work is the most important thing that you can do to get into law school.

Well, it isn't. You have to resist! Up to a point, legal experience is valuable and the mentoring and good will of practicing lawyers can never hurt you. But neither of these things will make up for poor undergraduate grades. If your mentor is serious about helping you, he or she will make it possible for you to study.

Co-Op Programs

If you attend one of the many universities with a co-op education program, you'll have the opportunity to gain career-related experience by working at a full- or part-time job. It is usually possible to earn academic credit as well. The work experience is considered so valuable that on many campuses students in engineering and other technical fields are required to participate in the co-op program.

Co-op jobs are most plentiful, and most rewarding, for technical majors. Firms looking for accountants, for example, can hire upperclass students and expect them to do almost everything that college-graduate accountants can do. Although they pay the students well by student standards, they pay less than they would have to pay career employees. (One advantage of being an accounting major is that it is usually fairly easy to get an accounting co- op job.) Not the least of the values of the co-op program to such students is that it makes it easier to get postgraduate employment: a new graduate can simply apply to a firm that is already familiar with his or her abilities. Participants in co-op programs have higher placement rates than other college graduates and, at least on some campuses, higher starting salaries.

Even if you are not an accounting or business major, co-op programs often have jobs available in lawyers' offices, in the legal firms of large corporations, or in the offices of regulated businesses and industries. In fact, many businesses prefer to leave all their college student hiring to co-op programs. One reason for this is that the co-op programs screen the applicants. You usually have to qualify for co-op by having, and maintaining, good grades, and you always have to pay a fee.

Once you are accepted into the program, a co-op counselor will provide a list of available jobs. (In addition to nearby part-time employment, the counselor will probably also have full-time jobs and jobs at remote location; if you secure one of these, you will probably have to delay your college graduation.) The counselor will help you draw up your résumé and give you some tips on doing well on job interviews. On some campuses, the co-op programs run valuable not-for-credit courses on such topics as dressing for success, writing job applications, and business etiquette.

Armed with this assistance, you apply for the jobs you are interested in. You will have to compete with other co-op students in an application process that will include interviews but will largely be decided by grades. Competition may or may not be keen, depending on the kind of job, local employment conditions, and the number of students at your institution who are seeking such work. In my recent experience at Bradley, the co-op job developers turned up four or five law firm jobs each year, and some of them went begging.

Once you have the job, the firm will assign someone to supervise you and to report to your college. Try to make a good impression on this executive because he or she will be the best person to describe your work experience in a letter of recommendation, and also because co-op jobs are theoretically ongoing and you'll want to be invited back. It is common for students to keep the same part-time jobs for several years or to work full-time for the same firms for several intervals during their college years, but the firm can decline to re-hire any co-op at the end of any semester.

If you are a social science or humanities major who does not have the technical training of an accountant or engineer, and you are employed in a law firm or corporate office, you can expect your work to consist largely of general office duties. Coffee-making is standard, as is photocopying, running errands, filing, and in general, fetching and carrying. Perform this work with a good will, even after it becomes boring. It has to be done.

But remember, the co-op employer has also promised to teach you something. At a minimum you should be in a position to see what the professionals in the office actually do, and there should be someone to answer your questions. After a while you should be given at least some opportunity to do responsible work. At a law firm, this can include some rudimentary legal research or legal drafting. Expect this work to be closely supervised at first, and do not show impatience if an older employee checks every step. If you perform well, you'll be given more independence.

The best co-op jobs provide extremely good mentoring opportunities. Some firms provide regular seminars, during which the students meet informally with professionals. Others have formal programs of speakers and office tours. Smaller businesses and firms can't afford formal programs, but they may still be very good at introducing young people to the professional world.

If you feel that you're doing nothing but busywork, and not learning anything, tactfully complain to your supervisor. If that doesn't help, complain to the co-op faculty adviser. Occasionally, co-op jobs don't work out. As with any job, however, don't be in a hurry to quit unless you have a better alternative.

Internships

State and local governments, many federal agencies, political party organizations, and campaign committees offer part-time or summer internships. So do many good-government voluntary organizations and private lobbying outfits; one of my students, for example, spent an educationally valuable summer in Springfield working for a group that represented Illinois banks. Newspapers, magazines, and a variety of other businesses also offer internships. Unlike co-op jobs, which are meant to be ongoing, most internships are one-shot deals; you'll work for a semester, or a summer, with no possibility of re-employment. Also unlike co-op jobs, internships are usually unpaid.

It's usually fairly easy for a student with good grades to secure an internship in a prosecutor's or public defender's office, an urban police department, an administrative department of a city government, a state agency, or a state legislative committee. Internships with federal agencies are sometimes more competitive. These are also more likely to be too far away for part-time work.

To obtain a part-time internship, you will need to sign up for the appropriate course. On some campuses, internships are required of students in certain majors, most commonly journalism, social work, or criminal justice studies. On other campuses, they are open only to students with good grades. Some internships may be restricted to students majoring in certain subjects. Your prelaw adviser or your academic adviser can tell you about your options; your college catalog will list the appropriate course numbers, the eligibility rules, and the names of the instructors.

Most colleges require you to sign up at least a semester in advance, and you should always speak to the instructor before you register. If you have any special scheduling requirements, any handicaps, or any other conditions that may affect your employment, make sure that the instructor knows about them. Find out where you will be working (for it is the instructor's responsibility to find you an opening), what you are likely to be doing, and how much time will be required. Ask for the names of other students who have worked in the same office, and then contact them to see if they found the experience worthwhile. Before you commit yourself, make sure that you can make feasible travel arrangements if you have to travel any distance from campus.

In most cases, you will have to obtain a summer internship yourself. Allow seven or eight months for the process. Academic and prelaw advisers usually keep track of such opportunities. They post advertising handbills on bulletin boards near their offices and may make flyers and brochures available. They may also list possible internships in newsletters and on electronic bulletin boards. Your college placement center might also keep track of opportunities. Prelaw clubs and mentors also often pass along information that they receive. I also know of cases where ministers and chaplains received leaflets advertising internships in law-relevant fields and passed them along to students. From whatever source you receive it, there will be an address or a telephone number. Request an application and, when it arrives, follow the instructions.

Internships with political parties, good-government groups or publications are similarly advertised on posters and flyers. They may also be advertised in political magazines or school newspapers. You may also hear about them from individuals who work for these organizations, or from older students who have held such internships in the past. You can call the local office of the Sierra Club, or any political group, and ask if they have any such opportunities. Internships with business groups are harder to find. They are often unadvertised; the group's full-time staff recruits students through an old-boy network that may include college professors but is often limited to the families and friends of people "in the trade." Ask your prelaw adviser and any professors you feel comfortable with if they know of any internship opportunities in their fields. And ask your parents, relatives, and family friends.

For both summer and part-time internships, the course instructor will monitor your performance. You will meet with him or her, discuss what you are learning, and eventually write a paper or two. Sometimes the instructor will meet with several interns at once. From your individual or group conferences, you should obtain some guidance about what to look for in your work experience. Sometimes the instructor will provide, or will require you to find, detailed information about the work of your agency or organization.

At work, you will do whatever needs to be done. In most cases, this will include that famous general office work. Expect (surprise, surprise) to make coffee. But like a co-op job, the internship is supposed to teach you something. Internship employers have even more of a responsibility to you because, unlike co-op employers, they're not paying you. Most recognize this responsibility, and some make extensive promises. The Illinois Attorney General's office is not an extreme example when it advertises that "typical internship assignments include: performing legal research in the law library; working with consumers who complain about unfair business practices; [and] assisting lawyers with case study and legal writing."

Hold them to their promises! As with co-op jobs, sometimes internships don't work out. But in contrast to co-op jobs, such complaints are rare. It's much more common for interns to complain that they are being worked to death. They're given responsible chores, all right—but chores that take much longer than their commitment of 15 hours a week.

The reason for this is that the government agencies that take interns are famously understaffed and overworked. When they obtain the services of bright and energetic young people—who, remember, are working for free or for very little—they load these volunteers with as much work as they will bear. Because of this well-known tendency, internships in public prosecutors' offices and similar government agencies are *perceived* by the law schools as extremely good experience. But as with all jobs, don't let the work interfere with your studying. If you can afford to commit the time, summer internships are probably better than part-time work in this regard.

Not all students can afford to spend a summer without earning money. For that matter, some have to forego even part-time internships because they need paying work. If you are in this position, ask the course instructor if some support is available, either from the agency or from the college. Sometimes small grants are available, or time for internships can be built into the college financial aid package. Also, investigate whatever internships you can find with business organizations. Pressure groups and similar private organizations sometimes provide better pay.

4

The Law School Admission Test

The Law School Admission Test, or LSAT, is required for admission to all law schools accredited by the American Bar Association. It is the only other variable to be spoken of in the same breath as grades as a major factor in determining whether or not a candidate is admitted to a law school. Almost without exception, my students approach it with fear and trembling.

They've been spooked. Students who have taken the test often return with horror stories. Some experienced overheated exam rooms, poor lighting, or noisy distractions. Others had to work with high fevers or dripping sinuses. One poor fellow had to hold a broken pair of glasses against his forehead with his left hand while he worked. Another young man arrived late and had to sit in the only available chair, in an aisle where the proctors kept tripping over his legs while he worked. When he finished, he joked that his score would be so low they'd offer him an athletic scholarship.

Without fail, someone is sure to bring up that legendary Sad Sack—that cousin's girlfriend's roommate or roommate's girlfriend's cousin whom everyone has heard of—who put the answer to question 13 on line reserved for question 14. Then he put the answer to question 14 on the line for question 15 . . . question 15 on line 16 . . . and so on, not catching his error until a split second before the proctor announced that time was up. Even though no one seems to have actually met this character, everyone is worried that such a mistake could actually happen, because the LSAT is a single make-or-break event. Couldn't all the hard work and all the good grades be canceled out by a single unavoidable bad performance?

In real life, probably not. The LSAT counts and it is important to do well on it. But it doesn't pose the kind of irrational danger you may think it does. It is extremely unlikely that otherwise well-qualified candidates will have their application status drastically reduced by the LSAT. It is much more likely that their status will be confirmed, or even improved. To understand why this is so, you need to know something about the way the law schools use the test.

The Purpose of the LSAT

Remember, the main objective of law schools is to predict which candidates will be able to do law school work. Nowadays, the undergraduate grade-point average is the single best predictor of success in law school. But before World War II, undergraduate courses of study were not standardized and many colleges were not accredited. Grading standards varied widely, so colleges could not reliably be compared with each other. As a result of this variation, undergraduate GPAs were not always dependable predictors of law school success.

For this reason, law schools developed a single standardized test for all applicants to take, on the basis of which they could be ranked and compared. The LSAT was first used in 1948–49 and has been a routine part of the law school application process since the 1960s. The Law School Admission Council, a nonprofit association of law schools, later created an organization, the Law School Admission Services, or Law Services (as it is universally known) to administer the LSAT, do research on the application process, and perform a variety of other administrative and statistical chores for the law schools. Law Services claims that the present LSAT measures skills

> . . . that are considered essential for success in law school: the ability to read and comprehend complex texts with accuracy and insight, organize and manage information and draw reasonable inferences from it, reason critically, and analyze and evaluate the reasoning and argument of others.

Law Services has conducted research that demonstrates that the LSAT correlates with and predicts freshman law school grades. The better you do on the LSAT the better you will tend to do in your freshman year of law school.

This correlation is weak, however, and Law Services fills its publications with warnings against overreliance on the test: "The LSAT does not measure every discipline-related skill necessary for academic work, nor does it measure other factors important to academic success . . . [s]cores should be viewed as approximate indicators rather than exact measures of an applicant's abilities."

Moreover, grades have become more useful. Now that undergraduate colleges are all accredited and their programs are nationally standardized, law schools can feel confident that grades earned at one college can be compared (perhaps with a little adjustment) to grades earned at another college. And recent studies have indicated that the undergraduate grade-point average is now a better predictor of law school success than the LSAT.

Why, then, do law schools continue to use the LSAT? There are several answers. One is that "the combination of a student's LSAT scores and undergraduate grade point average yields a better prediction of law school success than either measure when used alone." Law schools combine the two numbers in different ways, most weighing grades more heavily, but a few emphasizing the test. They claim improved predictive power for their admissions formulas when compared with either number used alone.

The gain appears to be small, however, and some law school administrators have questioned whether continued use of the LSAT is worth its cost. They fear that widespread use of cramming and test-preparation courses is reducing the predictive power of the LSAT. And they are sensitive to charges that the LSAT, like all standardized tests, is culturally biased: it is said to favor white, middle-class males, and to work against poorer students, African Americans and members of other minorities who are less familiar with mainstream culture, have less experience with standardized tests, and are less likely to be able to afford the expensive cram courses that might help them catch up.

For all these reasons, many law schools have decreased their reliance on the LSAT (though the trend to do so may have ended). That's good news for students who have, or hope to achieve, good grades. And it should calm some of the fears of students with performance anxiety.

But law schools are unlikely to dispense with the test entirely. To some extent, this is simply a matter of inertia, for all organizations resist change.

But there are other reasons. Some law school administrators fear that in the future the predictive power of grades may decline. They remember the widespread concern over the grade inflation of the 1970s, when all the students at some institutions seemed to earn only As and Bs while the students at other schools approximated the normal distribution, and they fear that the present debate over multiculturalism and decanonization may again lead to widespread disparities between schools. They hesitate to abandon their 45 years of experience with the LSAT (and to disband the organization of testing specialists and administrators that now administers it) when they may need a uniform, reliable predictor in the future.

The most selective of law schools consistently receive applications from thousands of well-qualified applicants each year. They need some way to rank students all of whom have superb grades. For these law schools, the LSAT functions as another hurdle or obstacle, another needle's eye that each candidate has to pass through.

The LSAT can be used for political cover. The exact score that the test provides for each applicant seems mathematically precise, and comparisons on the basis of these exact scores seem more objective and impartial than they actually are. Numbers seem "scientific," and people are more willing to accept decisions made on "scientific" grounds than decisions that are marked by personal discretion. Consider the following hypothetical conversation between the dean of a state-supported law school and an influential state senator whose legislative committee controls the law school budget:

> **SENATOR:** How come you admitted Julia and Mary to your freshman class, and rejected my son Johnny?
>
> **DEAN:** Well, senator, as you can see on this printout, Julia had a 158 LSAT score, Mary had a 157, and your son had only a 156. *I* didn't rank them, the *test* ranked them. . . .

It seems objective. It seems fair. Numbers don't lie . . . right? The test takes the personal element out of the rejection letters. Of course, Law Services keeps insisting that the test isn't capable of such precision, that it should never be used as the sole criterion for the admit/reject decision, and that it "should not be given undue weight solely because its use is convenient." But no bureaucrat readily gives up such a useful shield.

Finally, some supporters of the test have turned the affirmative action argument around, arguing that African Americans and members of other traditionally disfavored minorities are less likely to make good grades, even when they possess considerable ability, either because they face bias or because they suffer from poorer preparation because of bias in the past. If we are to have more minority lawyers, the argument runs, minority prelaws need some way other than grades to demonstrate to law schools that they have the necessary intellectual skills. The LSAT provides such an opportunity.

This is merely a specialized case of a general argument: law schools won't admit an applicant unless he or she provides some effort of law-school related intellectual skills. The more chances a candidate has to do this, the fairer the application process is. As long as the LSAT has some predictive value, eliminating it would make the process less, not more, fair.

How Much Does It Count?

It counts. The LSAT and the GPA are the two "numbers" that determine most law school admissions.

Most law schools are candid about the weight given to these two numbers. Boston University "places primary emphasis on an applicant's undergraduate record and score on the Law School Admission Test," considering other factors "where appropriate." Marquette Law School says that "the two factors which weigh most significantly in the selection process are the academic record and the results of the LSAT. The admissions committee, however, also considers non-numerical factors." All those other "factors"—work experience, letters of recommendation, essays, and so on—only make a difference in marginal or nontypical cases. The University of Illinois Law School makes this point clearly:

> Applications for admission will be evaluated by giving significant and, in many cases, controlling weight to the applicant's undergraduate grade-point average and score on the Law School Admission Test. When examining the applications of applicants *whose grades and test scores do not automatically determine their acceptance or rejection*, the Admission Committee attempts to identify students whose numerical records appear to underpredict their likelihood of success in law school and students whose admission would contribute to the diversity essential in achieving variety and richness in the educational experience. . . . [emphasis added]

But very few law schools are so slavish in their adherence to a numerical formula that they will allow a poor test score to hurt an applicant with good grades. To understand why this is so, you need to know a piece of good news: LSAT scores tend to correlate with grades. That is, if you have good grades you are likely to earn a good LSAT score. For these easy cases, it really doesn't matter which number a law school decides to weigh more heavily. A good test score reinforces the good impression made by a high GPA; conversely, a low test score, added to a low GPA, simply reinforces the conclusion that the candidate doesn't possess the skills necessary for law school.

But what if you are one of the hard cases—if, that is, your grades and LSAT scores point in different directions? If you have good grades and a poor LSAT score, how should the law school evaluate you? Since grades are earned over three or more years and reflect your performance in a variety of situations, as evaluated by a large number of "evaluation monitors" (a fancy word for professors who grade your work), doesn't it make sense to conclude that grades are a more accurate reflection of your intellectual skills than a pencil-and-paper test which is given only once, on a Saturday morning when you may or may not be at your best? Of course it does. Most law schools have drawn this conclusion, and weigh grades more heavily in such a case.

If your grades are poor and your LSAT is significantly better, however, it points to a different conclusion. A low GPA doesn't mean *you don't* have intellectual skills. You can't prove a negative. The low GPA means that you haven't yet demonstrated these skills. There could be some reason for that other than stupidity. The LSAT, with all its weaknesses, is a test, a task, an opportunity for you to demonstrate what you can do. The test is independent of grades in the sense that a high score is evidence that you can do law school work no matter how poor an impression your grades have made. It's a second chance. In such a case, a thoughtful law school admission committee will weigh the test more heavily, especially if you can provide some plausible reason why your grades were low. (I have already mentioned one possible reason: racial prejudice, or the lingering effects of previous racial discrimination.) This is the only practical way for most traditional applicants to compensate for poor undergraduate grades.

When to Take the Test

The LSAT is offered four times a year, on a Monday in June and on Saturdays in early October (or late September), December, and February. Your prelaw adviser will know the exact dates a year or more in advance. You need to register four or five weeks in advance; there is always a deadline, and Law Services charges a late fee (currently $47) if you don't make it. Law Services reports your score about six weeks after you take the test.

Since test preparation courses are designed to work best if they are completed within a few months of the test itself, you should plan on a spring course if you intend to take the June test, a summer course for the October test, and so on. And you'd better start saving your pennies. In 1995–96, the fee for the basic LSAT is $78. There are additional charges for reporting the score. Test-prep courses can cost as much as $800. You will also have to pay for test-prep materials, transportation to the test site, and much, much more.

Law Services recommends that traditional students take the LSAT in June at the end of the junior year. In my experience, this is optimum for almost all traditional students. June is an unhectic time of year and there is little danger of blizzards or hurricanes interfering with travel plans. You will know your score in plenty of time to plan an application strategy, secure application forms, fill them out and mail them by December, to take advantage of the benefits of applying early. You have the October test date in reserve if you need to take the test over, or if you have an illness or accident.

If you can't take the test in June, you should plan on October. You'll still have time to get your applications in the mail by December. But plan carefully; October tends to be a hectic time of the year for college seniors. And there isn't any fallback position.

If you take the test in December, or retake it then after an initial poor showing, your position is, as the military says, deteriorating. You won't know your score until after the first of the year. Therefore, you must choose either to apply to law schools "blind"—and run the risk of applying to schools you won't have the numbers to get into or of not applying to schools that *are* within reach—or else delaying your application. Usually, you will be best off applying blind, but to more schools. You'll have to spend more money in application fees, and put in more time filling out application forms.

If you are re-taking the test in December and applying blind, be sure to mark all your application forms HOLD FOR DECEMBER TEST. Otherwise a law school may evaluate you on your earlier (and hopefully poorer) score and reject you without waiting for the results of the retest.

The February test date is little used. It is there mainly for nontraditionals who work on getting into law school over a longer period of time, students with special circumstances, and people who aren't sure they want to go to law school and just want to see how well they can do. February is not a good choice for traditional students, not even for a re-test. Some law schools now refuse to consider applicants who take the test in February for admission the following autumn.

Registering for the LSAT

You need a copy of Law Services' free *Information Book*, which has the necessary registration forms bound inside. Prelaw advisers receive a shipment of these books each year, usually in February or March. They will either have copies on hand or know where on campus they are distributed. College testing centers, continuing education centers, education offices on military bases, graduate school offices, and placement services all often have copies available. Or you can contact Law Services directly, using their automated service number, (215) 968-1001.

Be sure you have the book for the year in which you expect to take the test. An annual book is good for four test dates, beginning in June; the 1997–98 book, for example, is available in March of 1997, and is good for four tests beginning with June of 1997 and ending with February of 1998. There will be a new book, with a different-colored cover, for each subsequent years.

The *Information Book* contains a lot of useful and well-written information about the test and the application process generally. You should read it carefully and keep it for reference. Since it is clearly written, you'll probably find the registration form easy to fill out. Although Law Services periodically sends prelaw advisers booklets with suggested answers to student questions about registration, I find that I get very few such questions. Here are some of the tricky parts:

- *PIN Number.* Law Services wants you to pick a four-digit personal identification number. It will be your password, and you will need it whenever you communicate with them. Whatever number you pick, write it down! If you leave this entry blank, Law Services will assign you a number; it will be sent along with your admission ticket.

- *Ethnic Description.* If you are an African American or a member of another traditionally disadvantaged minority, you ought not to hesitate to identify yourself as such. Because qualified "protected category" law students are much in demand, identifying yourself is much more likely to help, rather than to hinder, your application.

- *Mailing Address.* Law Services will send your score, as well as your ticket, to this address, so be sure that you will still be living there six weeks after you take the test. If you have any uncertainty, put down your parents' address or some other permanent location. If you don't get your score—if, for example, a spiteful ex-lover destroys your mail—there is a procedure for obtaining a replacement. Contact your prelaw adviser.

- **State of Permanent Residence.** If you are a traditional student, this will probably be the location of your parents' home. Law schools and financial institutions may use this address to determine your eligibility for in-state tuition or for certain financial aid programs.

- **Test Center Code.** You must choose where you will take the test. The form has spaces for first and second choices. A list of test sites and their code numbers is found elsewhere in the *Information Book*. If you are a traditional student, you should take the test on your own familiar campus. Your second choice can be the site closest to your parents' home, or some other familiar location. If these options are not available, try to pick locations easily reachable from wherever you are living. You want to avoid a long and exhausting commute before you take a long and exhausting exam.

- **Release of Information.** If you check this box Law Services will make your score available to the prelaw adviser at your home institution. Since you want to work closely with your prelaw adviser throughout the application process, you should check the box. This is especially important if you attend a large, impersonal university where the prelaw adviser may not know you. If you are a nontraditional and you check the box, Law Services will report your score to the prelaw adviser of the college from which you graduated. That prelaw adviser will probably be willing to help you, at least to the extent of answering specific questions, on a time-available basis.

- **LSDAS.** You can sign up for the Law School Data Assembly Service on the same form that you use to register for the LSAT. You should do so if you plan to apply to law school within 12 months of the date that you take the test. You don't need to do anything more than register at this time, and list all the undergraduate, graduate, and professional schools you have attended. Eventually, you'll have to send LSDAS transcripts from each of these schools, which they will summarize and forward to the law schools you apply to. I'll explain how this works in chapter 8.

- **Publications.** You can also use the registration form to get copies of Law Services' publications. If you don't already have one, you should buy a copy of the *Official Guide To Law Schools*. (I'll have more to say about it in the next chapter.) You should also check the box for a free copy of *Financial Aid for Law School* and, if appropriate, *Thinking about Law School: A Minority Guide*. If you decide to prepare for the LSAT on your own, without taking a cram course, you should also buy some of the preparation materials Law Services offers.

- *Fees.*   The application process is not cheap. If nothing else, you can try to avoid that $47 late fee and the fee for changing your test site after you've chosen one. If money is a major problem, read the section in the *Information Book* about fee waivers. The process of applying for a waiver is tedious and requires documentation. And it must be completed nine or ten weeks before the test date. But Law Services will usually honor a legitimate request.

- *Special Arrangements.*   Law Services will make special arrangements for people in remote locations, Saturday Sabbath observers, left-handed persons, and persons with certain handicaps. If you are handicapped, don't be afraid to ask for special consideration (see chapter 13). Allow extra time, because Law Services may require paperwork to document your special needs.

Once you've mailed off the registration form—along with your check—put the *Information Book* in a safe place. You'll need the information about the test and the sample questions when you prepare, and you'll need the various other forms in the book later on in the application process.

Within four weeks of your registration, Law Services will send you an admission ticket. Check it carefully. Make sure that your name is spelled the same way on your ticket as it is on the identification cards in your wallet and that all the descriptive and test center information is accurate. People have been excluded from the test because the information on their tickets was incorrect. Note particularly that Law Services may have changed the location of the test center. If you find errors or have any questions, call Law Services at (215) 968-1001. You should also call if you don't receive your ticket "within four weeks or by the Monday prior to the test date."

Structure of the Test

For all the fear and trembling that it inspires, the test is remarkably banal. The LSAT "consists of five 35-minute sections of multiple choice questions, in three different item [question] types, and one 30-minute writing sample." Four of the five multiple-choice sections are graded, the fifth being used "to pretest new test items and to equate new test forms." The essay, on a topic explicitly stated, is not graded. A copy is sent to each of the law schools you apply to.

The three types of multiple-choice questions are probably all familiar to you from other standardized tests that claim to measure verbal and reasoning skills. The reading comprehension sections require you to read brief paragraphs and then answer questions about what you have read. Various kinds of puzzles and brain-teasers are used to measure analytic and logical reasoning ability.

Preparing for the Test

Until quite recently, test advocates denied that preparation could influence a test taker's score. They claimed that the LSAT measures aptitudes, which are innate and inherited and can't be changed, rather than things that are learned. As evidence to support this claim, they pointed to the fact that most students who retake the LSAT earn scores on the retake that are within a few points of the scores on their first exams.

However, contrary evidence has developed. We now know that any student's standardized test scores tend to correlate; that is, that a student who does well on one standardized test tends to do well on all such tests that he or she takes, regardless of what the tests are supposed to measure. This seems to indicate that tests measure (at least in part) some test-taking skill or talent. If such a skill exists, it should be perfectible through practice, just as a skill for playing the piano or hitting a baseball is perfectible.

Often people who take the test say that specific preparation has been helpful. Students may point to college symbolic logic courses, or math courses with similar content, as being helpful preparation for the questions that are supposed to measure logical reasoning. In my experience, the students who do well on reading comprehension questions tend to have large vocabularies, and no one is born with a large vocabulary. We learn words by reading.

If these suggestions are not enough, prelaw advisers have direct experience of students who improve their scores dramatically if they engage in a systematic course of preparation between a first test and a retest. I often see improvements of as much as 25 percentiles. In recent years, Law Services has been doing its own statistical studies, and it publishes a table listing the fate of "repeaters." Substantial improvement is the exception, but it does occur.

Faced with such evidence, Law Services now grudgingly admits that preparation can sometimes help:

> Because the LSAT does not test specific knowledge attained in course
> work, you cannot "study," in the traditional sense, in preparation for the
> test. However, it is possible to prepare by becoming familiar with the types
> of questions you will encounter on the LSAT. This will help you do your
> best when you take the test.

They now warn that "very few people achieve their full potential without
preparing at all," and they sell their own test-preparation materials.

The private prep courses probably go too far, however, when they
suggest that test scores are simply a function of preparation. They argue
that the more preparation you undertake, the better you will do, implying
that if you work hard enough before the test you will get a perfect score.
In my experience, there seem to be innate limits. Practice can improve an
LSAT score just as it can improve the ability to play the piano: a moder-
ately talented guy can learn to knock out tunes for his friends, and a more
talented person can improve enough to become a professional musician.
But only a few people can perform at the virtuoso level. No matter how
many hours duffers put in at the keyboard, there is a level of skill above
which they will not rise. Still, even though test preparation will not put
everyone in the top five percent of test takers, almost everyone will benefit from test preparation to some degree.

But what is proper preparation? Since the LSAT doesn't test specific
content, your college study skills may not be appropriate. Experts agree
on three points. One, alluded to in the Law Services statement quoted
above, is that familiarization and experience with the kinds of questions
you will be asked, the pencil-and-paper test format, and the time limits
that will be imposed will make it possible for you to do better. There are
strategic considerations for approaching the test as a whole. For example,
since there is no penalty for guessing, you should never leave a question
unanswered. There are also strategies for approaching specific kinds
of questions. For example, the standard reading comprehension "unit,"
which requires you to read a paragraph and answer questions about it, is
best approached by reading the questions first, then reading the paragraph with an eye to seeking the answers. There's a little trick to this; it
takes some experience. But the test-taking skill may amount to nothing
more than habitually using such tricks.

Along these lines, Thomas O. White, one of the developers of the LSAT,
has recently observed that the only skill that such tests reliably measure
is the skill involved in choosing the right answer from among the four
incorrect answers designed to fool you. This skill is unrelated to the

concepts and texts that the LSAT questions purport to be "about." In his thoughtful 1991 book, *Inside the LSAT*, White argues that student preparation should focus on perfecting this question-analyzing skill, and he provides a course of exercises for this purpose.

The second agreed-on point is that performance is improved by practice. Skills are improved by using them. Just as you can't improve your piano playing by reading about the piano or staring at the keyboard or watching somebody else lecture, so you can't improve your test-taking skill except by using it.

The third point is that the value of preparation is partly psychological. Confident students do better. Students who have never taken lengthy exams, have no experience with the kinds of questions used on the LSAT, or who are simply nervous, will improve their self- confidence simply from having practiced and done well on dry runs.

Test Preparation Courses

Proper preparation, then, is preparation that builds on the three principles of familiarization, practice, and psychological boosting. At their best, test preparation courses are taught by specialists in testing who explain the various kinds of questions and suggest strategies for approaching them (familiarization), supply practice material and assign significant amounts of homework (practice), and guide you through increasingly realistic rehearsals or dry runs, with a great deal of attention and praise as your performance improves (boosting). Candidates for prep courses include students

1. with a history of doing poorly on standardized tests, who need to learn the fundamentals of test-taking;

2. who are unfamiliar with the kinds of questions used on the LSAT;

3. who have little self-discipline and can't depend on their own resources to do the necessary practicing; or

4. who have little self-confidence and who will benefit from the psychological boosting.

In my experience, students who benefit the most from prep courses have usually self-identified themselves as members of groups three or four.

Let me add a word about group four: many excellent students are insecure about their abilities. Many such students opt to take a prep course defensively, for no better reason than that they know other students are taking them and they are afraid of being at a competitive disadvantage. I see nothing wrong with this. Granted, it's expensive. You can prepare on your own for a fraction of the cost of a prep course. But psychological preparation is just as valuable as real improvement in technical abilities. If you are an insecure person who worries about things, it's far better to take the course and not really need it than to skip it and spend your time worrying that you have missed something.

A good test prep course will be offered by an experienced outfit. Some are offered by universities themselves. Near Bradley, for example, both Illinois State and Northern Illinois University have offered prep courses. Most courses, however, are now offered by specialized companies that use college classrooms during off-hours and publicize their offerings through college channels. You'll come across solicitations on college bulletin boards or in the school newspaper from a dozen or more competing companies. Sometimes prelaw clubs or prelaw advisers will endorse particular offerings.

Look for a course offered close to home and ending within six weeks or so of the test date you have chosen. A good course will provide ample practice material and be offered on a schedule that will allow you time to do homework and have the homework critiqued by the teacher. Expect to work regularly, an hour or two each evening, for perhaps four evenings a week.

The Stanley H. Kaplan organization, which has a reputation for consistently high quality test preparation (and which, in some years, has claimed to have prepared as many as half of all the candidates who took the LSAT), requires you to attend class for an evening a week for eight weeks. Realistic diagnostic tests are provided at the beginning and end of the program, classes are small, homework is integral, and students are motivated to do the homework by peer pressure and by the knowledge that they won't get their money's worth if they don't practice. Kaplan is a large enough company to arrange for offerings in every part of the country, so there is most likely a Kaplan offering on or near your campus. And their advertising is extensive—some would say omnipresent. You can obtain specific information on offerings by calling them at (800) KAP-TEST or by visiting their homepage, http://www.kaplan.com/etc/lsat/law_index.html.

At the moment, Kaplan's chief competitor is the smaller and newer Princeton Review. Though the two companies are feuding, their offerings are more similar than they are dissimilar. Princeton Review stresses small classes and computerized analysis of performance. It also offers a guarantee of extra help; if you complete the program as required and don't improve, you can repeat the course before you try again. You can reach Princeton Review at (800) 865-7737 or online at http://www.review.com/law/law_homepage.html.

Since the Princeton Review is a smaller and hungrier company, there may be some of the Avis effect: Princeton Review may "try harder" to satisfy customers than the industry-leading Goliath. But in my experience, there is little to choose between these two national competitors. Through the years my students have consistently had good luck with the Kaplan offerings. Since Princeton Review has been available, students have had pretty regular good luck with *their* offerings also.

The two companies have other competitors and, if you live in a large city or attend a large university, you may have a choice of several. Ask older students about their experiences. You can't count on having as good an experience as other students, but you *can* avoid repeating someone else's disaster. Courses that resemble the big two in structure, are offered over several weeks, and provide references are likely to work best. Courses that are offered "intensively" over a single weekend (or even on a single Saturday afternoon) are much cheaper, but have little to recommend them otherwise. Their teachers can provide familiarization with the three question types, but there's no time for practice or for psychological reinforcement. Nor do they provide the regular scheduling that helps students discipline themselves.

Preparing on Your Own

There are no secrets in the test preparation business and you should beware of any company that promises to teach you some unheralded method or system. All any prep course can do is explain the question types, encourage you to practice, and provide positive feedback. You can learn about questions and test-taking strategies from readily available published material, some of it put out by Law Services. And you can buy ample practice material. You can practice on your own if you

- generally do well on standardized tests and have little difficulty mastering new question types;

- are a disciplined person who can stick to a regular practice schedule; and

- have enough self-confidence not to need to take a prep course defensively.

I tell my students to evaluate themselves by working through the practice material provided in the *Information Book*. Do you feel that you understand what each question asks you to do? Did you get most of the question right? Did your performance improve as you became more familiar with the task? If you answer these questions affirmatively, you have probably satisfied the first condition.

Law Services makes available old LSATs; you can order them at the time you sign up for the LSAT, at a cost (in 1995–96) of $6 each or three for $14. The "Triple-Prep Plus" kit contains three tests, explanations, and a set of questions used for the ungraded essay. At the moment, it costs $16. These offerings also include a realistic computer answer sheet that can be photocopied and used over and over.

These old tests are ideal for diagnostic or dry-run purposes. They provide not only questions, but *sections* of questions, enough to be worked against time limits under realistic conditions. But Law Services doesn't provide the masses of questions that you will need for your regular evening practice. For this, you should acquire one or more of the practice books put out by large test-prep companies and available in your college bookstore. Look for books with a recent copyright date, with practice questions that resemble in difficulty those in the *Information Book*. There's no need to confine yourself to a single book. Unlike prep courses, printed materials are quite cheap.

The Black Pearl Company currently offers a course mainly on videotape. "The Advantage: Managing The LSAT" course includes seven-and-a-half hours of videotaped instruction, printed supplements, and three old LSAT tests, of which experts have dissected and analyzed each question. Black Pearl developed the course for universities, and at least 25 have adopted the course and make it available to their students. But Black Pearl also sells the package directly to students. You can contact them at 308 Earles Lane, Newtown Square, PA, 19073, or (800) 854-2111.

This may be a useful option for students at small, isolated campuses who do not have access to a formal prep course, or for people who cannot afford the offerings of the proprietary companies. But note: I include it here under self-preparation. The "Advantage" course doesn't provide formal structure or incentives to practice. You will need the self-discipline to work regularly on your own.

Computerized test-prep materials are now becoming available. Some can be downloaded from college mainframes; others are available on disk. When you work in this way, the computer can keep track of your speed and measure the time elapsed. If you have trouble with a question, you can call up an explanation on the spot. This can be helpful during the early stages of your preparation, when you are mainly working on familiarization and developing the testtaking strategies that you will use. But you should try to do at least some of your practice on pencil and paper. In the last stages of your preparation, you should work as much as possible on realistic answer sheets, against a time limit kept by a timer. The time limit on the real test is intentionally designed to make you hurry. To be successful, you'll have to develop a feel for how much time you can spend on each question. You'll need a rhythm; this is as much a matter of moving your hands on the paper as it is of mental concentration. This rhythm will only develop if you work under realistic pencil-and-paper conditions.

Law Services did a formal statistical study of preparation methods used by candidates who took the LSAT in 1990–91. "The most popular method of preparation," they concluded, "was use of the sample questions in the *Law Services Information Book*, followed closely by a book not published by Law Services and [i.e. in addition to] the sample test." In other words, most candidates prepared on their own. (Commercial test prep courses were used by as many as 40 percent; that option has become more popular since 1990–91.)

Whatever method you choose, you should work at it regularly and diligently. Find a quiet place. (Exception: include a full dry run or two, early on a weekend morning, in a classroom, sitting in an uncomfortable chair.) There's good evidence that noise, and especially rock music, interferes with study, and some evidence that Mozart and similar serious music enhances study. Don't eat or drink while you work; it interferes with the development of the rhythm. Besides, you won't be able to eat during the test. Plan to finish within six weeks of the date that you will take the test. If you have trouble keeping to your schedule, you will have to draw on whatever motivational techniques you've used in the past to stick to a diet or athletic training schedule or to memorize French verbs.

Many students have told me that the practice is much easier if there is someone to share it with. The old training-buddy philosophy is used by many gyms and weight-loss programs. If you have several friends who are taking the LSAT at the same time, you can share the cost of the preparation materials and mutually support each other.

The parallel to athletic training is useful in another respect. Whatever else it is, the LSAT is a morning of grueling physical exertion. Students have compared it to a distance race. You will have to concentrate for more than three hours, with only a brief break. Physical conditioning is valuable. In post-test critiques, some candidates have suggested including a sensible program of aerobic workouts as part of the test prep effort. A twenty-minute jog or swim every other day will help you sleep well during your training.

But we can learn one caution from athletic training as well: you need to avoid overdoing it. If you find yourself exhausted all the time, if you are working practice questions in your dreams, or if your friends complain that you never take a break, you are probably overtraining. If you jog or swim regularly and you find that you are able to do less and less as the test date draws nearer, you should shorten your practice sessions. Don't stop altogether. Just cut back.

Taking the Test

You've heard the advice over and over: get a good night's sleep. Eat breakfast. Wear loose and comfortable clothing and avoid dangling jewelry. Get to the test center early. Try to get a seat out of traffic, out of direct sunlight and not too close to a heating vent. Above all, *don't worry about it!*

All of this is good advice. But if you are a habitual worrier who can't sleep or keep anything down before a test, the advice won't do you any good. By this stage in your life you probably have a routine for dealing with anxiety. You should follow it. Don't make any sudden changes. If you regularly wake up with two cups of coffee, do so on the morning of the LSAT. If you never drink coffee, don't let somebody talk you into starting just before you take the test.

There's one exception to this rule: try to avoid drugs that make you drowsy. In this category are many over-the-counter remedies, including antihistamines, as well as most tranquilizers. If you are taking prescription medication that interferes with your alertness, talk to your doctor well before the LSAT.

If you haven't been able to pick a test center close to home you'll need to plan for a commute. Don't assume that there won't be traffic on a Saturday morning. Allow plenty of time. And think about what you'll do if your car won't start. Consider carpooling with friends or using public transportation. If the commute must be a long one, consider traveling to the test site the night before and sleeping over. But beware: if this means that you'll stay with a friend you haven't seen for months, you'll have to find some way to avoid staying up all night and talking.

The proctors will not admit you to the test center without the ticket that Law Services sent you when you registered. (If you registered late you will have an "alternative authorization," perhaps a telegram, that is the equivalent of a ticket.) Law Services also requires one form of identification, preferably with a photo, "positive or descriptive enough so that the test center supervisor has no doubt as to the authenticity of your identification." They suggest a driver's licence, student ID, employee ID, or current passport; they will not accept a social security card or credit card.

The proctors may assign you to a seat. Though you can't choose for yourself, you may be able to make a tactful adjustment if you arrive early, before the test center fills up. If you are allowed to choose, look for a well-lit corner.

Law Services wants you to bring several number 2 pencils and a good eraser. Don't plan on sharpening pencils; there won't be time. Instead, carry a mechanical pencil or two as a backup, the kind that has continuously-feeding lead. It doesn't work as well as a good, sharp wooden pencil. But the point won't break and leave you weaponless. The proctors may supply special pens for the essay part (perhaps so they can be sure that you actually wrote it during the time allowed) but you will not be able to use these pens for the multiple choice sections. You may want to bring candy, gum, or antacids with you. Except for a coughdrop if you are coughing loudly enough to be annoying, they won't let you eat during the test itself. But there will be a break near the halfway point. Bring a wristwatch or clock, but be sure it is noiseless. Proctors are authorized to exclude beeping or clanging timepieces.

Avoid bringing anything else, especially items of value. The proctors will probably make you leave any bulky items outside. You don't want to spoil your concentration by worrying about having your property stepped on or stolen.

Here are some miscellaneous test-taking tips:

- Settle into your rhythm and try to stay in it.

- Never answer from your own knowledge or experience. Some questions may include, as attractive wrong answers, choices that appear to be politically correct or desirable.

- Read all the choices before answering a multiple-choice question.

- If an answer appears to be correct with qualifications, it is wrong.

- Keep an eye on the answer sheet. Every five questions, scan up the column to make sure that the previous four lines each contain one, and only one, marked circle.

- If you first write the answer on the test booklet, next to the question number, and then transfer the answer to the answer sheet, you will minimize the chances of writing the answer on the wrong line.

- Try not to make any stray marks on the answer sheet. You won't have time to erase them.

You've probably come across these tips while practicing. The proctors will announce the time five minutes before the end of each section. Don't panic if you aren't able to get every question fully reasoned out before you run out of time. But reserve a half-minute or so to guess, or to fill in at random the answer lines for the questions you haven't had time to finish. You should never leave a question unanswered.

During the break, get up and move around. Do stretching exercises or climb a few flights of stairs. Sip a little coffee or soda, but don't gulp down barrels of fluids. And take the advice of the late Duke of Windsor and never pass up a chance to use the bathroom.

A Word on Cheating

Bradley's testing center personnel, who administer the LSAT on our campus, tell me that of all the outfits that offer standardized testing, Law Services is by far the most security conscious. They have very elaborate rules (summarized in the *Information Book*) and may require, among other things, thumbprints and signatures. In fact, they warn that security procedures may double the time you will have to spend at the test site. *Don't mess with the security rules!* Don't talk back to the proctors, don't argue, and don't make jokes. They have the power to kick you out.

In recent years, testing companies have become increasingly worried about cheating. (Rumors of security problems may explain why they have not progressed much toward their eventual goal of replacing all paper-and-pencil tests with more sophisticated, but more vulnerable, computerized versions.) The number of cases that Law Services investigated for "misconduct" rose to 132 in 1993, from 70 in 1992, 31 in 1991, and 19 in 1990. As a result, proctors have been given increased training in detecting and processing cheaters. Law Services may also try to detect cheating by analyzing exam papers themselves.

Law Services' statement on misconduct is printed in the *Information Book*. If a determination is made, after due process, that you have been cheating, then Law Services will report that fact to any law school that you apply to—forever. It is highly unlikely that any law school will admit you under such circumstances.

Reports

Law Services will send you a "candidate report" within six weeks, under normal circumstances. If the report is late, it may mean that Law Services has placed a hold on your file; this, in turn, may mean that you are suspected of cheating. But it probably doesn't. Most delays are caused by routine administrative problems.

The candidate report contains a copy of your machine-graded answer sheet, a list of your responses taken from this answer sheet, and a list of the correct (or "credited") answer for each question. *Check each of the questions marked wrong* to make sure that the answer the machine recorded for you is actually the one that you marked on your answer sheet. Mistakes have been made. If the computer graded you incorrectly, you need to contact Law Services within 90 days, following the procedure described in the *Information Book*.

You have the right to challenge a question that seems to contain an "error or ambiguity . . . that affects your response." Law Services has developed an arbitration procedure to deal with challenged questions. You must call the attention of the test center supervisor to the challenged item as soon as you finish the test, and then write immediately to Law Services, Test Development and Research Division, Box 40, 661 Penn St., Newtown, PA, 18940-0040, identifying the question by section and number, and explaining in detail why you believe there is an error.

Most challenges are found to be without merit. For this reason, and because the test requires concentration and rhythm, you shouldn't waste time during the test itself looking for ambiguities to challenge. But if you have what you think is a legitimate gripe, don't hesitate to call it to the attention of the test supervisor. Challenges have occasionally been upheld. Law Services excluded one question judged "unsound" and re-scored the September, 1989, test. As a result, the scores of about 15 percent of the testtakers were raised by one point each. This represents a significant improvement.

If You Did Worse Than Expected . . .

If you leave the test site knowing that your performance was a disaster, you have the option of requesting that your exam not be scored. About eight percent of test takers ask to have their scores cancelled in this way. You can do this in one of three ways. Within five working days, you can write, FAX or overnight-express a letter to Law Services, *ATTN:* Score Cancellation, Box 2000-T, 661 Penn St., Newtown, PA, 18940-0995, including your name, address, social security number, or nine-digit Law Services identification number, the test date, test center code (from the *Information Book*) and address, and a statement that you want your score cancelled. The test center supervisor will give you a form that you can use instead of a letter for this purpose, but you must still send it to Law Services on your own.

Or you can cancel by filling out a box on the answer sheet itself before you turn in your paper. This is certainly easier, and saves postage. But canceling at this time may be a panic response, and any request to cancel, once made, is irrevocable. For this reason, I recommend that you not cancel on the test form. Instead, you should go home and think about it.

If you cancel, your paper will not be graded and you will never know how well you actually did. And you will have wasted the cost and trouble; you'll have to do it all over again. Since, in my experience, worried test-takers often can't predict how well they actually did, you should cancel only if you are sure that your performance was a disaster. If you froze and left most of the questions unanswered, then you are in this category. So is the apocryphal Sad Sack I mentioned earlier who messed up the answer sheet. Otherwise, you are best off letting the test be scored.

If you don't request cancellation in one of these three ways, your grade will be recorded. It can never afterward be expunged. Even if you take the test over, your second score will not replace the first. Law Services will report all the scores you earned within the last five years to every law school you apply to.

Even if you did very poorly, you ought not to rush into taking the test over. You're in the position of a poker player who has to decide whether drawing a card will improve his hand. Above all, you don't want to weaken your position. You are likely to do better the second time you take the test. Few do worse. But according to Law Services, you are unlikely to do very much better. (A table summarizing the fate of "repeaters" is in the *Information Book*.) Law Services says that

... research indicates that when an applicant has taken the LSAT more than once, the average of the scores has more predictive validity than any one of the scores *unless special circumstances are present.* Otherwise, a decision to use one of the separate scores rather than the average is probably unwise. [Emphasis in original]

If the two scores are close together, this is what the law schools will do. The second test will simply confirm the conclusion of the first that your abilities were properly measured, that they lie roughly in this range, and that the test is therefore a good predictor of your likely success in law school. If you score at the fortieth percentile the first time, and the forty-second percentile the second time, you've just confirmed the conclusion that your abilities lie in this range, distinctly below average. At all costs, you want to avoid giving this impression.

However, if the two scores differ markedly—if, for example, the second score moves you from the fortieth to the sixtieth percentile—then law schools will probably assume that special circumstances were present, that there was some problem or handicap that kept you from doing well the first time, and that the second test score better captures your abilities. So one variable to consider is whether or not you are likely to do signifi-cantly better the second time.

How realistic is it to assume that you can make this improvement? Think back to the day of the test, and ask yourself the following questions:

- Was I sick during the test? Was I feverish, fuzzy-minded, or fum-bling with Kleenex and coughdrops?

- Was I off my stride because of antihistamines or other drugs?

- Was I exhausted?

- Was I under some unusual emotional strain?

- Did I have some mechanical problem? (One student had to work with a torn muscle in his right arm and wound up doing much of the test left-handed.)

- Were there distractions in the test room?

- Did I leave a lot of questions unanswered?

- Was there one kind of question I just didn't understand?

- Did I need a lot of time to decipher the questions before I began to write?

- Did I do less preparation than my friends?

- Is there some form of useful preparation that I didn't do this time, that I could do before a retest?

You should conclude that the first test will approximate your retest score unless you can honestly answer yes to some of these questions, or know of some other tangible, specific reason why it does not represent your best effort. Be honest with yourself. Your test score won't improve by magic.

But it may improve if you can identify some specific problem and fix it. If you suffered from a lack of preparation, then you have to prepare. If your problem was caused by fatigue, or strain, or worry, then you will have to deal with these things before a retest. If you can do so, there is a good chance of substantial improvement. And you should approach the retest in a positive state of mind. After all, the flu is unlikely to strike twice, the mate whose infidelity was wrecking your concentration is unlikely to be around, and the poor initial showing should help you discipline yourself to practice.

But what if you can't point to some specific problem that affected your test performance? In this case, whether you should take the test over depends on how damning the first performance actually was. This, in turn, will depend on your overall application position.

At one extreme are the candidates whose scores are absolute disasters— typically at the twentieth percentile or below. If you are in this group, your options will narrow drastically. If your grades are very good—that is, if you have the 3.7 GPA normally needed for a top law school—then you may be able to get into a less selective school on grades alone. If you are willing to step down, your prelaw adviser can help you put together an application list of law schools that de-emphasize the test.

But few students have this option. Because grades and test scores correlate, most students with poor LSAT scores have poor grades as well. If you are in this category, you have no choice. You must take the test over, and you must do significantly better, or you won't be able to go to law school at all.

At the other extreme there are students who have the grades for a top law school but whose test scores, though good, aren't quite high enough. They're at, say, the sixtieth percentile instead of the eighty-fifth or ninetieth percentile. The choice here is to take the test over, hoping for the rise of a few points needed to catch on at Harvard or Yale, or to stand pat and step down to a less selective law school.

In such cases, I usually recommend taking the test over—but only if the student's record is truly outstanding otherwise. A retest could result in one of three outcomes:

- The student improves enough to catch Harvard's eye.

- The student scores roughly the same as on the first try, leaving him law-school bound, but to a less selective school. Thus, he remains where he would have been had he not taken the retest.

- The student does significantly worse. This is unlikely. But even so, his good grades should get him in somewhere.

Such a student can't lose by taking a retest.

These are the extremes. But most of the students who ask me about retests aren't at the extremes. They're in the middle. They have marginal grades and their test scores are also marginal. They didn't feel particularly confident while they were taking the test . . . but no, they can't point to specific reasons for not doing their best. An improvement in the test score may make the difference between admission and rejection. But spending more time on grades, or choosing schools to apply to more carefully, may be better uses for the available time.

Marginal candidates will have to make judgment calls. I always tell them to reassess their overall application positions. When law schools consider marginal candidates they consider such other variables as letters of recommendation, essays, work experience, and personal background. If an applicant is strong in the "other qualifications" category, he or she may well be accepted with a lower LSAT score. Some law schools consider favorably a candidate whose grades improved substantially over time, even if the overall GPA is still relatively low.

I'll be discussing these variables in later chapters. If you re a marginal applicant, you should consider them before deciding whether to retake the LSAT. And you should speak to your prelaw adviser, to try to get a feel for how particular law schools will view your record.

If you decide to retake the test, what I said above still goes: practice, be prepared, and do your damnedest. If you decide not to retake the test, you will need to strengthen whatever other aspects of your record can be strengthened. I advise students to try to get a single straight-A semester: a record of four or five A's, a 4.0. Then you can write something like this on your law school applications:

> I know my LSAT score is rather low. I do poorly on standardized tests. But please consider my record this _____ semester. These grades are what I'm capable of.

You've given the law schools something to look at, an accomplishment that signals an ability to do law school work. That may distract the admission committee from your slightly-too-low test score. It won't get you into Harvard. But it may be the best way to play a marginal hand.

5

Making Your List:
Getting Information

There are 178 ABA-accredited law schools. You could theoretically maximize your chances of acceptance by applying to all of them. But each one requires you to pay an application fee, fill out a time-consuming application form, and file letters of recommendation and other supporting documents. Even if you have the money, there isn't time to apply to all of them.

Nor should you. My own personal recordholder is the young woman who applied to about 35 law schools in 1990–91. She was accepted by about twenty of them. All she accomplished with all this effort and expense was to postpone the hard decision—the choice of which school to attend—from before she applied to afterward. You'll need to apply to more than one law school, and later on I'll give you some tips on deciding how many. But competitive applicants don't have to apply to more than 15 properly chosen schools. The key phrase in that sentence is "properly chosen"; the only way to get accepted to the right law school for you is to make sure that all of the schools on your application list offer the qualities and programs you're seeking, together with a reasonable chance of acceptance. In Chapters 6 and 7, I'll list some of the things you should consider when you put together your application list.

To make a proper list, you'll need information: about the size, location, and programs of each of the law schools you're considering; about how selective each one is, about how students live on each of the campuses; and about how successful each one is in placing its graduates. This information isn't available in any single location. It's scattered among many published sources and informants. You'll have to collect it. You can find some of it in commonly available books, but you'll also have to dig information out of the minds of law students, lawyers, prelaw advisers, law school representatives, and other informants.

Since you need to collect a lot of information, you'll have to work at it systematically. Many traditional applicants devote their junior years, or the summer between their junior and senior years, to this task. This is an ideal time to visit at least some of the law schools you're considering. But you shouldn't postpone gathering information until the end of your college years. Unique sources pop up at unexpected times. Every time you meet a law student or attend a lecture given by a lawyer, you have an opportunity to learn something about law schools. It's never too soon to begin. You can work at gathering information all through your college years. If you have friends who are also planning to go to law school, or if you're a member of a prelaw club, you can divide the workload and collect information together.

You will need some way to keep track of it all. The most organized student I know bought a special notebook during his freshman year and carried it with him at all times. Whenever he heard something about a law school, he wrote it down. After he outgrew the first notebook, he bought a loose-leaf binder and organized his information by school. To this scrapbook, he added information from publications. Every few months he spent an evening cross-referencing it. By the time he applied to law school, he had six fat binders full of data. When he graduated, he passed his files on to younger friends. You don't need to be as thoroughly organized—or as compulsive—as this young man. But if you can develop some system to keep track of and share the information you gather, you will find it much easier to choose the right law schools when the time comes.

What follows in this chapter is a list of various readily available sources, in no particular order, and a description of what, in my experience, you can expect to learn from each. No single source will provide all the information you'll need. And each source has its blind spots and pitfalls, its distortions and deliberate omissions. Actually, the task of collecting and sorting out all this information is good training in reading systematically and thinking critically!

Screening Publications

Since there are 178 schools to be researched, you'll find it handy to have a single source that provides thumbnail sketches of each of them and is arranged to make comparison easy. The best single browsing source is *The Official Guide To U.S. Law Schools*, which is put out annually by Law Services itself "in cooperation with the American Bar Association and the Association of American Law Schools." The *Official Guide*, as I'll refer to it, is the horse's mouth of information about law schools. It contains a two-page article on each accredited law school, covering such topics as facilities, admissions policy, programs of study, joint degrees and other specialized programs, student activities, profiles of students currently enrolled, expenses and financial aid, housing, and placement. The *Official Guide* provides a mailing address and telephone number for the admissions office of each school. In tabular form, it compares schools, state by state, on such variables as the size of the student body and the faculty, and the number of books in the library. Finally, and most important, for most of the schools it discusses, the *Official Guide* provides information about the LSAT scores and GPAs of students recently admitted; this information, usually presented in graphs called "grids," can be used to calculate your chances of getting accepted. I'll explain how to use these grids in Chapter 6.

The *Official Guide* is the handiest browsing source I know. It provides a quick way to skim through the attributes of many law schools. But a word of caution: the information is provided by the law schools themselves. It's "official" information in that it is what the law schools want you to know. As I'll explain in Chapter 6, the grids may overstate the qualifications of the students. And you won't read about any weak spots in the curriculum.

With this cautionary note, the *Official Guide* is invaluable. You can begin by browsing in the library's copy, but a new edition is published each year and when you get down to serious planning you will need an up-to-date copy of your own. You may find it in some college bookstores or you can order it from Law Services. You can check the box on the registration form for the LSAT, as I described in Chapter 4. Or you can get a Law Services Information Book from your prelaw adviser and send the publications form, with a check, to Law Services, Box 2400, 661 Penn Street, Newtown, PA, 18940-0977; if you have a major credit card, you can call (215) 968-1001. The 1996 edition was $15.

Barron's Guide To Law Schools covers much of the same ground as the *Official Guide*. Here, too, you will find brief profiles of all the accredited schools, and here, too, are handy comparison tables. *Barron's Guide* contains some information not in the *Official Guide*; for example, it has a comparison table listing the proportion of women in each law school's student body. Because the information has been edited by Barron's researchers instead of simply being supplied by the law schools, you may find the entries more clearly written and candid. *Barron's Guide* also includes information on the LSAT and a sample test, as well as numerous tips on the applications process. Unlike the *Official Guide, Barron's Guide* is available at most shopping-mall bookstores. But *Barron's Guide* is not revised annually and may not be as up-to-date. Moreover, *Barron's Guide* doesn't contain the invaluable admission grids. It's a useful screening document and supplement, but again, when you get down to detailed planning you will need the *Official Guide*.

Since 1993 the Princeton Review has put out the *Student Access Guide to the Best Law Schools*. A new edition is available each fall. The book includes brief profiles of 170 law schools, in addition to a mass of useful information about the LSAT, law school curriculums, the admissions process, financial aid, and similar matters. Some of the information comes from the law schools themselves. Information is also gathered from surveys of administrators and law students. Princeton Review makes an attempt to identify the best and worst schools on such criteria as quality of life and quality of teaching. Since the book is published by Random House, it should be widely available in bookstores. The cost in 1996 was $20.

Your prelaw adviser may have a set of "Profiles" software prepared by the Midwest Association of Prelaw Advisers, or MAPLA. "Profiles" is a database with fairly extensive narrative descriptions of law schools; the data includes information on faculty, student qualifications, journals, minority programs, placement, and so on. The database can be searched to print profiles of individual schools or lists of schools based on special programs, joint degrees, geographic region, class sizes, tuition level, and the like. MAPLA profiles is available for purchase in Windows application only; it can be purchased directly from Micron Systems Corp., ATTN: MAPLA Profiles Software, Box 605, Washington Crossing, PA, 18977, or 1- 800-784-0033 with a major credit card. In 1996, the direct sale price was $35.

The American Bar Association publishes an annual survey of its own, *A Review Of Legal Education In The United States*: Law Schools And Bar Admission Requirements. Single copies are currently free from the American Bar Association Section on Legal Education, 750 North Lake Shore Drive, Chicago, IL, 60611. It contains statistical information about law schools in tabular form: student enrollment numbers, faculty size, tuition, library size, and availability of part-time and joint degree programs. Most, if not all, of this information is available in the two publications I've described above. The *Review's* unique value is to law students, not prelaws, because it gives details of bar admission requirements.

Law Schools Online

The screening documents provide thumbnail sketches of many law schools arranged for easy, if superficial, comparison. But how do you get details about the offerings of any one law school?

At present, law schools are moving rapidly into the world of the Internet. Many have established homepages on the World Wide Web, though some of these pages are still "under construction." More law schools are expected to do so in the future. Typically, the homepages list the kinds of information available in the printed catalog; some also have lists of current events on campus. Many homepages have links that allow you to communicate directly with a law school representative, or to order printed catalogs and application forms.

Your computer can be a good place to start your research on particular schools, but, as is generally true of the Internet, it can be difficult to find the necessary information. Because the electronic world is changing so rapidly, I can't give you any firm research guidelines here. At the moment, many law school homepages are accessible through the Yahoo directory (http://www.yahoo.com) under the heading "government/law/law_schools/ LSAC_ member." About 65 are listed there. (This directory also lists three Canadian law schools and at least one training program for paralegals.)

Typically, a law school's homepage is accessible through the homepage of the larger university of which it is a part. You can look for the University of Pennsylvania, for example, not the University of Pennsylvania Law School. If you search in this way, you will be able to collect information on the university as a whole—its programs, resources, and student life— as well as on the law school itself. The Yahoo search directory lists universities in alphabetical order under the index headings "Education/ Universities—U.S." The World Wide Web Servers directory lists universities regionally, grouped by state. In either case, once you have keyed in to the university's homepage, look for a link to the constituent colleges, or to programs.

What You Can Learn from Catalogs

To get a full picture of any law school, you will have to consult its catalog or bulletin. Your campus probably maintains collections of old catalogs, and prelaw advisers sometimes keep catalogs in their offices. Here at Bradley the political science club maintains a collection and the library has a set on microfiche. Fraternities and sororities often have collections as well. You can use these reference sources for browsing, but many law schools are changing rapidly. If you're serious about a school, you should obtain a copy of its current catalog. You can call, e-mail, or write to the address for the school's admissions office given in the *Official Guide*, or to the address printed on the school's advertising poster on your prelaw adviser's bulletin board. If the school has a poster, you can often save a few pennies by using the postage-paid postcards stapled to it. And you can sometimes order a catalog directly online, through a link on the law school's homepage.

Allow two or three weeks if you call, six weeks if you write. If the catalog hasn't arrived and you haven't gotten a postcard saying that you'll get one as soon as new ones are printed, write or call again. Law school admissions offices are more efficient than they used to be, but requests for publications can still sometimes get lost.

The catalog is the absolute authority for the school's admission requirements, deadlines, fees, courses of study and graduation requirements, course offerings, academic policies, and similar rules. Some catalogs are very soberly printed in black and white typeface, to encourage you to think of them as contracts specifying what you'll have to do as a law student. Law schools provide many pages of detailed information on the qualifications and activities of their faculties, their unique special programs, and their physical facilities and resources. Application forms will be bound in them or mailed in the same envelope. Catalogs are also a form of advertising. Many are now printed on slick paper, awash with color photos of gleaming modern buildings, smiling happy students, and the marvels of local scenery. At professional meetings, prelaw advisers sometimes make jokes about catalogs that appear to be designed by the same people who do the brochures for tourist sites, retirement condominiums, and investment real estate.

That doesn't mean that the information inside is incorrect. It will always be factually accurate, especially on curriculum requirements. But it's what the law school wants you to know, presented in the most attractive way. On student life, catalogs are often, shall we say, rosy. If you see a photo of students frolicking in a pool, you can assume that there will actually be a pool there. But you can't assume that as a law student you'll have much time to swim in it. Similarly, catalogs simply leave out what is unattractive. You can't go to them to determine whether student life is stressful because class instruction emphasizes pressure. Nor will the catalog tell you if the campus has a parking problem, or a crime problem, or if there's poor morale among the faculty.

Other Law School Publications

Law schools sometimes publish leaflets, brochures, and even videotapes. Like the catalogs, these specialized materials are combinations of information and promotion. Some of them are pure advertising fluff; one recent promotional videotape I received alternates attractive shots of the cityscape around the law school with interviews with sweatshirt-clad law students earnestly explaining how much the faculty cares, really *cares* about them. I'm not sure what you can learn from such things, although the pictures are attractive and the soundtrack contains very upbeat music.

The leaflets and brochures may also describe special programs and facilities not fully discussed in the catalogs. Many law schools have special brochures on financial aid, minority programs, and similar matters that are not of concern to all applicants. As with catalogs, the leaflets will be factually accurate but won't dwell on the school's shortcomings. (One law school takes great pride in pointing out that its new building, which houses classrooms and libraries, is fully wheelchair-accessible. But it doesn't mention that the cafeteria, which is in a separate, older, building, is accessible only with difficulty.)

Sometimes law schools send bunches of these specialized brochures along with their catalogs. To be sure that you will get everything you need, you should mention any special needs or interests when you order the catalog.

Law schools also publish newsletters and magazines directed at alumni and philanthropic organizations; these often discuss recent campus activities, awards and honors won by faculty members, and notable achievements of students. You may occasionally come across otherwise obscure information. In one issue of *Southwestern Law*, the demographic profile of Southwestern University Law School's most recent freshman class, details of minority enrollment, and recent bar exam success rates, can be found hidden among reports on alumni association activities, profiles of photogenic students, and annual fund drive reports. Valparaiso

Law School's newsletter sometimes contains a discussion of campus placement activities. Many law schools have been opening new buildings recently; they are often extensively photographed and described in alumni publications.

Don't be overly impressed by a newsletter's reports of the achievements of faculty and students. All law schools can point to a record of accomplishment and you don't yet have the knowledge to tell which honors and distinctions are important and which are not. Nevertheless, the newsletters can give you an idea of what, and how much, is going on on campus. In my experience, newsletters are especially valuable for their discussion of clinical programs, moot courts, and similar student activities.

If you show an interest in some law schools, they will put you on their mailing list, and you will receive these newsletters in the mail. If you have friends or relatives who are attorneys, ask them to pass along any newsletters they may receive.

Formal Classes

Some colleges offer for-credit classes in subjects relating to legal practice. Bradley, for example, has offered a class in law as a career for three semester hours of political science credit.

Of more immediate value, some campuses have not-for-credit courses in such useful subjects as résumé-writing, preparing for job interviews, dressing for success, and the like. Although these courses are most useful to students seeking jobs with large corporations, much of what you will have to do to get into law school is similar.

These career courses are often taught by adjunct professionals—that is, by working lawyers or business professionals who teach part-time. Or they are taught by regular faculty members but enriched with guest speakers who work in law or business. Some of these courses will give you an opportunity to talk to young lawyers who can answer your career-related questions.

Law Students and Lawyers

Just as with buying a new car, word of mouth is important. You should never pass up an opportunity to talk to someone who has been there.

If you have friends or relatives who are lawyers or law students, you are ahead of the game. If you are a member of a social fraternity or sorority, try to keep in touch with alumni members. Phi Alpha Delta social events are excellent places to network. If you're a nontraditional applicant and somewhat older, you have an advantage: you will be able to approach lawyers as generational equals, perhaps at your place of business, at church, or at voluntary groups that you belong to. If you have such contacts, you're in a position to create your own advisory board and return to the same experts whenever questions arise. Like most people, lawyers and law students will be most candid when speaking informally to people they know well.

Prelaw clubs and prelaw advisers often maintain mailing lists of recent alumni and may arrange panel discussions to bring them to campus. When I asked the members of Bradley's prelaw club which of their activities in the past year they found the most valuable, they overwhelmingly mentioned an evening program that brought four law students to campus to talk about their experiences in law school. If you hear about such a program, you should take advantage of the opportunity to listen to the speakers and ask questions.

Law students can speak with authority about prelaw education. Students who are alumni of your own undergraduate college can discuss which courses they found especially helpful when they got to law school, or which courses they wish they had taken—or wish they had studied harder in.

Law students can't always tell if they're receiving a good legal education, but they are well placed to know if they're getting a bad education. If classes are overcrowded, if there aren't enough books in the library, or if there is excessive pressure and competition, law students will know it. If a law school claims expertise in some specialty but actually offers very few courses in it, law students will know, and will be angry.

Law students are also the absolute experts on living conditions at their law schools. They know from personal experience whether it's possible to rent a reasonably priced apartment, whether the campus has a parking problem, or whether the fear of street crime keeps women students from going to the library after dark. If you encourage law students to talk about their experiences, this kind of information will emerge. But be careful: a certain amount of grumbling is normal and healthy, and a lot of the things that law students complain about are either unimportant (poor food in the cafeteria) or not really defects (great masses of homework; demanding professors with high standards).

Don't expect law students to know much about law schools other than their own. Some law students travel and some meet students from other schools, for example in moot court competitions. And I know of one law student who had two siblings who had attended two other law schools and for whom comparative law school one-upmanship was a staple topic of family conversations. But these are the exceptions. Most students have little contact with law schools other than their own. When asked, they tend to rely on the same rumor and hearsay that everyone else relies on.

Young lawyers can also talk with authority about these things. They may also be in a position to compare the quality of law schools, because they work with other lawyers who have come from many different schools and they soon learn which of them have had high-quality educations. Finally, young lawyers can talk about their experiences in legal practice. Ask them to speak about their specialties and whether they feel that their educations properly prepared them for the work they are doing.

Older lawyers are excellent sources of information about different kinds of legal practice and about the institutional and social aspects of professional life. Most belong to professional and political organizations. Many keep in touch with their legal alma maters and become involved in recruiting and promotional efforts. They may be able to tell you whom to contact in the admissions office, or introduce you to other lawyers who have even more information about a given school. But don't rely on older lawyers' memories to learn what it's like to study law. Law schools have changed dramatically in the past 20 years.

Because so much information on law schools is subjective, you should avoid giving undue weight to any one informant. You ought not to apply to a law school just because you were impressed with one of its alumni; conversely, you shouldn't shun a school simply because a student grumbled about his living conditions. The key here is to try to talk to as many people as you can. If you are in a position to gather information over a long period of time, you will find it possible to talk to many.

Once you begin collecting information systematically, you will probably find that much of it comes from law school recruiters.

Recruiters and Where to Meet Them

Most law schools have people on their staffs whose job it is to publicize the school's good points, hand out publications, answer your questions, and encourage you to apply. These representatives may be law professors, or even currently enrolled law students who receive law school funds to travel to their alma maters for the hometown law school fair. Usually, however, they are full-time professionals specializing in enrollment management. Their formal titles vary; I will refer to them as recruiters, representatives, or reps.

Law schools *want* you to talk to their reps. Reps will often come directly to your campus; last year, 15 came to Bradley. The prelaw adviser, the prelaw club, or the placement center will maintain a calendar and arrange for reps to speak to interested students. At Bradley, we try to provide a quiet lounge for an hour or two on a Wednesday or Thursday afternoon (a time when most students are free); students can come in and ask the rep questions individually or in small groups.

Reps are available at the annual open houses that many law schools hold, and they also attend college and university law school fairs. Larger universities typically attract more recruiters, although as many as 20 have attended Bradley's small September fair. Most of the reps at a campus fair come from law schools in the region. (If there's a recruiter from a school far out of the immediate area, a school that your prelaw adviser tells you has not drawn any of your college's graduates in recent years, he is probably there because that law school is trying to increase its geographic diversity by enrolling more students from your region. Your application may be viewed unusually favorably at such a school.)

If your campus does not hold a law school fair, ask your prelaw adviser about neighboring campuses. Law Services sends prelaw advisers an annual *Recruitment Calendar*; though it's admittedly incomplete, the 1995–96 edition lists almost 150 events. If you are a nontraditional student, ask the prelaw adviser at your alma mater, or at the nearest university, when the fair will be held. No one will object if you come and ask a few questions.

You can also speak to reps at one of the national law school forums that the Law School Admission Council sponsors each year. In 1995–96, forums were held in Atlanta, Boston, Chicago, Houston, Los Angeles, and New York. As opposed to campus fairs, which tend to be regional, the forums are of national scope. Representatives of 100 or more law schools are typically on hand.

Reps like to talk about the strong points of their schools and are knowledgeable about course offerings, special programs, unusually good faculty members, and similar details. If they're astute, they will know something about their students, especially those who are alumni of your college. (I often learn about my former advisees from law school reps.) They may have promotional videotapes and other advertising materials to show you, and usually bring catalogs and other publications with them.

Many have been trained to emphasize one or two things that distinguish their law schools from other law schools; therefore, they can often discuss truly unique educational programs. A rep can explain what you'll be studying if you want to specialize in, say, environmental protection law, and how his or her school differs from other schools with this emphasis. He or she can also tell you how many students take this option and what kind of placement history they have. Catalogs are often vague about such details.

You'll get the most useful information if you do some preparation before the interview. If you can say, "Your catalog said you specialize in environmental law, but you have fewer courses in it than ____ law school," you'll get more specific information than if you just say, "Uh, does your school have environmental law?" Reps have told me that they're more likely to be candid when they're talking to people who have demonstrated an interest in their schools by having done research.

Reps can also discuss student life, including such details as class size, financial aid, and the availability of housing. But remember, the rep is not an impartial informant. Reps work for law schools and their job is to try to present their schools in the best light. They will not volunteer details of the campus's crime problem or parking problem. If you tactfully ask a rep direct questions about such things, you will probably get honest but vague answers. Similarly, don't expect definitive answers about your chances of admission. If you explain your status and grades to a rep and are discouraged from applying—if, for example, the rep gently suggests that you take extra coursework or graduate work to improve your grades before you apply—then you can assume that your chance of admission isn't very good. But the reverse isn't true. If you are encouraged to apply, don't assume that you are assured of acceptance. It's part of the rep's job to encourage you to apply. Law schools like to have the luxury of a large applicant pool from which they can choose the best-qualified students with the maximum geographic and ethnic diversity. Unless your application status is hopeless, the rep wants to put you in this pool.

Whenever you talk to a recruiter, you will be asked to put your name and address on a list or to fill out a card. You may observe the recruiter taking notes about your conversation. Don't panic. This does not mean that your interview is part of the application process or that it will "count" in any way. The rep is going to put you on a mailing list for follow-up contact; if you've asked detailed questions you can expect to get more information in the mail (perhaps some of those specialized brochures I mentioned above) or a letter from a specialized rep, such as a minority group adviser. The rep also monitors his or her own performance by keeping track of what kinds of questions students ask. If people keep asking the same question—perhaps, for example, about the incidence of date rape on campus—the existence of widespread concern will be reported to the rep's superiors.

However, you shouldn't assume that you can be sloppy because the interview doesn't "count." Reps always note their impressions of the people they talk to. If you are really obnoxious, it will be remembered, and may even be mentioned to someone whose opinion really does count. Law schools are small organizations. Their employees all talk to each other. Truly shocking or humorous details may make their way to professors who sit on the admissions committee, and you don't want to become famous as the kid at the recruiting luncheon whose idea of humor was to make mashed potatoes come out of his nose. Whenever you speak to any law school employee, you should be inoffensive and polite. I'll give you some tips below in Chapter 12.

Visits

I encourage my students to visit the law schools that they are seriously interested in. There's no substitute for being on the ground and seeing for yourself what the law school is like. Don't feel that you are intruding. Law schools want you to come. "Our viewbook cannot possibly compare with the actual Gonzaga experience," says Gonzaga University Law School's catalog: "Come and meet our students and faculty, tour the campus, experience a first-year class, and discuss financial considerations for attendance with a School of Law financial aid counselor."

Some law schools have annual open house programs, one- or two-day affairs meant to attract large numbers of people to campus at one time. Open houses provide the tours, speakers, and classroom visits that Gonzaga lists in the above quotes (although more and more law schools offer only "simulated" classes), and meetings with law professors and students, as well as with recruiters. There are often special small group sessions or workshops for candidates with special needs or problems; if you're a member of a minority group, for example, you will have an opportunity to get together with other minority candidates and minority law students. Some law schools offer receptions or luncheons and a few even make overnight accommodations available.

Some law schools have several open houses through the year. Others concentrate on October and November, considered the prime recruitment periods. Your campus prelaw adviser will have scheduling information for nearby law schools. If you request a catalog from a law school you'll probably get announcements for the next several programs.

Some law schools have also started "outreach" programs. These are designed to promote the law school among minority group members and others whom the law school is making a special effort to attract. Schools with outreach programs take extra steps to publicize their open houses, by means of special mailings to prelaw advisers and undergraduate minority student organizations and fraternities, and sometimes to community groups as well. You may find details of open house programs on church and social group bulletin boards, or in advertisements and activities listings in your campus newspaper.

You will be able to see more of the law school and talk to more people if you visit during an open house. But as with any open house, the law school is prepared for your visit and on its best behavior. The floors are carefully swept and the skeletons the law school is ashamed of have been carefully stored in dark, locked closets. Moreover, there are often crowds at open house programs. You may find it difficult to get all your questions answered.

If you visit individually, the reps may have more time to spend with you and you may get a glimpse of the law school's ordinary routine. But because you can't intrude too much on the working life of the school, you may not be able to visit classes, get a complete tour of the facilities, or talk to faculty members or students.

Because of scheduling problems, most of you will probably have to arrange individual visits. You can reduce expenses by going in small groups with your friends, with the campus prelaw club, or with your parents. Each year, a rep from IIT/Chicago-Kent Law School arranges for Bradley's prelaw club to visit three or four Chicago-area law schools during a single day trip. Four Bradley fraternity brothers took a tour of five or six Eastern law schools during one spring break, driving from city to city and staying overnight at local chapters of their national fraternity. (If you're a nontraditional applicant and you are planning to attend law school to improve your career opportunities with the firm at which you are currently employed, some of your application expenses, including travel, may be tax-deductible. Check with your accountant.)

You should always call the law school admissions office for an appointment. At a minimum, this guarantees that there will be a rep available to speak to you. Admissions offices are usually very accommodating and will work around your schedule. But you should honor any request to choose another day: they try to avoid disruption during law school final exams or when some special event is scheduled. If you have some special need or interest, mention it when you make your appointment. The admissions office will try to answer your questions about, say, financial aid for minorities, if it knows in advance that the questions will be asked. Find out where visitors are supposed to park.

Try to arrive early—if possible, at the beginning of the school day. Walk around before your appointment. Check out the parking, the pedestrian route from the subway, or the other transportation arrangements. Try to get some idea of what it's like to move around on the campus. Are buildings close together? Are they laid out logically? Don't be put off if the buildings are old, but look to see if they're well cared for. At the start of business in the morning, the rest rooms should be clean. Institutions often respond to financial problems by cutting back on maintenance. Vandalism, beyond the amount normal in large cities, can be a sign of student disaffection or of poor relations with the neighboring community. Try to determine whether problems are chronic or temporary. If traffic is tied up because the law school is building a new building, the problem may evaporate before you arrive.

If the school has student housing, does it seem neat and well kept? Walk around in the neighborhood. Is there a great deal of foot traffic? Are there small businesses—bookstores, say, or movie houses—that indicate a thriving cultural life? Or is the neighborhood nearly deserted, populated only by a few furtive figures hurrying past boarded-up storefronts?

Sit in the cafeteria as students arrive. Do they look healthy? Are there groups of alert people endlessly discussing and debating, with books and notes spread out in front of them? Or do the students look harassed and fearful? Do they tend to sit alone? Do they seem distrustful when you try to make conversation? Law is best studied where there is a vibrant intellectual climate, and the best law schools find ways to encourage students to talk about legal issues with each other and with faculty members.

Take the time to look at the school's facilities. The library should be open early; in fact, many law libraries are open around the clock. Whatever books or equipment the school provides should be accessible and in use.

Look at the bulletin boards in the classroom buildings and library. Among the posters offering to sell used cars there should be advertisements for numerous activities, some course-related (speakers, exhibits), others career-related (book and software company advertising, law firm recruitment visits), and still others simply social (law fraternity activities, intramural sports, picnics and dances, even movie and theater nights). If the school is a vibrant intellectual community there will be a place where students post cartoons and joke memos. The only way you'll be able to find out about the existence of such valuable services as a night escort program for women will be to see it advertised on a bulletin board or in a publication.

Buy a city newspaper. It may have information about local problems. In 1994, complaints about the Dean of the University of Hawaii Law School—that he was politically pressured to admit the friends and relatives of state political leaders—were extensively reported in the Honolulu *Advertiser*. Newspapers contain classified ads for apartments and rooms, and ads for supermarkets and restaurants; from them, you can make an assessment of the local cost of living. Saturday newspapers often contain advertisements for local places of worship. Collect whatever student publications you can find. They're not intended for promotional purposes and they often contain candid discussions of campus problems. I once saw a headline that said "BUDGET CUTS THREATEN FACULTY LAYOFFS."

You will meet with a campus representative who will have a prepared presentation about the school's good points, and who should be able to answer your questions. You'll be able to collect information about special programs and features, and you should also ask the rep to discuss any problems you've observed. If you have reservations about the quality of student life, you can also ask to speak to some students. If none are available, ask for the phone numbers of student organizations.

The representative will provide a tour of the campus. Although the tour will focus on whatever facilities the law school is proudest of, you should keep your eyes open. Sometimes you can spot a crack in the facade, an indication that things aren't as wonderful as they look. I was visiting a law library one day when I heard a student loudly complaining to a librarian that for the third time that semester an article he needed to read had been ripped out of a law journal. Vandalized research material is a classic sign of cutthroat competition among students—whichever one gets to the material first sabotages the efforts of the others.

Several years ago, when computers were still a novelty, one of my students was visiting a law school that boasted a microcomputer lab for student use. While her tour guide was rhapsodizing on the value of the new machines, she idly turned on one that was not in use and tinkered with the keyboard. She noticed that it had some sticky keys. When she typed "MAN" it consistently came out "MAAN," or even "MAAAN." She looked over the shoulder of a student who was working. His machine did the same thing. Being well versed in computer technology, she readily diagnosed the problem. Later, she casually mentioned to the recruiter that the computer lab was due for a visit from the maintenance technician, who should come around periodically and lubricate the keyboards with a silicon spray.

The recruiter responded, "What technician?"

If you stay late or return to the campus after dark, you should study the campus's security arrangements. Access to school buildings should be controlled. In big cities, security personnel should be visible. Unless the weather is very bad, there should be some pedestrian life until at least ten or eleven o'clock. Don't be upset if you see only people in groups, or women walking only with escorts (who usually wear orange vests or armbands, or some other identifying insignia). That doesn't mean that crime is rampant; it means that they're sensibly protecting themselves against the unpredictable residuum of crime that exists everywhere. But a campus should not appear totally deserted after dark on a week night.

Remember, all these are just impressions. Don't be too quick to write a school off. All cities have some noise, pollution, and crime. All law schools are hectic, busy places and a certain amount of congestion and stress is both normal and desirable. But as you travel from school to school, you can compare one with another.

6

Making Your List: Setting Your Priorities

Let's perform a little experiment. First, name the law school you would attend if you could choose any one you wanted.

Perhaps you named a distinguished law school with a national reputation or a law school known to be strong in the specialty you want to study. Or perhaps you named the school that one of your parents attended. But you came up with a *name*, right? If you're like most applicants, you've given a great deal of thought to this question. You've read through that law school's catalog, you've spoken to some of its students and alumni, and perhaps you've even visited.

Now, what school will be your second choice? Did you find it harder to come up with a name? List your third and fourth choices. And your fifth, sixth and seventh. If you're like most applicants, you quickly run out of names. You've given very little thought to other schools that you might have to fall back on.

Many applicants don't know what they will do if they don't get accepted by their first choice schools. They wind up applying to a nearby local law school with a night program, or whichever schools their friends are applying to, or schools chosen at random. These schools, about which they know little, often don't have the programs and features they want.

If this is your attitude, you're taking a big risk. You may have to settle for a school that is not your first choice. You may have to settle for your last choice. This means, first of all, that you'd better have a last choice. One reason candidates fail is that they don't apply to enough law schools. Your application list should include some schools that you're pretty sure will accept you.

But if you're going to have a productive and enjoyable law school experience, these insurance schools need to be as carefully chosen as your top choices. You can have a happy and productive law school experience at a local school that has the programs and specialties you want and is situated in a comfortable location, even if the school doesn't have much of a reputation. But you won't be happy or well-educated if you wind up at a school that offers few programs, has poor quality instruction, and is located in an unpleasant, inconvenient, or dangerous setting.

In the next chapter, I will show you how to put together a list of law schools at varying levels of selectivity. You should attend the most selective law school you get admitted to that has the particular combination of programs and qualities that you want. You can be confident of attending a compatible law school only if you make sure before you apply that all the law schools on your application list—insurance schools as well as top choices—have the programs and qualities that you want. Or most of those programs and qualities. Or, at the very least, your top priorities. So you should know in advance that the things you will need to have a good law school experience are present at all the schools you apply to.

Here is the best method to use to decide which law schools to apply to: first, go through all your information and make a list of all the schools that have the programs and qualities you want. Consider as many schools as you can. Work from the *Official Guide*; it contains the names of all the accredited law schools. When you make this first list—call it your preferred list—don't worry about which of these law schools you have the numbers to get into. And don't worry if your preferred list is very long. You're not going to apply to all of these schools. Just list the schools you'd be happy going to. Second, read Chapter 7 and calculate your chances of admission to each of these schools. Following the guidelines in Chapter 7, decide how many schools to apply to. Third, prune your preferred list into your application list. You'll wind up with five to fifteen schools, at varying levels of selectivity, all of which you'd be happy attending.

The Right Law School for You

To use this method, you'll have to decide in advance which qualities and programs are important to you. You have your own particular educational goals, and you'll have to decide for yourself what kinds of places you will feel comfortable living in. Though I'll list a number of variables you should consider, I can't tell you what you should consider important; you are a unique individual and you'll have to set your own priorities.

One student had spent most of his life studying an unusual form of martial arts and had come to depend on his daily practice sessions for relaxation and unwinding, as well as for exercise. When he chose a law school, it was of primary importance to him to live in a city where he could continue to study this particular sport. This isn't something of concern to most people. But it was vital to him.

For some people, the cultural tone of the community—its offerings of music and other performing arts—is of vital importance; for other people it is not. Some candidates are concerned about schools for their children. Handicapped students must be concerned about accessibility. Some people want to be near their families, while others need to stay far away.

Take a pad of paper and make a list of the things that are important to you. Don't feel embarrassed if your list seems unusual. For one thing, it probably isn't. You aren't the first person who needs to live close to your Significant Other who is attending medical school, or who can't live happily without being near a body of water or without being able to see mountains in the distance. You are certainly not alone in having allergies or ailments that keep you from living in certain parts of the country.

Besides, no one will see the list but you.

Now, in no particular order, here are some variables that everyone should consider.

Location

How you will live while you are a law student will largely be determined by where your law school is located. The law school's location will also play a role in determining where you will practice law. So you should give some thought to what part of the country you want to live in.

Place-Bound Applicants

A place-bound candidate is one who can't leave some particular city or state. Most are nontraditionals who have family obligations that can't be put on hold. I knew a woman who was going through a protracted divorce and who was under court order not to move her children out of the state. I've met other applicants who could afford to go to law school only at night and didn't dare give up day jobs where they had understanding employers. If you have a handicap that requires access to a large medical center, you will have to live in one of the few large cities that has such facilities. If you have allergies, or if you absolutely can't stand cold weather, you will be restricted in where you are able to live.

If you're truly place-bound, the selection of a law school will be very simple: you'll have to go to one in the place you can't leave. If that place is Chicago, you'll have a choice of six or seven law schools. If it's out on the Great Plains somewhere, your choice will be much more limited. This limitation will make it quite difficult to find the best law school for you. You'll have to choose from a few schools, instead of from 178.

For this reason, I encourage students to keep an open mind. There are good reasons for staying put. You may have a personal reason, perhaps a sick parent. Or you may need to take advantage of the substantial tuition discount your state university offers in-state residents. (The Illinois state schools, for example, charge roughly a third of the tuition cost of equivalent private schools.)

But many applicants who say they're place-bound are merely avoiding inconveniences. They don't want to be too far away from parents who do laundry or they don't want the hassle of making new friends, learning the geography of a new place, or mastering unfamiliar regional customs. Many of these candidates are limiting themselves unnecessarily. Some, I suspect, are simply overwhelmed by the prospect of choosing law schools from a list of 178, so they bring the task within manageable proportions by arbitrarily limiting themselves to the few schools in a small, familiar region.

If you think you are place-bound, sit down and list your reasons for wanting to remain in one place. If you are truly immobile, one controlling reason will dominate all your planning. If you hem and haw and keep coming up with another marginal advantage of your home region, you aren't really place-bound. It's to your advantage to try to transcend your limitations by considering many law schools, not just the ones close to home.

If You Know Where You Want to Practice Law

Contrary to what you may have heard, you aren't required to study law in the state in which you will practice. If you graduate from any ABA-accredited law school, you are authorized to take the bar exam in any state. Nor do you need to go to a local law school to learn the idiosyncrasies of local law. True, you will have to know local law to pass the bar exam. But few law schools, even the ones at the bottom of the status rankings, spend much time on local law anymore. They are required to follow the ABA-prescribed national curriculum and they emphasize legal concepts that are useful everywhere. After you graduate from law school, you'll get a job, relocate if necessary, begin work at your new firm, and then take a cram course in local law offered by a local proprietary school. You'll take the cram course even if you've gone to a local law school. *Then* you'll take the local bar exam.

Still, there are some advantages to studying law in the state in which you will practice. Simply by living in a community you'll learn a lot about its geography, history, and peculiar local customs. This knowledge will be useful when you begin practice. Although top law firms tend to recruit nationally, most of the legal employers in a given city recruit only locally. Attending a local school offers a way in to the local status ladder and old-boy networks. The University of Texas, for example, has traditionally educated the Texas establishment that tends to dominate the state's commercial and political life. If you're sure that you want a conventional business or real estate practice in Chicago, you could do worse than to attend De Paul law school, the alma mater of many of that city's most powerful business and political leaders. Temple University Law School has played a similar role in the legal life of Philadelphia.

The old-boy and status-ladder connections are becoming more important now that many law firms are hiring law students on a part-time basis for summer jobs and then choosing new full-time associates from the ranks of young lawyers who were former summer employees. Many more of these summer opportunities will be available in the immediate community near your law school.

These advantages are mostly for people who want to work with established firms and who will do traditional kinds of business or government-oriented law. If you want some unusual specialty—entertainment law, for example—then studying where you intend to practice is less important. If you're going to study a still-emerging specialty, career patterns and employment patterns are much less fixed and affected by tradition. And if you have the numbers to attend one of the most selective law schools, you're likely to be able to secure legal employment anywhere.

If You Don't Know Where You Want to Live

If you aren't sure where you want to live and practice, don't despair. One strategy is to pick schools in growing, dynamic parts of the country. Although business lawyers aren't as dependent on the prosperity of their communities as, say, engineers (because lawyers can always do bankruptcies and liquidations when the economy turns bad), there are always more—and better—opportunities in a growing region than in a declining one.

Alternatively, you can pick an area where you feel comfortable living. If your hobby is sailing, you'll want to be near water; if its skiing, near snow and mountains. You probably won't get much chance to ski or sail while you're going to law school, but it might be nice to have the option. And you increase the likelihood that you'll be able to live there after you graduate.

Finally, you can choose a location to maximize your chance of admission. Many state law schools are still legally required to give preference to residents of their states. But these law schools also offer a substantial financial saving; consequently, they attract so many in-state resident applicants that they're in a position to be very selective. If you're a marginal applicant, you probably won't get much benefit from your resident status. If you come from a less-populated part of the country and can afford a private law school, you're more attractive to regional and local schools out of your area that are seeking geographic diversity.

Whatever you do, you aren't making a lifetime commitment. You can always leave a city or region when you graduate from law school. If you can't find anything in this discussion that seems important to you, you may as well indulge your wanderlust. One recent Bradley graduate decided to attend law school in an Eastern city, even though she didn't plan to spend her life there, so she could experience "a little Sodom and Gomorrah before I settle down."

Urban vs. Rural

Almost all law schools are located in big cities or state capitals. Even when their parent universities are in the suburbs, law school campuses are usually downtown. Law is intimately connected with the community's business and political life and is best studied where those activities are carried on most intensely. In big cities, law schools find it easiest to raise funds, recruit professors and adjunct faculty members, locate guest speakers, and schedule internships, clinical work and part-time jobs for their students.

Big cities have drawbacks, however. They're noisy, dirty, and crime-ridden. Traffic, parking, and security precautions make big city life extremely burdensome. Some people are unable to accustom themselves to the pace.

If you've never had the experience of a big city, I urge you to give it a try before deciding that you can't adjust to it. A summer job or a month at an urban summer school, perhaps after your sophomore year of college, should be an adequate test. If you can live for three years in the heart of a downtown, you will have many more opportunities than if you can't.

But if you can't, you can't. I know one young man with severe asthma and another who simply wasn't able to adjust to nighttime urban noises, even after a whole summer of trying. A rural campus is preferable to permanent lung damage.

Few law schools are actually in the boondocks, however. If you want a slower pace, the best choices will be state universities located in relatively small, though not tiny, communities. The University of Illinois at Champaign-Urbana and the University of Iowa at Iowa City are examples. Both of these excellent law schools are part of very large state universities that, in turn, are located in dynamic smaller cities.

Or you can look for smaller schools in even smaller towns. The Vermont Law School is located in South Royalton, "a typical New England Village" located about 35 miles from the state capitol and a somewhat longer car ride from Burlington. Capitalizing on its smallness, the school advertises an emphasis on teaching and creativity resembling that of a liberal arts college.

Full or Part-Time Programs

If at all possible, you should attend law school on a full-time basis. You'll save time, because part-time programs typically take four or more years, and you'll simply get more out of your law school education. Part-timers find it difficult to participate in student activities and often have little contact with other students.

I recommend that students attend during the day, even if it means borrowing money to do it. But if you're a nontraditional and have family obligations, this may not be possible. Finally, because part-time programs are usually easier to get into, some of you may have to choose between part-time study and no law school at all.

If you must be a part-timer, your range of options will decline substantially. Only about 80 schools have part-time programs (and some of these are small). Since part-time programs differ considerably one from another, read the catalogs carefully. Before you begin, make sure you know exactly what is expected of you, how long it will take, and how good the placement record is for students who have preceded you.

Big vs. Small

In contrast with good liberal arts colleges, law schools have higher student-faculty ratios and, at least in first-year subjects, much larger classes. And some are even bigger and more impersonal than others. Georgetown University Law Center, with 2,016 students and 84 full time faculty members, has a much different tone than Washington and Lee, with 371 students and 32 faculty members. If you feel you need some degree of personal attention and nurturing, you are more likely to get it at a smaller school that advertises an attempt at personal contact. You can't always tell what the tone of the school is from talking to a recruiter or reading a catalog. If you visit, however, you may be able to see whether small-group interaction is taking place. Ask the rep whether you can sit in on a third-year course or seminar. It should contain more discussion and more student-generated give and take than the typical first year class. If you talk to law students, ask them if they ever have trouble getting their questions answered.

Big schools aren't necessarily inferior. In fact, they are superior in most respects. The bigger a school is, the more courses and specialties it can offer. The larger the student body, the more diverse will be the social and professional life, and the better will be the contacts and networking possibilities. Most of the top law schools are fairly sizeable, and some are among the largest. Georgetown is very well regarded. Harvard has about 1,785 full- and part-time students, Virginia 1,142, Columbia 1,050. Recent enrollment figures, faculty sizes, and a variety of other demographic data can be found in the *Official Guide*.

How You Will Live There

In comparison to undergraduate colleges, all law schools are high-pressure places. Although few law professors still persecute and humiliate their students in the style made familiar in the movie "The Paper Chase," the nature of legal study guarantees long hours and a lot of work. Law courses are always graded and opportunities, in law school itself and in job placement, are always strongly linked to grades. (One student said that law school was just a three-year continuation of the three years of hard work he spent trying to get into law school.) Clinical work, summer jobs, law review editing, and other non-classroom activities are also extremely time-consuming. But they'll help you in your career. Law is not a field of study for people who can't take some pressure.

That said, some law schools are worse than others. This is extremely hard to measure; law students can talk about the pressure they feel, but they're not in a good position to compare their schools with others. And there aren't good comparative statistics on such things as student suicides and breakdowns.

Since more law students drop out than flunk out, attrition rates can reveal the existence of problems with student morale. The size of each law school's first-, second- and third-year classes can be found in the American Bar Association's annual *Review of Legal Education* (see Chapter 5.) With the exception of a few local and night programs that still anticipate high flunkout rates, law schools try to keep their attrition to less than 10 percent between the first and second years. If it's much higher than that at a school you are considering, ask the school's recruiter to explain why. There may be a good reason. The sophomore class may have been smaller to begin with, for some law schools are expanding. If the recruiter can't provide a good reason, ask whether such attrition is typical. If so, it may mean that the school's educational climate is discouraging.

Student Activities

If you're good at forensics and want to practice some form of law that requires extensive courtroom advocacy, you should investigate the possibility of continuing your speech or debate activities in law school. All law schools require some participation in moot courts and similar simulations. Some are very active in regional and national moot court competitions. In recent years, William and Mary's Marshall-Wythe School of Law has been particularly strong in national competitions.

Although no law school offers varsity sports, most have physical fitness facilities and many have at least student-organized athletic contests. They also offer a variety of social and affinity organizations. Some schools have more such activities than others, and some are more successful than others in creating a sense of participation and community.

Religious Fellowship

The legal profession has been plagued through the years by well-publicized ethical problems. Each year, it seems, there are scandals and prosecutions, with previously well-regarded attorneys falling in disgrace. Some would argue that there's no room for a person with deeply held religious beliefs or high moral standards among the sharks and hucksters. They say that the notion of a religious lawyer is an oxymoron, a contradiction in terms like hastening slowly, or army intelligence, or student athlete.

This is nonsense. There are many lawyers of extremely high integrity. If you are a religious person with high moral standards, the legal profession needs and will welcome you.

That said, however, you may feel uncomfortable on some campuses because you'll find a lack of kindred spirits, facilities for worship, or connection to the religious institutions in the larger community. You can't assume that a law school will have a religious tone, or provide religious facilities, simply because it is part of a university that is run or subsidized by a religious body.

Most law schools do provide some opportunities for religious fellowship. For example, the University of Illinois College of Law, Wake Forest University Law School, and many other schools have active Christian Legal Societies. These organizations can be discovered by reading bulletin boards and other announcements (another reason for visiting and seeing for yourself), by talking to students and alumni, and by recommendations from religious leaders in your church. You may want to investigate Pepperdine University Law School, which prides itself on maintaining a "Christian emphasis" and being part of a Christian community, and where you may find like-minded students. Don't feel that your religious beliefs will compel you to get an inferior legal education: Pepperdine is a highly selective law school, part of a distinguished university with a nationally known MBA program, in a scenic and popular location. Regent University School of Law, which is associated with the Christian Broadcasting Network, advertises that it tries to teach law "in the context of a historical and Biblical foundation," and attracts many students with religiously conservative political views.

Jewish students with traditional views may be interested in Cardozo Law School. Although the law school attracts a diverse student population, it is part of Yeshiva University, which has a variety of programs of interest to orthodox Jews. Whatever your faith, most religious students will find it easiest to find religious facilities and clergy in a large and diverse city.

Minority Enrollment

Here is a thumbnail sketch of law school bigotry: until after World War II, the more established law schools were effectively restricted to white male students. Many maintained quotas limiting the number of Jews and Catholics. To serve these deprived minorities, night law schools and other marginal operations sprang up. Some became identified with particular ethnic communities; they were known as, say, Irish schools, or Jewish schools.

Things have changed. Anti-ethnic quotas largely vanished by the 1960s. Although African-American and other protected group members are presently underrepresented at almost all law schools, they are eagerly recruited and their numbers are growing. You need not fear that your membership in a traditionally deprived group will keep you from attending a good law school. In fact, as I'll explain in Chapter 13, you'll probably find that it will help you. Some schools pride themselves on ethnic diversity. The newly accredited District of Columbia Law School, for example, is "particularly committed to admitting students from groups, such as minorities and women, which have traditionally been, and remain, underrepresented in the Bar."

Formal discrimination against women has all but disappeared, and now 40 percent of all law students are female. Nevertheless, some law schools are considered more hospitable to women than others. Using such criteria as the percentages of women who made the law review staff (or otherwise excelled) and the percentages of tenured faculty members who were female, law professor Linda Hirshman ranked top law schools on their friendliness to women in the September, 1995, issue of *Glamour* magazine. In the order in which they are friendly to women, the top law schools are said to be Duke, Iowa, Stanford, NYU, Minnesota, Columbia, Cornell, Illinois, Pennsylvania, and Yale.

The push for diversity has proceeded so far that it is difficult to find homogeneity even when you're looking for it. The old ethnic identifications have largely disappeared. But there are exceptions. I've mentioned Cardozo. Howard University Law School has traditionally been the educator of African Americans who will become civil rights lawyers. And a few other law schools still retain their historically African American character. For example, the student body at Southern University Law Center in Baton Rouge, Louisiana, is about 60 percent African American.

Clinical Programs

In the 1960s and 1970s most law schools responded to criticism that legal education had become too abstract and theoretical by creating clinical programs that would involve students in real court cases. Some clinics put students to work dealing with the problems of impoverished clients. All clinical programs provide practice in interviewing, counseling, and negotiating. In many states, law students are allowed to perform many legal tasks under the supervision of a member of the Bar.

Clinical programs are a valuable part of every lawyer's education, but they are most important for students who will eventually practice family law, criminal law, or litigation, or who will work in smaller firms or legal aid societies. Since clinical programs vary in quality, you should be sure that the schools on your preferred list have strong programs if you intend to practice in these areas.

Law schools indicate the scope of their clinical offerings in their catalogs. A good program reflects a significant commitment of resources, employs specialized teachers, and provides options. Cardozo Law School, for example, offers seven clinics dealing with such subjects as criminal law and appeals, taxation, immigration law, and mediation. It also has extensive internship programs, placing students in judicial clerkships, prosecutor's offices, and appellate court administration.

Specialized Programs

A specialized program, sometimes called a concentration or emphasis, is a group of related courses, sometimes coupled with internships, clinical activities, or travel—all designed to prepare you for some specialized area of legal practice.

Until quite recently, there was no such thing as a specialized program. Legal education was directed at teaching students to "think like lawyers," on the assumption that knowing a certain method would prepare a lawyer to untangle any legal subject or case. As a result, all law students used to get the same education. There were no formal majors, as in undergraduate schools, and there were no programs to train specialists, like those in medical education. Many law schools allowed no elective courses at all except in the senior year, when law students were permitted to choose seminars in complex subjects like taxation.

However, legal practice has become specialized. Lawyers are increasingly involved in arcane and previously remote areas like sports and entertainment. They're extending the profession internationally, by working for multinational corporations. And they're having to deal with increasingly complex statutes, like the Environmental Protection Act or the Tax Code. The amount of specialized information that a sports or environmental or tax lawyer must know in order to do his or her job has increased enormously.

As a result, law schools have begun to accept the existence of specialized areas within the law. There is still no such thing as a law school major and all law students are required to take the same core of traditional courses heavily oriented toward conventional property and commercial law. But beyond that core, schools often offer groups of courses in specialized fields.

If you aspire to have a traditional business or litigation career, or if you already know what your niche will be in life, you don't need to worry about a specialty. You can ignore this criterion. But if you know that you want to enter a particular specialty—like entertainment law or environmental protection law—you should attend a law school that is strong in that field. Doing so will help ground you in your subject and should make you more attractive to the specialized law firms (or the government bodies or the multinational corporations) that you will want to join.

Not every law school offers every specialty. You'll have to do some research. Some specialties are common. For example, about 70 law schools have demonstrated a strong interest in international law, which largely deals with the legal environment of multinational corporations. Other specialties are extremely rare, offered by only a few schools. St. John's Law School, for example, is known for its pioneering program in sports law. Washington University in St. Louis is well known for its excellent program in environmental law. State law schools tend to offer specialties useful in the state itself, both as a community service and also because the specialized teachers and resources are available. Thus, North Dakota emphasizes agricultural law and Oklahoma offers courses in oil and natural gas law.

Many law schools list their specialized programs in the *Official Guide*. But for details, you'll have to read catalogs. You should also look at the list of journals that the law school publishes, as well as at the list of student associations. University of Houston Law Center has organizations of students interested in aeronautics and space law, health law, and admiralty, among others. You can also ask law school reps. Your prelaw advisor may have lists of schools offering some common specialties. These can quickly become dated, however.

Some programs are better than others. At a minimum, a law school should offer courses taught by specialized faculty members. At least some of the specialists should be full-time faculty, as opposed to part-timers (or "adjuncts"); the full-timers are around more and may be more involved in law school activities. But there should be some adjuncts. They are practicing lawyers and will bring their up-to-date experience into the classroom. If appropriate, there should be interdisciplinary coursework. A program in law and economics, for example, should provide courses taught (or team-taught) by economists as well as courses taught by lawyers. Some of the courses should be seminars. Beyond that, a program should offer appropriate clinical experience, contact with professionals working in the specialty, student activities, and library resources. A definite plus for any specialized program is a student-edited scholarly journal.

When you visit the campus, ask to speak to students specializing in the field that interests you . Ask them about their activities. There should be contact among the students in a given specialty beyond classroom activities. If you speak to a young lawyer working in a specialty, ask her if she feels that her school adequately prepared her for the work she is now doing. And always ask law school reps about the placement rates for recent specialized graduates. A good placement service is an important part of any specialized program—and often the hardest part to get useful information on.

If you don't know what kind of specialty you want to go into, don't despair. Because all first year law school students are required to take the same courses, you don't have to commit yourself to a specialty until the second year. The best thing to do is to go to a large law school that offers many specialties, and keep your eyes and ears open.

Joint Degree Programs

Unlike a specialized program, which is part of a law school curriculum, a joint degree program is a joint venture. You will study in the law school as well as in another graduate college, usually one that is part of the law school's parent university, and you will work toward a law degree and a second advanced degree at the same time. The second degree is sometimes a Ph.D. or another professional degree. Most commonly it is an MPA, for people who want to go into public administration, or an MBA, for people who want to work as lawyers for large corporations. But other joint degree programs exist, and some are quite exotic. Duke University offers a degree in forestry, and the University of Illinois offers one in veterinary medicine.

In joint degree programs you will study law and other subjects either simultaneously or on an alternating basis. The program will take longer than three years to complete, most often four or five years. But the joint program is designed to take less time than pursuing the two degrees separately.

Joint degree programs are of value for people aiming at legal specialties for which extensive education is appropriate. To understand the legal environment of hospitals, doctors, and drug companies, it's valuable to be both a lawyer and a doctor. There are similar niches for lawyers who are also economists, or scientists, or scholars of foreign cultures and languages. Extra degrees also come in handy if you're applying for a job with a government body or a large corporation. Big organizations sometimes insist on stringent formal qualifications as a way of reducing a large number of job applicants to a manageable number. They often favor applicants who have MBAs or MPAs as well as legal credentials.

But joint degree programs aren't for everyone. If you're interested in a traditional business or litigation career, and if you expect to work for a smaller firm or be self-employed, you'll get little benefit from a second degree. You shouldn't apply for a joint degree program unless you anticipate some career use for the second degree.

7

Making Your List: Calculating Your Chances

You should attend the most highly regarded law school you can get into that has the features and programs that you want. If your undergraduate record is very good, you can aspire to one of the best regarded—and consequently most selective—of the law schools on your preferred list. Even if you're not admitted to one of the top law schools, you should be able to go to a very good school in the next rank. If your record is marginal, you'll have to settle for a less selective law school, one closer to the bottom of the status ranking. If, like most applicants, your record falls between these extremes, you can aspire to a high midrange law school, but you should protect yourself against failure by applying to lower-ranking schools as well. In this chapter, I'll explain how to determine the selectivity of the law schools on your preferred list and I'll show you how to calculate your chances of admission to each of them from the information you have available. I'll also give you some guidelines for deciding how many of the law schools on your preferred list you should apply to.

How Law Schools Are Usually Rated

You've probably come across many ranking systems for law schools. The best known is the annual ranking put out by *U.S. News and World Report* magazine, usually in March. It groups some schools in the "top 25" and distributes the others into four tiers. A widely used ranking was published by *National Jurist* magazine in April/May, 1994; your adviser may have a copy. And there are many others.

Law schools can be ranked according to objective criteria. You'll see rankings based on the number of books in each law school's library, the qualifications and accomplishments of faculty members (as measured by how many books and articles they have produced), the quality of their facilities, and similar "countable" variables. Other rankings are based on the law schools' reputations, usually as measured by a survey of law school deans or other knowledgeable persons. *The National Jurist* ranking is based on "student satisfaction" as measured by a survey of law students.

However, little of this has any direct bearing on the quality of education that a student is likely to receive. The world-famous research libraries possessed by Illinois and Yale (among others) are primarily of value to graduate students or scholars; although law students are required to do extensive research, they can manage quite well with the minimal library holdings that the American Bar Association requires all accredited law schools to possess. And because of these accreditation requirements, all law schools build their curriculums around the same basic courses. All teach most first-year and second-year courses by the "Socratic" method in large lecture sessions. All now have legal writing and clinical training programs.

Although the highest-rated schools have more well-known faculty members and are centers of legal scholarship, they don't necessarily provide better teaching. The nightmarish, high-pressure freshman contracts course in the movie *The Paper Chase* was offered at Harvard. Professor Kingsfield, the remote and downright scary teacher, was represented as a lawyer of high professional reputation, the consultant of appellate judges. Yet many lawyers who attended law schools of more modest reputation can usually recall some concerned and hardworking teachers who had the ability to make difficult material *more* understandable.

If this is so, are there any career-relevant advantages to attending a better law school? The answer is yes. The better a law school is, the more likely it is to offer *consistent* strength: to have all its courses taught by competent, if not inspired, people who have the time and resources to be effective teachers. The better law schools offer extensive arrays of specialized programs; although they may not cover every specialty in the fast-changing legal world, they are most likely to provide well-qualified faculty members in the specialties that they do offer.

Because they possess these resources, the better law schools sometimes offer unique opportunities. Although all schools have clinical programs and all law students have some opportunity to work on real cases under supervision, only at Harvard can students—a very few students—work on the cases of noted appellate advocate Alan Dershowitz. All law schools publish student-edited law reviews, but only at the top schools can students work on reviews that are regularly read and quoted by appellate judges. It is mainly at the top schools that specialized reviews in cutting-edge newly emerging legal specialties—women's law; Hispanic-oriented law; law and ecology—are begun.

If nothing else, the simple fact that some law schools are thought to be better allows them to attract better students. Good fellow students are more important than good teachers—they will arouse your curiosity, stimulate you to work hard, and even answer most of your questions. They will become lifelong friends and colleagues. And because top schools can choose their entering classes from a large pool of applicants—sometimes 30 or more for each vacancy—all of whom are of extremely high quality, they can gain the benefits of diversity, as well as of individual talent.

Top law firms tend to recruit from top law schools because they know that this is where high-quality students can consistently be found. For the same reason, many appellate judges fill their prestigious clerkships only from among the top graduates of the same schools. Certain kinds of legal jobs—teaching at a top law school, working for a blue-chip New York law firm—are almost impossible to attain unless you attend a top law school. And the prestige of being a graduate of a top school will make it easier for you to secure legal employment nationwide.

You've probably noticed that this argument is circular: because these law schools have the reputation of being better, people treat them as though they *are* better. They then attract the better students . . . whose performance and eventual successes make the school look better . . . which perpetuates the school's reputation . . . which generates more success . . . which attracts more of the better students. . .

In other words, there's a house of mirrors here. Perhaps there's nothing underlying a law school's reputation for quality except a history of having such a reputation. Status may be based on nothing but perceptions. But it exists nevertheless. Top law schools *do* draw better students and faculty members; they *do* increase the career options available to their graduates.

Therefore, if you have the grades and LSAT score to qualify for one of the nation's top law schools, you should consider attending it even if it has an unattractive location or other drawbacks. You'll get a similar, though proportionally smaller, reputational advantage if you attend a school at the second rank, and even at the third rank.

Some of this quality advantage is based on things that can be counted or measured. Mostly, however, as the Supreme Court observed in *Sweatt v Painter*, the qualities "which make for greatness in a law school" are "incapable of measurement." Though intangible, such things as "the reputation of the faculty, experience of the administration, position and influence of the alumni, standing in the community, traditions and prestige" strongly affect the fate of a school's students. How can you tell which schools are better when you are dealing with intangibles?

A Useful Rating System

The published ratings won't help you very much. They purport to identify the country's 10 best law schools, or 50 best. Some publications even rank all of them, beginning with number 1 and running on through number 66, which is in some way better than number 67, and finishing with number 178, the country's single worst law school. These rankings assume that one law school is superior to another in the same way that one football team can be said to be superior to another. But there's no tournament or league in which, say, Harvard Law will compete with Stanford Law, and no scoring method that can be used to award one or the other a larger number of points.

For these reasons, it's nonsense to rank schools cardinally, such that there's exactly one top-ranked school, and one 66th, and one 78th. Harvard and Stanford are so similar, and offer their students so many of the same advantages, that it's better to consider them as two members of a group of excellent schools than to argue about which of them is marginally superior.

But there *are* career-relevant differences between the group that includes Harvard and Stanford and a group of local law schools with fewer (and less well qualified) full-time faculty members, fewer resources, and a student body chosen primarily from the neighboring community. Law schools can be clustered in quality groups. The schools within each group offer students similar career-related advantages, although they may differ widely in other respects. Overall, some groups are superior to others.

At the very top are law schools that almost everyone agrees are the best in the country. I list them in alphabetical order: University of California Boalt Hall (Berkeley), Chicago, Columbia, Harvard, Michigan, Stanford,

Yale. No matter how law schools are ranked, these schools appear at the top of every list. A graduate of any one of them will have whatever advantages a top school can provide. He or she will have the largest number of career options.

If you're familiar with most published rankings, you probably expect a list of the top ten law schools. I've listed only seven. I haven't made a top-ten list because, as prelaw advisers like to say, there are 20 or more law schools that think they're in the top ten. Below the rank of undisputed best schools, there's second group we can call the top-ten wannabees. These are very good law schools indeed, and in most respects are indistinguishable from the Group I schools above them. Again, I list some in alphabetical order: UCLA, Cornell, Duke, Illinois, Minnesota, NYU, Northwestern, Penn, Texas, Virginia, Wisconsin. Groups I and II together make up a bit over 10 percent of all law schools, and enroll about 13 percent of all freshman law students.

Below the top two groups what you tend to find are not inferior schools so much as incomplete or inconsistent schools. Group III is made up of good-quality law schools that offer students many advantages but that lack the faculty depth, or the full range of specializations, or the nationwide reputation for superior quality that Group I and II schools possess. Group III schools try to be national, in the sense that they recruit students from all over the country. Few, however, are as diverse as Harvard or Stanford. At many, there's a preponderance of students from the local region. Some of the students at Group III schools wanted to go to Group I and II schools but were unable to get admitted.

Group III schools offer some unique advantages. Some are state law schools that are the traditional channels leading to membership in the local elite; well-regarded state law firms, state government agencies, and research institutions recruit graduates of these schools. In this category are California (Davis), Iowa, and Washington. Some private schools also have unique regional reputations, such as Tulane and Vanderbilt.

In this category, too, are well-regarded smaller schools with unique specialized programs. The University of Oklahoma, for example, is a pioneer in legal studies relating to Native Americans.

Group III schools attract fewer well-qualified applicants and are consequently relatively easier to get into than schools in Groups I and II. But the key word in that sentence is "relatively." Reps from Group III law schools routinely tell me that they receive two, three, or four applicants for each place in the entering class.

Group IV is a transitional category. Schools at this level resemble Group III schools; they have the ability to provide a strong basic education and usually offer some specialties. Often, however, the lesser quality of the student body begins to make itself felt and the educational climate is not as vibrant. Resources are more limited. The schools in urban areas are more likely to have part-time programs and to depend heavily on part-time instructors. At this level are the state universities in smaller states and the second-line state universities of some larger states, as well as smaller private schools. Though they aspire to diverse student bodies, most Group IV law schools are thought of as regional and draw their students primarily from nearby.

Remember, the regard in which a law school is held is mostly a function of its reputation. Reputations lag behind accomplishments. Some Group IV schools are extremely dynamic places and properly characterized as up-and-coming. The reputation simply hasn't caught up yet. Such a school is a sleeper: it can't provide the prestige of a more established school, and its career advantages are still limited, but it can provide a superior education.

I would place Southern Illinois University Law School in this category. It is a new and quite small program, and as yet has little national reputation. But because Illinois has a shortage of public law school places offering the in-state tuition discount, Southern has consistently attracted superior students—students whose grades and LSAT scores often qualify them for a more prestigious school. As a result, the educational climate is vibrant and alive. I've been quite impressed with the graduates I've met.

Dynamic Group IV (and most Group III) schools are trying to improve their reputations by recruiting more students from outside their immediate regions, encouraging faculty members to write for publication, and becoming innovators in such areas as computer applications. Some have had considerable success. Though easier to get into than schools in the higher groups, most have raised their admissions standards in recent years.

If your grades and LSAT scores are poor and you can't aspire to a higher-rated school, your chance of getting a good legal education will depend on identifying one of these Group IV sleepers. Your prelaw adviser may know about some in your immediate region. If you visit, look for enthusiastic students, young and energetic full-time faculty members, and an overall tone of high morale. The law school recruiter will be able to point to a record of improvement: a new building, higher entering class LSAT scores each year, writeups in national publications, and the like.

Group V schools are often hard to distinguish from those in Group IV. Sometimes they're similar in facilities, but lack the dynamic atmosphere. Most Group V schools are local, not in the sense that they teach local law but because they attract most of their students from the immediate region and expect most of them to remain in the area after graduation. They are most likely to accommodate themselves to place-bound and nontraditional students by offering part-time programs. Since older local law schools have been in business in the same area for a long time, they have extensive networks of alumni nearby and can sometimes offer unique opportunities for local careers. Yet aside from a few talented people who are there to take advantage of these opportunities, students at Group V schools are either place-bound or unable to get accepted anywhere else.

For most applicants, Group V schools are insurance schools. Entrance requirements are low in comparison with schools in the higher groups, but still substantial. Though it's still rare to find a student who didn't have at least a 3.0 undergraduate GPA, local law schools are most likely to provide second chances for slow starters. They may allow candidates with poor records to enroll in their evening divisions even if their numbers aren't good enough for admission to the full-time program.

Calculating Your Odds from Grids

The most important determinants of whether or not you will be admitted to any law school are your numbers—your undergraduate GPA and your LSAT score. The more highly regarded a law school is, the higher your numbers have to be to be reasonably sure of being admitted. How can you tell what your chances are at each of the schools on your preferred list?

The task is easiest if the school you are considering is one of the roughly 110 schools that publish detailed information about the fate of last year's applicant pool in the *Official Guide*. This information is in a table titled APPLICANT GROUP FOR THE _____ ACADEMIC YEAR, which is always located at the lower right-hand corner of the law school's two-page entry in the *Official Guide*. Prelaw advisers call these tables grids; a sample is printed as Figure 1.

FIGURE 1   A Grid

Applicant Group for the 1996–97 Academic Year

Undergraduate GPA

LSAT Percentile Scores	3.8+	3.6–3.79	3.4–3.59	3.2–3.39	3.0–3.19	2.8–2.99
91–99						
81–90		37/25				
71–80						
61–70						
51–60						
41–50						
31–40						

The vertical axis measures the LSAT scores of the people who applied for admission to that law school the previous year. Applicants with the highest LSAT scores are on the top line of the table. Some schools present their data using the numerical test scores that range between 120 and 180. Others, however, present their data using LSAT percentile scores. Your LSAT score report contains a table for converting numerical LSAT scores to their percentile equivalents.

The horizontal axis measures the undergraduate GPAs of the people who applied to that school the previous year. Applicants with the highest GPAs are in the column at the far left. Different schools break the numerical continuums into different categories. One school may groups GPAs in the following categories:

3.41–3.6

3.21–3.4

3.01–3.2

while another uses a different set of categories:

3.51–3.75

3.26–3.5

3.01–3.25

A few law schools put the LSAT scores on the horizontal axis, and the grades on the vertical axis. All grids are the same in overall structure: the best-qualified applicants are in the cell in the top left hand corner of the table. And the worst applicants, those with the lowest grades and test scores, are at the lower right.

To use the grid, you read up the table until you come to the line that contains your own LSAT score. Then you read across, from left to right, until you come to the column that contains your undergraduate GPA.

In Figure 1, I've given you a set of numbers in only one cell, that for students whose grades range between 3.6 and 3.79 and whose test scores are between the 81st and 90th percentiles (about 159 to 164, according to the conversion table). There are two numbers, 37/25. The left hand number, sometimes marked "APP," is the number of students with GPA and LSAT scores in that category who *applied* to the law school during the previous year's application cycle. In this example, there were 37. The right hand number, sometimes marked "ACC," is the number of applicants in that bracket who were *accepted*. There were 25. The 25 were chosen from the 37, and represent about 67 percent of applicants. In other words, roughly two out of three candidates with those numbers were accepted at that law school the previous year.

FIGURE 2   Some 1996–97 Applicant Distributions at Hypothetical Law School

Undergraduate GPA

LSAT Percentile Scores	3.8+	3.6–3.79	3.4–3.59	3.2–3.39	3.0–3.19	2.8–2.99
91–99						
81–90	42/41					
71–80						
61–70						
51–60				50/25		
41–50						
31–40					19/1	

How can you use these numbers? Consider a hypothetical law school that publishes the partial grid in Figure 2. Suppose you're a student with a 3.8 GPA and an LSAT score at the 87th percentile—a student with outstanding qualifications. Referring to the grid, you find that 42 students with qualifications in this category applied last year. Of them, 41 were accepted. Assuming that this year will be like last year, you can feel confident of being accepted at this school. Perhaps that's an understatement: you've almost got a lock on admission. True, nothing is certain. This year may be more difficult than last year, and even last year there was one student in this category who didn't make it. Still, as long as you get a decent break on the year, and you don't mess up some other part of the application process—as long as you don't forget to submit some required form before the deadline, or get a poor letter of recommendation, or insult the Dean—you're as certain of admission to this school as you can be.

I would define this school as an *insurance school* for you, a school at which you can have maximal confidence of acceptance. Some applicants won't have insurance schools; many will have insurance schools only in Group V. But if you want to be a lawyer, any law school is better than no law school. If you've got the numbers, there should always be at least two insurance schools on your application list.

Now look at Figure 2 again. Assume you're a student with a 3.35 GPA and an LSAT score at the 60th percentile. According to the grid, 50 such students applied to Hypothetical Law School last year, and 25 were accepted: half, exactly. You aren't certain of being accepted. But you have a fighting chance. You're *competitive* for that school. I would refer to it as a *possible school* for you.

I tell my students to consider themselves competitive for a school if roughly 40 percent of the applicants in their categories were accepted. To assess your actual chances, you should consider whether your numbers are toward the top of the cell you are in, or toward the bottom. At Hypothetical Law School, the cell you are in contains students with GPAs ranging between 3.2 and 3.39. So your 3.35 puts you towards the top of your grade group. Similarly, your LSAT percentile score of 60 puts you at the top of the 51–60 range.

Since the law school will choose from among many students who have roughly the same numbers, it will necessarily consider other factors. Your chances will greatly improve if you can present yourself well on the formal application: if you can write a good essay, get good letters of reference, present desirable work experience and extracurricular activities, or in some other way distinguish yourself from the others in your cell. I'll give you some tips for presenting yourself as well as possible in Chapters 9, 10, and 11.

Here are some other things that may give you an edge at schools at which you are competitive:

- If you are applying to a state school, make sure your application identifies you as an in-state resident.

- Make sure you identify yourself as a "legacy" if you apply to a school that one of your parents attended, especially if it is a private school to which your parents have donated money. As schools increasingly face budget problems, keeping contributors happy is becoming increasingly important.

- If you can pay your own way to law school, consider applying to schools that are known to be extremely expensive. Applications to such schools declined in the early 1990s, while applications to inexpensive public schools grew dramatically. I see this as evidence that more and more applicants have to consider costs when they plan their legal educations.

- Try to get whatever benefit there is in applying early (see Chapter 9).

- If appropriate, identify yourself as a sought-after protected group member. Affirmative action programs are still thriving (see Chapter 13).

- Finally, be particularly careful to make sure that your application is complete, neat, and in proper form. When a committee has to choose between a number of candidates who have very similar qualifications, it may be tempted to simplify its decision making by becoming extremely picky about its formal rules. It can then eliminate applicants who make trivial errors or omit even unimportant pieces of information.

You will probably find that you are competitive for a number of schools at roughly the same quality level: at all the Group III schools on your preferred list, for example. You should apply to some of these, and make your application as strong as it can be. If this year is anything like last year—that is, if the law schools you apply to don't suddenly receive many more applications or have an unusually well-qualified applicant pool— you have a good chance of winding up at this level.

Now, look at Figure 2 again. Suppose you've got a 3.0 average and an LSAT score at the 40th percentile. At good old Hypothetical, 19 people with such qualifications applied last year, and only one was accepted. These are long odds. You are unlikely to be accepted. I call schools at which your odds are less than two in five *wish schools.* Ordinarily, you shouldn't apply to them.

But there are exceptions. The benefits of attending a top law school are so great that it's worth at least trying, even if your numbers make admission unlikely. If you present yourself properly and exploit some of the edge factors I described above, there's always the chance that there's something in your background that the school will feel it needs to make its student body more diverse. It doesn't cost that much to try.

Second, if a school offers some unique advantage to you—if, for example, it has a unique specialized program or is in an ideal location—then to you the cost of applying is well offset by the reward if you are admitted.

In either case, you will need to do your damnedest on the subjective parts of the applications, and you will also need to pray for a break. If the school has a bad year and gets fewer qualified applicants, and consequently has to become less selective, or if you turn out to be the only applicant from, say, rural Nebraska, you could get lucky.

But you must never, never put all your eggs in any basket marked "long shot." It's one thing to pray for a break, but it's something else entirely to plan your life around the expectation of getting one.

There's a third time when you should apply to a wish school—or, better, several wish schools—and that's when you have no alternative. If you're like the person in the third example, the student with a 3.0 average and an LSAT score at the 40th percentile, you won't have any insurance schools. You won't find any schools at which the odds are in your favor. If you want to go to law school, you'll have to try to bring home a long shot.

Before you give up entirely, though, there's one more thing you should know about grids. Sometimes they make schools look more selective than they actually are. We know that this happens but we're not sure how often.

Remember, the information on the grids is supplied to the *Official Guide* by the law schools themselves. Because a law school's main asset is its reputation, and it will attract better students by seeming to already have better students, law schools have an incentive to make their student bodies look more elite than they actually are. They can't actually lie about student qualifications. But they can present the data in ways that favor them the most.

Sometimes, under or near a school's grid, there will be a statement in fine print, something like this: "This profile includes 97.5 percent of all applicants admitted." Okay, so 2.5 percent of the admittees are omitted. Who might they be? Some schools omit candidates accepted under affirmative action and outreach efforts, who tend to have lower formal qualifications. (Some law schools carefully note that they include such students in their grids.) They may also exclude foreign and transfer students, as well as older nontraditionals whose applications are hard to compare to those of traditional students.

Grids also may omit applicants who are accepted late. Law schools always admit more students than they have room for, assuming that some admittees won't be able to attend for financial or personal reasons and others will decide to attend other law schools. Less well regarded law schools are aware that they are used as insurance schools and they expect to be turned down a lot. But they can't predict exactly how often, so they keep waiting lists. (I'll have something to say about your chances if you're wait-listed in Chapter 14.) Wait-listed candidates aren't admitted until after first-choice admittees decline to attend—not until May at most law schools, and sometimes not until well into the summer. I know of one candidate who was admitted three days before fall classes were to begin.

Late admittees have lower numbers than the turn-downs they replace; that's why they were wait-listed. If the law school bases its grid on information available in, say, early May, it includes the turndowns among those accepted. But it doesn't include the inferior applicants who were wait-listed and later admitted to replace them. The law school's grid will look better qualified than its fall entering class.

Calculating Your Odds Without Grids

Now you know why I advised you in Chapter 5 to buy an up-to-date copy of the *Official Guide*. The grids are extremely valuable.

Still, about 65 law schools don't publish them. How do you calculate your odds of admission to one of these schools?

Most schools provide at least partial information, either in the *Official Guide* or in their catalogs. Some, while not describing last year's applicant pool, identify ranges of scores within which you can rate your chances as good, competitive, or poor. Look for a graphic, or a statement like this:

If your GPA is above x and your LSAT score is at the yth percentile or higher, you have an excellent chance of being admitted. If your GPA is below m and your LSAT score is at the nth percentile or lower, you are unlikely to be admitted. If your numbers fall in between these extremes, you have a chance to be admitted.

You can use such a statement as you would a grid and put the school on your insurance list, your possible list, or your wish list.

Some schools publish only an average: "Our freshman class had a median undergraduate GPA of 3.5 and a median LSAT score at the 70th percentile." If you've taken a statistics course, you know that an average isn't very useful without the standard deviation, which law schools almost never provide. A 3.5 average could describe ten students with 4.0 GPAs and ten students with 3.0 GPAs. Or it could describe ten students with 3.49 GPAs and ten with 3.51 GPAs.

If the law school supplies only vague information, or no information at all, you'll have to rely on whatever you can learn elsewhere about how applicants have fared in previous years. Some of the law schools that don't publish grids belong reputationally in Groups I and II: Chicago, Georgetown, and Harvard, among others. If you apply to one of these schools, you can simply assume that superb numbers are an essential but not necessarily sufficient qualification for admission. Always treat these extremely selective schools as long shots.

The MAPLA profiles software, which was mentioned in Chapter 5 and which your prelaw adviser may have, contains some information on selectivity. Based on this information, the Career Center at Boston College is currently maintaining a site on the World Wide Web called the B.C. Online Law School Locator. The locator groups together over 160 law schools into categories based on the median LSAT scores and GPAs of accepted applicants in a matrix. It also includes links to some law school online sites.

For less well-regarded schools that don't publish grids, your prelaw adviser may know how alumni of your college have done and may also have off-the-record information about how given schools make their decisions. If you visit the law school, you can ask the admissions representative to rate your chances as excellent, good, or poor. As I explained in Chapter 5, you can't learn much from a rep's encouragement. But if you are discouraged from applying, you should conclude that your chances are poor.

If your GPA and test scores diverge, you'll find it helpful to know whether the law schools you are considering emphasize grades more heavily than the LSAT, or vice versa. You can deduce this information from the admission formula that a law school uses. Law Services will send you a list of formulas when it sends you your LSDAS report. You'll learn how to evaluate them in Chapter 8.

Whatever bits and pieces of information you can collect for such a school, you're unlikely to be able to calculate your odds of admission as precisely as you can for a school that publishes a grid. It's best to allow a margin of error. Don't use such a school as insurance. Lengthen your application list instead.

Tips for Putting Together Your Application List

Now you have to decide which of the schools on your preferred list you will apply to. I'm convinced that one main reason for candidate failure is the failure to apply to enough law schools. According to Law Services, the average applicant applies to four or five law schools. I advise you to consider this a minimum number. Depending on your qualifications, the point of diminishing returns is somewhere between seven and fifteen schools. If you've chosen 15 schools properly you'll gain little additional security by adding a 16th, unless you are a marginal applicant.

Average Applicants

If you're an average applicant, your numbers are good enough for you to get accepted somewhere, but not really competitive for a school in Group I or Group II. So it's important to choose enough of the right schools to maximize your chances of getting in somewhere, and to optimize your chances of winding up at the highest possible level of reputational quality.

You should pick two insurance schools, two or three schools at which you are competitive, and, if you have some good reason for wanting to attend, one or more wish schools. Your list will contain at least four schools, and optimally five to seven. The schools will be distributed across at least three levels of selectivity.

If you're a nervous type, you can apply to more insurance schools. But since these schools are all, by definition, schools at which your odds of acceptance are good, you're simply increasing the likelihood that you'll get accepted to more than one school within the same quality range.

You can also apply to more schools at which you are competitive. Consider doing so if you

- had trouble calculating the odds of admission at some of your schools (see the previous section);
- don't have an edge at any of them;
- can't decide which of them is your first choice; or
- aren't applying to any wish schools.

Group I or Group II Applicants

If your numbers qualify you for a Group I or Group II school, you will have to calculate differently. So many top candidates apply to these highly regarded schools that admission is never based on numbers alone. Of the more than 1,500 Harvard applicants in 1990–91 who had GPAs above 3.5 and LSAT scores above the 96th percentile, only 36 percent were accepted. Top schools pick and choose from among top candidates and rely heavily both on subjective factors you can control—like the quality of your essays—and factors you can't control—like your demographic profile and the location of your home of record. Therefore, even for candidates with top numbers, acceptance is always chancy.

I recommend that if you have the numbers for a top school, you should apply to several top schools—five or more, if you have the time to fill out the forms. You must still apply to two insurance schools; for you, these will probably be very good schools carefully chosen from the Group III schools on your preferred list. Your application list will have at least seven schools on it. All of Group I plus some of Group II plus two insurance schools adds up to perhaps 15 law schools.

Marginal Applicants

If you are a marginal applicant with numbers distinctly below average, you may be able to go to law school if you persevere, but you may not be able to attend a school on your preferred list. You won't have any insurance schools; at best, you are poorly competitive. Reread what I said above about making the subjective parts of your application as strong as possible. I'll give you some suggestions in Chapter 9 below for explaining away or compensating for your shortcomings.

To maximize the possibility that you will find an admissions committee willing to give you a chance, you should apply to many schools from among those in Groups IV and V that promise in their catalogs to look at the "complete individual" rather than relying on "mere numbers." Investigate schools in unpopular regions. Expect to apply to at least 15 schools. Applying to more won't hurt.

8

The Law School Data Assembly Service

As Law Services describes it, their Law School Data Assembly Service "provides a means of centralizing and standardizing undergraduate academic records to simplify the law school admission process." You have to register for the LSDAS and follow its rules. You don't have a choice. With only two exceptions, all ABA-accredited Law Schools require you to submit your undergraduate transcripts to them only through the LSDAS.

An "Assembly Service"

The LSDAS performs a variety of statistical and record-keeping chores for the law schools. Among other things, it's the administrative way the law schools you apply to learn about your LSAT score. But from your perspective, the LSDAS has one main task: it takes information from the transcripts that you send it and puts the information into a standard form so it can be easily compared with the academic records of other law school applicants. For example, it converts grades to a standard four-point system, allowing 1.0 for each D, 2.0 for each C, and so on. After conversion, grades earned at schools that use a standard A through F grading system can be compared with those earned at schools that use other grading systems.

After "assembling" your academic information, the LSDAS sends a report to each of the law schools you've applied to. The report contains

- standard name and address information;

- the converted grades, expressed in a standard year-by-year and college-by-college table;

- photocopies of each of the college transcripts you've sent to the LSDAS;

- your most recent LSAT score;

- up to 12 earlier LSAT scores, if you've taken the test more than once;

- photocopies of your most recent LSAT writing sample;

- photocopies of the writing samples from earlier LSATs if you've taken the test more than once, with a maximum of two;

- a list of "all law schools reporting your prior matriculation or intent to matriculate and the year in which such reports were made (only if such information has been reported)";

- photocopies of certain special documents, "such as a letter from a certified professional regarding a handicap or a letter from Law Services regarding conditions during a particular test administration" (i.e. an explanation that something went wrong, such that your LSAT score may not be reliable); and

- whatever index numbers the law school you're applying to has asked the LSDAS to calculate for you, for use in its rolling admission setup (about which more below).

In theory, the LSDAS report gives the law school all the "hard" or "countable" information it needs to compare you with other applicants, in a format that's easy for the law school to use.

Though it eases the burdens of the law schools, the LSDAS increases your workload. Law Services is not the Central Intelligence Agency. It "assembles" and manipulates only the information that you make available. You must supply the requested information, and you must check up on the LSDAS to make sure that it is doing its work properly.

Registering for the LSDAS

Law Services prefers that you register for the LSDAS when you register to take the LSAT. As I mentioned in Chapter 4, you use the same form; you need only check the LSDAS box, tell Law Services how many law schools you will apply to, pay the LSDAS fee in addition to the LSAT fee (currently $79 plus $7 for each law school you want an LSDAS report sent to except the first, which is free), and list all the undergraduate, graduate, and professional schools that you have attended. You should do this if you expect to apply to law school within a year of taking the LSAT, as the LSDAS fee is good for 12 months. If for some reason you need to extend the period, there is a form in the *Information Book* that you can use to renew your LSDAS registration for another 12 months. The current renewal fee is $47.

If you're following the procedure I've described in the previous chapters, you won't finalize your application list until you know your LSAT score. Therefore, you won't know how many law schools you are going to apply to at the time you register for the LSAT. You can still register for the LSDAS; you don't need to list the law schools you'll apply to on your registration form. Nor are you limited to applying only to the number of schools that you pay for when you register. Simply pay for the minimum number of schools that you will apply to. (There will certainly be your top choice, two or three other possible schools from your preferred list, and two insurance schools.) Later, after you finalize your application list, you can increase the number of schools to which you want reports sent by filling out the "Order Form for Additional LSDAS Law School Reports," which is found in the *Information Book*. The cost of later additions is $10 per law school. Mail the form and the additional fee to Law Services in the special envelope provided; it is addressed ATTN: Additional Report Form.

If you don't register for the LSDAS when you sign up for the LSAT, you can register at any time. You use the "Law Services Order Form" in the *Information Book*, the same form that you use to register for the LSAT, omitting the LSAT sections and filling out only the LSDAS part.

Whenever you sign up for the LSDAS, you'll be asked to identify all the undergraduate, graduate, and professional schools you have attended. For each of these schools, you enter the assigned four-digit "college code;" these codes can be found in Appendix E of the *Information Book*. There are enough machine-readable boxes on the "Law Services Order Form" for you to list your present undergraduate school, a professional or graduate school, and up to three other schools you have previously attended. If you've attended more schools, Law Services requires you to list them on an additional non-machine-readable form, also located in the *Information Book*, titled "Academic Record Form."

You must make sure that Law Services knows about *all* the schools you have attended since you graduated from high school. If you omit a school and Law Services later discovers the omission, they will suspect you of what they call "misconduct." Specifically, you may be accused of trying to make your record look better than it is by concealing some previous poor performance, poor behavior, scandal, or even criminality. Law Services has a procedure, described in the *Information Book*, for investigating suspicions of candidate misconduct, and can impose a range of punishments. Read this section carefully. The punishment can be severe enough to destroy your ambitions. There's no way to get into law school except through Law Services. You don't want to be on their bad side.

After you register for the LSDAS, you'll have to submit a transcript from each of the colleges, universities, and professional schools that you've attended. Law Services won't accept a transcript that you submit directly. So you can't just photocopy your most recent report card. Instead, you must visit or write to the registrar of each school you've attended and arrange to have a transcript "bear[ing] the official seal of the registrar . . . sent directly from the registrar's office to Law Services." As you may already have guessed, Law Services wants you to use a special form for this purpose. Postcard-sized transcript request forms are bound into the back of your *Information Book*; you fill one out for each college and ask the registrar to staple it to the forwarded transcript. Expect to pay a small fee at each college.

If you can't obtain a transcript, perhaps because a college has gone out of business, there is, what else, a special form in the *Information Book*. You must explain why you can't obtain a transcript on the "Academic Records Form."

The LSDAS does not summarize the records of foreign universities with grading systems unlike those of American schools. If you did part of your undergraduate work at a foreign school, check to see if it is among the "participating schools" listed in Appendix E of the *Information Book*. If it is, treat it like an American school. If it's not, the best course of action is to arrange for the foreign school to send transcripts both to the LSDAS (using the postcard-sized form) and also directly to each of the law schools you are applying to.

If you did all of your work at a foreign college—to be precise, a school that is not in the United States, Puerto Rico or Canada, or among the few foreign "participating schools" listed in Appendix E of the *Information Book*—you are not eligible to subscribe to the LSDAS. You must contact each of the law schools you intend to apply to, explain the problem, and determine how they want you to proceed. This is one of the special circumstances that justifies seeking an informational interview with a law school official (see Chapter 12). You'll probably be asked to arrange to have official copies of your foreign transcripts sent directly to the law school.

If you're a traditional student, you should arrange to have your transcripts forwarded to LSDAS over the summer at the end of your junior year. The law school will evaluate you on six completed semesters of academic work. If you expect to improve your GPA substantially during your senior year, you can delay requesting your transcript until late in the fall semester of your senior year, or request it early but ask the registrar to delay sending it until the fall grades are available. You will then be evaluated on seven semesters of work. Because you'll forfeit the early application advantage that will be discussed in Chapter 9, you shouldn't take this course of action unless you expect your GPA to improve substantially.

If you've sent LSDAS transcripts covering six semesters of work and you later decide you want a seventh semester added, all you need to do is ask your college registrar to send LSDAS a seven-semester transcript. (Depending on your college's policy, you'll probably have to pay another small fee.) When Law Services gets this updated transcript, it will re-evaluate your file and send your law schools updated reports. Believe it or not, you don't need to fill out a form to request this update from Law Services. They do it automatically.

However, an updated report won't help you if the law school has already made its admit/reject decision before the updated report arrives. Therefore, if you think at the time you mail off your law school applications that you will want to add a seventh semester's grades, you should mark your applications "Hold For Fall Grades." If you do this you need to make sure that you follow through and have the additional transcript sent.

After Law Services has received transcripts from all the colleges, universities, and professional schools you listed on the registration form, it will perform its various manipulations and send you a printout identified as your Master Law School Report. The Master Report is your copy of what the law schools will receive; it includes The Law Services summary of the academic and biographic information you've provided (on the registration form, and from the various transcripts), your LSAT scores, and reports of any prior law school matriculations. (Some graduate work may not be listed.) It's your responsibility to *check this information carefully*. Errors have been made. If you detect one, "you should note the error directly on the report"—using contrasting-colored ink, for clarity—"and return it to Law Services, Academic Record Analysis, Box 2700, 661 Penn Street, Newtown, PA, 18940-0964." I suggest that you keep a copy and send the original back certified mail, requesting a return receipt. This is an important document. Law Services will notify you of corrections.

If you don t receive the Master Report within a few weeks of ordering your transcripts, you can query about the status of your file by calling Law Services at (215)968- 1001. The most common reason for a delay is that colleges are sometimes slow at sending out transcripts.

How Law Schools Will Learn About You

You don't have to worry that reports will be sent to law schools before transcripts arrive or corrections are made. In fact, Law Services won't send any reports to law schools at this point, even though you've paid for them, because Law Services doesn't know where to send them. You haven't told Law Services which law schools you're applying to.

Nor will you. You don't directly request Law Services to send out a report. Instead, when the law school receives your application, it will request a report directly from Law Services. Law Services will check to make sure that your file is complete and your fees are paid, and then it will send its report, similar to the Master Report, directly to the law school.

Once you've actually begun applying to law schools, and the law schools have begun to request these reports, Law Services will send you a monthly LSDAS update report. The report will list all the schools to which Law Services has sent an LSDAS report about you, and it will also indicate any other changes that Law Services has made in your file—for example, the receipt of an updated transcript. (No report will be sent to you for any month in which there is no activity in your file.) Keep all these reports. They are evidence that law schools received LSDAS information about you.

(If you are unable to pay the required LSDAS fee, there is a procedure described in the *Information Book* for seeking a waiver; see Chapter 4. Your request is most likely to be granted if it is supported by a strong letter from a financial aid officer at your undergraduate college, or other official who is familiar with your financial situation.)

Admission Formulas and Index Numbers

Among the materials that Law Services will send you with the Master Law School Report is a list of "mathematical formulas used by law schools for which Law Services calculates admission indexes."

Although these mathematical formulas are a subject of much fascination among prelaw students, there's nothing mysterious about them. An admission formula is simply a convenient way for a law school to convert each applicant's GPA and LSAT score into a single weighted index number, which can then be compared to the index numbers of other applicants, past and present. Candidates can be ranked according to their index numbers. Or, as I'll explain in Chapter 9, a law school can establish an arbitrary minimum index number as a cutoff point in its rolling admission system, automatically accepting candidates with higher index numbers.

A typical admission index multiplies your LSAT score by some constant (which Law Services calls constant A), multiplies your GPA by a second constant (constant B), adds the two resulting numbers together, and then adds a third constant, constant C:

Index #= (LSAT × A) + (GPA × B) + C

Each law school develops its own formula with its own characteristic set of constants. It communicates this formula to Law Services, which puts it into the computer that generates LSDAS reports. If you apply to a law school that uses a formula—say, Hypothetical Law School—Law Services will apply Hypothetical's formula to your GPA and LSAT score and compute your index number for that school, when it assembles its report for Hypothetical. It will print that "index number for Hypothetical" *only* on the report form that it sends to Hypothetical.

That number *won't* appear on your Master LSDAS Report, because at the time Law Services prints the Master Report it doesn't know which law schools you are going to apply to. (Remember, it doesn't know until each law school requests a report on you.) Nor will it appear on your monthly update reports. But along with the Master Report, Law Services will send you a printed list of all the formulas currently in use. Since you know your GPA and LSAT scores, you can compute your own index numbers for the schools you apply to.

The index numbers won't tell you much, though. You don't know how high an index number has to be to qualify you for admission. Sometimes you can get an idea of where you stand by comparing your index number to those of candidates of previous years who were admitted. But formulas change from time to time as schools refine their admissions procedures, and all were changed in 1991–92 when Law Services adopted a new scoring system for the LSAT. Sometimes a law school representative will tell you how high your index number has to be to be competitive. Your prelaw adviser may also have useful information.

Since the formulas combine grades and LSAT scores in a weighted fashion—that is, emphasizing one more than the other—you can use them to determine which of the schools on your preferred list are "grade-heavy" and which are "test-heavy." The larger constant B is, the more weight that school gives to grades. The easiest way to determine this is to set an admission formula up on a spreadsheet program and see what happens to the index number when you vary the GPA and the LSAT score. If the index number climbs much faster when you increase the GPA, that school is "grade-heavy." If it increases faster when you increase the LSAT score while holding GPA constant, then the school is "test-heavy." If you are one of those nontypical people whose GPA and LSAT score are widely divergent, you can use this information when you are drawing up your application list.

A cautionary word is in order: each school's formula is unique and idiosyncratic. The index number you compute according to one school's formula has no meaning at another school. If you can't find an admission formula on the Master LSDAS sheet for a school you are considering applying to, it may mean that law school is less numbers-bound than most, or doesn't use a rolling admission system. It could also be an indication that the school really means what it says when it promises in its catalog to "go behind the numbers" and "judge each applicant as an individual." But it could also mean that the law school has a mathematical formula and computes its own index numbers, rather than delegating this task to Law Services.

9
Filling Out Law School Applications

Developing a Strategy

Application forms mostly require you to provide detailed lists of objective information: names and dates of schools attended, addresses where you've lived, employment history, and so on. You may not perceive a need for a strategy for filling them out. But beyond the specific information you provide, the admissions officials will judge you in part on the overall impression your paperwork makes. They'll read between the lines. They will look at the forms to try to deduce what your personality is like and whether you have the disciplined intellect, the good work habits, the painstaking attention to detail, and the good communications skills that you will need to succeed in law school.

For this reason you should give some thought to how each piece of paper will look to the officials who will read it. You can't entirely control the information, but you do have some freedom to phrase and arrange it in a way that will make it look like it came from the desk of a mature and capable person who is intelligent, hardworking, and thorough, and can write clearly and well.

To some extent, how you will do this will depend on how good your qualifications are. If you're applying to an insurance school, you should view the paperwork—and every other aspect of the application process—

defensively. Since your superior GPA and LSAT score should be sufficient to get you admitted, the paperwork can't help you. If you're lucky, it will barely be glanced at. But the paperwork can hurt you if it's sloppy, incomplete, or not on time. The personal statement can hurt you if it reveals you to be a windy and tedious character, or mean-spirited and dishonest. Beyond providing the required information and being neat and thorough, your best course is to say little, and take every opportunity to focus attention on your superior numbers.

But if you're applying to a possible school or a wish school, your numbers may not be sufficient. If the law school "goes beyond numbers" to "judge you as a whole person," your paperwork will be scrutinized with some care. You can use it to try to explain away some of your shortcomings. Or you can use it to document some alternative accomplishments or assets that indicate that you have the qualities for success in law school.

If you're applying to a top law school, you'll need to have superior numbers. But the numbers themselves will not guarantee you admission. You'll have to distinguish yourself in some way from all the other applicants who also have superb numbers. Your paperwork is very important; it gives you an opportunity to describe your unique personality—so unique that any entering class will be a poorer place if you are not in it. You do this by documenting overall strength or some unusual and very impressive accomplishment. And you do it by writing an essay in a unique, personal voice.

Before you start filling out any forms, sit down and think about your strengths. What is it that makes you truly unique? And, most important, how will you demonstrate this uniqueness to someone you've never met. You can't simply assert that you are, say, extremely persistent. But you can make sure that your paperwork prominently features occasions when you overcame some obstacle or achieved some goal against long odds. A good college record despite poor high school preparation is one bit of evidence; a letter from a coach describing how you once ran a race while you were injured is a second.

Obtaining Forms

All the necessary application forms are bound into or included with each law school's catalog. Most law schools don't often revise their forms. Some reprint the same forms year after year, perhaps changing the date printed at the top or using different colored paper to distinguish each year's paperwork. But occasionally there are revisions. It's a good policy to make sure in advance that the forms you have in your possession will be accepted. If you have an old catalog, call the law school's admission office and ask if it has been up dated and request a new one if necessary.

If your numbers are *extremely* strong, ask the law school rep whether the school has an accelerated admission program. If it does, you may be asked to fill out a special abbreviated form, and promised that your application will be considered immediately upon receipt. Washington University in St. Louis, for example, has its Preferred Applicant Program. Unusually strong candidates are sent "a short application that the student can quickly complete." The personal statement and letters of recommendation are optional, and candidates who use this application are notified of the admit/reject decision within three weeks.

The advantage of accelerated programs are obvious: less work, less risk, and prompt consideration. If you qualify for such a program, you should by all means submit the accelerated admission forms. But you will only qualify if your numbers are very high for the school in question—in other words, only if the school is an insurance school for you. Nevertheless, knowing very early in the application year that you've been accepted to an insurance school will give you peace of mind and allow to work that much harder on your applications to your possible and wish schools.

The future of law school applications is online. Eventually, you'll be able to submit easy and fast electronic application forms. But that future has not yet arrived. We are just beginning to see application forms generated by computer. Law Multi-App, the leader in the field, sells a software package that can be used to generate acceptable application forms for participating schools. You provide the requested information by filling in the blanks just once. Then you tell the computer which schools you are applying to. The software replicates each school's admission form, filling in the information you have provided.

At the moment, 52 law schools accept Law Multi-App forms. If you are applying only to schools on Law Multi-App's list, the software will save you a lot of typing. But Law Multi-App does not generate financial aid forms, letter of recommendation forms, or various other special forms that some law schools use. So you will still need to obtain each school's set of printed forms. Law Multi-App can be contacted at (800) 515-2927 or at 635 North Chester Road, Swarthmore, PA, 19081. The most recent price was $47 plus $5 shipping for the full package; however, they offer less expensive options covering one, two, or three schools.

Some General Considerations

Law schools are always looking for painstaking attention to detail. Lawyers are expected to be careful, well-organized, and thorough. You need to demonstrate in your application that you are such a person.

For this reason, meeting deadlines counts. Following instructions counts. Completeness counts. Using the right form counts. Above all, *neatness counts*. If you were an admissions official, what would you conclude if you read a messy, handwritten form containing spelling errors and crossouts? What would you think if you read a form that was missing pages, or one on which some questions were left blank? Would you hire a sloppy lawyer?

Make a list of all the forms that each school wants you to fill out and return. Some schools have just one form, marked "Application for Admission." Others have an application and a number of supplemental forms—for residency, financial aid, and so on. Group the forms for each school together, perhaps in a manila folder. Later in this chapter I will give you a checklist of all the forms you'll have to fill out. I suggest that you photocopy it and attach a copy to the manila folder for each school. Use the checklist to make sure each application is complete before you mail it off.

Make photocopies of all the forms. You'll do rough drafts, and when you're sure that everything is the way you want it, you'll type the information neatly on the final copy of each form.

When you make the rough draft, *answer all the objective questions*. You don't volunteer information, but don't leave a question blank. Admissions officials must work their way through thousands of forms, and there is a powerful temptation to set aside any form that is "not complete," even if the omission is a minor one. It's a defensible way to reduce the workload.

Follow the instructions exactly. Don't write below a line marked "Do not write below this line." Date and sign everything that calls for a signature. And there are admissions officials out there who consider it a very serious flaw if you use a red typewriter ribbon when a blue or black one was called for.

Make sure the lists are complete. You may not think that an omission of some trivial bit of information can harm you. What does it matter if you've listed all of the apartments you rented while you were in college? Well, it doesn't. But suppose you leave out that tenement on Slum Street that you lived in for just three weeks before the roaches drove you out and an old teacher writes in a letter of recommendation, "Johnny wrote a remarkable term paper, considering that he was living at the time in one of those hovels on Slum Street." The admissions committee doesn't care where you lived. But the *omission* itself raises questions. Is there a reason why you didn't list it? Is there something you don't want the admissions committee to know?

Whenever you're asked to give an address, take the time to look up the zip code. If you're asked to list the name of an adviser, job supervisor, or other reference, include a phone number, area code first. By making it easy to contact people who know you, you give the impression that you have nothing to hide.

As a rule, *you should avoid volunteering information unless the information will do you some good*. If the law school asks you to account for all your time since your graduation from college, then you'll have to tell them about the six weeks you spent in a mental hospital suffering from clinical depression. But if the form doesn't ask about all your time, there's no need mention it. (Most forms don't go into such detail; they simply ask you to list all your jobs and all the schools you've attended.) If, on the other hand, you spent six weeks traveling in India and learning Urdu, you should find some way to work the experience into your application.

As much as possible, *you should try to answer all the questions on the application form itself*, typing your information only on the blank lines indicated. If the law school says you must answer a question in a given space, try to follow the instructions exactly.

Repeat information rather than referring back and forth. Cross-references can be confusing. You may find that you're asked to write the same addresses and phone numbers in more than one place.

If you're listing objective information, like the names, addresses, and dates that document your work experience, you may run out of room on the form. Even if you're only asked to describe your three most recent part-time jobs, for example, you may have trouble fitting the names and addresses of three employers, the dates of employment, the names and phone numbers of your immediate supervisors, and the descriptions of your duties into three or four skimpy lines.

In such cases, you must perform what newspaper editors call a "jump." Type as much of the information as you can neatly fit in on the application form itself; then type "See attached sheet" on the last line and finish answering the question on a blank piece of $8^1/_2$" by 11" paper. At the top of the blank sheet, type "Supplement to application of__," then type the number of the question that you're continuing and finish listing the requested information.

You shouldn't use a jump to prolong some essay or explanation beyond the limits that the law school has set. But you should use it to provide a complete answer to certain requests for information. In some cases, the law school may ask that you use a continuation jump sheet:

> 21. Are there any circumstances which might prevent you from devoting full time to the study of law? If so, check this box and provide an explanation on a separate 8½" × 11" sheet.

Whenever you make a jump you must make it clear, by typing "See attached sheet," that the information on the printed form is not complete by itself. Then you must identify the jump sheet clearly enough for the reader to connect it with the appropriate place on the printed form. Use the number of the question and some descriptive term as a heading:

> 22. Work experience (continued):

You're unlikely to need more than one jump sheet. But if you do, you should number them and refer to them in the plural on the main application form ("See attached sheets").

A Word on Honesty

You may have heard that it is common in some fields for job applicants to overstate their qualifications. A recent study by an employment screening firm in Texas concluded that about one of every two job applicants lies at least once on a résumé or application. College officials interviewed by the *New York Times* in 1995 said they were aware of widespread lying in the undergraduate admissions process; The University of Pennsylvania, for example, detects five or six fraudulent applications each year. Occasionally the media will report that someone—perhaps a government official—was fired (or expelled) for such dishonesty. But invariably we also hear that it is rare for a cheat to be exposed. In some fields, including journalism and sales, successful elders often reminisce about all the lies they had to tell to obtain that all-important first job. If everyone is doing it, you may ask, why shouldn't I?

Law school applications are different than job applications; there are good reasons to avoid lying on them. For one thing, lying can't do you much good. Your GPA and LSAT numbers are your main credentials, and they are not within your control. LSAT scores are sent to law schools directly by Law Services, and your grades are sent by your college, through the Law School Data Assembly Service. You can't get away with a lie that contradicts or is inconsistent with the transcripts and other records available to the admissions officials.

The damage that you can do to your career if you get caught in a direct lie is considerable. Actually, it's terminal: the punishment is dismissal from law school. True, law schools possess few investigative resources and they traditionally do little, if any, checking. But every once in a while there is a scandal, followed by a crackdown. In 1993 Law Services found that misconduct cases were increasing in numbers. "Inaccurate reporting of information, such as misrepresenting past academic history or falsifying letters of recommendation, are common charges. Fraudulent or altered records are also a problem." Since then Law Services has been working with law schools to share information and develop procedures that make it easier to detect this cheating.

To be licensed to practice law, you must satisfy the bar examiners of your state that you are of good moral character. This requirement distinguishes law from most other white-collar occupations, and some bar examiners take it very seriously. They have more investigative resources than any law school and in some states they conduct extensive background checks of bar aspirants. (I have received inquiries from bar examiners about the character of people I knew casually 15 or more years earlier.) They've been known to uncover evidence of lying on law school applications.

Finally, unlike most other professional occupations, law is a public career. You may want a government job some day, or an elective office. You're more likely to need a security clearance than, say, a cardiologist. Or you may simply become involved in some high-profile activity—a well-publicized lawsuit, perhaps— that will bring you under the scrutiny of the press.

For all these reasons you're best advised not to put anything on a law school application that could be revealed as a direct lie.

The Application Form

Law school applications vary. Some are one-page checklists that aren't much more detailed than the cards you fill out when you register at a motel. Others are six- or eight-page mini-psychobiographies that ask you to account for every minute of your life since age six. Depending on the schools you're applying to, you'll be asked for some or all of the following information.

Name

This is pretty simple, right? All you have to do is to put down your name. But trust the legal mind to have noticed that Nick Brown may not be the same person as N. Brown, or N. J. Brown, or N. Jeremiah Brown. Pick one way to write your name and stick to it. If you use a Jr. or a roman numeral after your name, be consistent. If there's any discrepancy between the name on your application and the name on your college transcripts, explain why at the end of the application in the blank space marked "Other Information."

You may come across a second line asking for a *former name* or an *other name by which you are known*. Perhaps you were adopted as a teenager, or you've Americanized the ethnic name on your birth certificate, or you've changed your family's Americanized name back to its original spelling, or you're a married woman who has taken her husband's name. If so, list the second name and, if required, explain the reason for the change.

Address

As with the LSAT registration form, you shouldn't use an address if the law school won't be able to reach you there for the full academic year. You may not learn about the final disposition of your application until late in the spring—even later if you're wait-listed. As a rule, it's best to ask all correspondence to be sent to a permanent address.

Law schools may ask you to list *former addresses*. The information could be used for background checks, but probably won't be. Law schools like to have geographic diversity in their student bodies, and if you've lived in some exotic or unusual location you should stress that information. Former addresses are also important in determining eligibility for in-state tuition discount and some financial aid programs.

Ethnicity

All forms now ask for optional *ethnic and racial identification*. You should check this box if you're an African American, Native American, Pacific Islander, Hispanic, Aleut, Inuit, or a member of some other protected category. If you're an otherwise well-qualified applicant, you will find yourself much in demand. Ask to be considered for any affirmative action programs that are available. In some cases, membership in a desired category has made the difference between acceptance and rejection. I'll have more to say about this in Chapter 13.

If you are not a member of a protected category, leave this question blank. Don't claim a status to which you are not entitled. "Falsifying ethnicity" is one of the common forms of cheating that Law Services is concerned about. And it's an easily detectible lie. Membership in a minority group can usually be confirmed by other biographical details: schools attended, voluntary associations joined, foreign languages spoken, and so on. (Candidates who are qualified for law school affirmative action programs were probably involved in college affirmative action programs.) Many law schools now routinely check.

Colleges, Universities, and Professional Schools

List all the schools you've attended, supplying the required addresses, dates of attendance, and degrees received. If you've completed most of the work for a degree and expect to finish before you begin your legal studies, type "(B.A. expected, May, 19—)" in parentheses.

As with registering for the LSDAS, it is important that you make the list complete. Omitting a school leaves you open to the suspicion that you're trying to conceal some dishonorable part of your background.

If there are no instructions to the contrary, list non-degree–granting programs (summer schools, Washington, D.C., semester participation, foreign study) along with degree-granting programs. But if the law school asks you to list them separately, do so.

Law schools usually want you to list colleges in the order in which you've attended them. If no specific order is requested, list them with the most recently-attended school first: graduate work on top, then the school where you got your undergraduate degree, then whatever other under-graduate schools you attended. The most impressive accomplishment will then be on the top line of the section, the line that the reader's eye naturally focuses on.

Work Experience

Again, unless otherwise requested, list the most recent job first. It is likely to be your most responsible and impressive position, and that's what you want the reader's eye to be drawn to.

If the law school requests you to list all the jobs you've ever held, you should do so. If you're a traditional student and you're describing part-time jobs, indicate how many hours you worked each week and how many weeks you worked each semester. If you held two or three jobs simul-taneously, mention this fact. If you want the law school to interpret your grades in light of the fact that you've always had to work to support yourself, you'll have to list enough jobs to document this consistently heavy burden.

If none of these conditions applies, you're best advised to list only the two or three most recent jobs, any jobs that required some unusual skill or ability, and any jobs you refer to elsewhere in your application.

Be accurate in providing the requested addresses, phone numbers, and dates of employment. Errors can be embarrassing. I know of one nontraditional applicant—call him Chris—who wrote that he'd worked for the Caterpillar Corporation between 1980 and 1986. His former job supervisor wrote a letter of recommendation that began, "I've known young Chris ever since he came to work here at Caterpillar in 1979." The supervisor later told me that a law school dean called him to ask about the discrepancy.

If you're a nontraditional applicant and you want your employment history to compensate for your low undergraduate grades, you'll have to make this section more extensive and impressive. You do this by describing your job duties, taking care to explain that doing a good job requires skills that are also necessary in law school. For example, if you are a sales manager, and you write, "Smathers Corporation, sales manager, 1986–95: planned regional sales campaigns, wrote training material, trained and supervised staff of six salespeople," you're actually saying that your work experience demonstrates planning and supervisory skills, as well as the ability to communicate clearly.

If your work experience is extensive you may want to attach your professional résumé. If your résumé documents professional growth and success—if, for example, it lists a series of increasingly higher-ranking jobs, or the assumption of more and more responsibility, or extensive professional education—then it is a much better description of your qualifications to study law than anything you can list on the application form. If you take this route, type "See attached résumé" on the application, and then treat the résumé as a jump sheet. Type "Attachment to the Application of ____," and the number of the question at the top.

If you're a nontraditional applicant it's a good idea to account for all of your time since your graduation from college. (Some law school applications explicitly request you to do this.) If there are gaps in your record, you leave yourself open to the suspicion that you are concealing some questionable activity or problematic event in your life.

This consideration is less important than it used to be, because the depressed state of the economy now makes it likely that business and professional persons will experience periods of unemployment through no fault of their own. But it is still more impressive to account for all your time, if you can do so. One woman typed, "The attached résumé describes my career activities since graduation, except for 1989–92, when I stayed home to care for my two small children," and then attached her résumé. Another woman, who had a record of sales jobs in the computer industry, wrote the following:

> The attached résumé shows that I was continuously employed in computer sales for more than ten years, except for 1993. I made an attempt to start my own consulting firm that year but my two corporate clients both moved their offices out of the area. Luckily, I was able to get my old job back.

There's a subtle plug in that statement: in the sales business, employers don't rehire former employees who were nonproductive.

Extracurricular Activities

Most schools ask you to list "college extracurricular activities or community activities." Some indicate that they want your list to be complete; others want you to list the three or four "that are most important to you." You are usually asked to describe the "extent of your participation," including the amount of responsibility you assumed, the offices you held, and the tasks you performed. Remember your strategy: you are trying to appear dependable, organized, hardworking, intelligent, interested in law, and the possessor of good communications skills. Well-written entries can suggest these things. In a brief but carefully organized entry, one sorority woman was able to document a history of growth and the assumption of greater and greater responsibility.

> Zeta Zeta Zeta sorority, six semesters (president, 1994–96; pledge mistress, 1992–94; organized committee to prepare homecoming decorations, 1992).

This modest entry is deceptive. It doesn't document growth or success, but in its quiet way it suggests steadiness, self-discipline, and social commitment:

> B. U. Prelaw club, 1994–96; organized three programs of outside speakers. Dramatic club, four semesters; roles in five plays, including the Artful Dodger in *Oliver!* Walker for President campaign, fall, 1994: performed general office work and canvassing. Peoria Area Headstart Project (A division of the Urban League, Inc.) 1994–96: tutored disadvantaged grade school children eight hours per week.

Unless you're instructed to limit yourself to a fixed number of activities, I suggest that you be exhaustive. Always include varsity sports participation:

Lacrosse team, three semesters; team captain, 1995–96

You can also include intramural sports if your participation was extensive or if you were involved in organizing or logistical chores, but you should omit occasional or irregular participation. Include volunteer work for charities, participation in church or synagogue activities beyond ordinary worship, and work for organizations like the Boy Scouts. Be sure to list any organizations that you will refer to in your essays, or elsewhere on the application, and any that may be referred to by the people who will write your letters of recommendation.

In some cases, application forms instruct you to list your activities chronologically, beginning with those you are still involved in. More commonly, you are left to devise your own organization, or simply instructed to list activities "in their order of importance to you." List them with the ones in which your participation has been most extensive first. Put the ones that are law-school-related toward the top: the forensics team and the Model United Nations should come before the church youth group. If you have a lot of activities, it's helpful to separate them into two groups, listing first the community activities (including political campaign or party work, charity fund drives, and so on) and later the campus activities.

If you're a nontraditional applicant, you can include voluntary groups connected to your employment. Being a member of a professional organization, a business group like the Rotary club, or a veterans' group like the American Legion demonstrates a commitment to the community and an ability to get along with other people.

Awards and Honors

List here any awards you've won that show that you possess skills useful in law school (writing ability, self-discipline) or traits desirable in lawyers (honesty, diligence, public-spiritedness). Scholastic honors, including scholarships, are especially desirable. You should also list college fraternity, athletic and other competitive prizes and awards, military decorations and professional or occupational recognition.

If you have a lot of awards, you can either try to be complete or else make a selection. As a rule, academic and individual awards are more important and should be mentioned first. Awards involving recognition by professional peers and educators are more impressive than those awarded by fellow students.

You should omit awards won before your college years that don't bear on your academic ability (e.g., voted high school class president), awards given for reasons that have nothing to do with the ability to do law school work (e.g., beauty contest awards given entirely on appearance or popularity), and awards that can properly be considered trivial ("fraternity brother of the month," when everyone knows that the award is rotated among all the active members).

If you're a nontraditional applicant and you want to emphasize your work experience on your application, listing honors you have earned for superior job performance is a good way to indicate that your career has been a success. In some professions there are lots of awards and it is fairly easy to establish a record of distinction. Sales careers, for example, often involve competition, awards, and prizes.

When you list an award, your achievement will be most easily intelligible if you can provide a very brief explanation of what the award was for, who awarded it, and how selective the award process was, as in the following examples:

Hometown University Dean's List (3.6 average or higher), six semesters
.Hometown University Horatio Alger Scholarship (one awarded each year, to a liberal arts student), 1995–96.
Smathers Corporation Top Salesman Award (one given each year to the highest-grossing salesman nationally) three years in a row, 1993–96.
American Legion of Illinois Citizenship Award (given each year to Illinois college students who perform"selfless public service") 1995–96.

In each of these examples, the explanation doesn't run more than a line or so, and features prominently some quality—scholarship, good citizenship, or motivation—that is desirable in a law student.

Personal Questions

All law schools ask detailed questions about criminal convictions, dishonorable discharges from the military, college or employer disciplinary actions, and even mental illnesses. As you can infer from such common instructional remarks as "Your application will be considered incomplete without this information" and "Superficial [explanations] lacking detail will substantially prejudice your application," law schools take these questions extremely seriously.

To give you some perspective on what is at stake, I reprint here the instructions on Widener University Law School's application form:

> If you have been a party to any criminal proceeding; been arrested, summoned, charged with, or convicted of a crime; been confined to a mental, penal or correctional institution; or if you have undergone mental treatment, your ability to be admitted to the practice of law—even after successful completion of your legal studies and graduation from law school—may be severely limited in one or more states or jurisdictions . . .
>
> Carefully review your application to make certain that all pertinent facts and information have been disclosed. Any discrepancies discovered after you matriculate could subject you to dismissal from the Law School. Questions asked on the application are also asked by bar examiners; some examiners check these answers against those on law school applications. Any discrepancies may adversely affect your admission to the bar. Of particular importance are juvenile or minor matters for which the court has sealed the records. *Many bar examiners take the position that the records are not sealed for purposes of admission to the bar.* [Emphasis in original]

Few law schools ask for all the information listed in this paragraph. Most ask only about felony convictions not expunged or pardoned. You need not volunteer what isn't asked for, but you must provide whatever information is requested. Information about criminal convictions, dishonorable discharges, and involuntary commitments to mental institutions can easily be checked against public records.

Don't feel, however, that a single blot on your record forever bars you from the practice of law. Many youthful indiscretions can be lived down. Uncharacteristic lapses in adults otherwise of good character are commonly ignored. And society now takes a much more liberal attitude toward many things that previously would have indicated poor moral character. Felony convictions for civil rights disobedience or draft resisting, divorces, non-marital pregnancies, and especially mental illnesses are all viewed much differently now than they were 30 years ago.

For this reason, if there is some skeleton in your closet, I recommend that you seek an informational interview with an admissions official at each law school that you apply to. Ask for a candid assessment of how the information is likely to be received, and whether other evidence can be submitted of good character and rehabilitation. The law school may ask you to seek further enlightenment from the bar examiners.

Some forms have a box that you can check if you want the law school to arrange such a *personal interview*. Use it if you have some special problem or there is something unusual in your background: if, for example, you have a partly foreign education or a handicap. If there's no such box, you should seek an interview by telephone. (I'll have more to say about these interviews in Chapter 12.)

The application may instruct you to list the names, titles, addresses, and even telephone numbers of the two to four people you will ask to write *letters of recommendation*. If you supply this information, the law school will know what letters are supposed to be in your file.

If you're asked to supply the *names and addresses of relatives who have attended the law school* you're applying to (or its parent university), the law school is signaling that it will consider your family background in the application process. You're fortunate if you are a "legacy"; there's a possibility that the law school will give you a marginal break because it doesn't want to offend your alumni relatives who are potential benefactors. If you have such an advantage, use it! Document the family relationship with the university as extensively as you can on the form. If your aunt attended the law school, ask her to write a letter to the law school explaining how she hopes you'll help her start (or continue) a multigenerational family tradition of attending that school. But don't expect much to come of it. Being a legacy won't make up for poor numbers.

Some law schools ask you to document your *family background* in some detail. Now that all law schools are more concerned to find academic merit in students, rather than good upper-class social connections, you may wonder why this information is still requested. You're not alone. No law school representative has been able to explain why this question is still asked. But providing this information can't hurt you. If your family is illustrious, some of the charm may rub off on you. And if your parents are of modest accomplishments, you're demonstrating that you're rising in life by developing and exercising your own talents.

Open-Ended Questions

Some law schools leave room on the form for a brief paragraph in which you can list *other qualifications*. Or they instruct you to use a jump sheet for this purpose. Typical questions ask for "any other factors concerning yourself that you think the admission committee should consider," or "any other unique personal qualities, talents and/or any activities . . . which indicate significant achievement." Don't list talents or character traits in the abstract. It isn't helpful for you to write "I am musically talented" or "I'm an extremely persistent person who never quits." Instead, list here any accomplishments that tend to provide evidence that you possess law-school-related talents or character traits. If not listed elsewhere on the application form, you should include

- fluency in a foreign language

- residence in a foreign country or extensive travel abroad

- computer or similar technical skills, beyond those commonly attained by liberal arts graduates

- publications

- publication or exhibition of photography or work in a similar art medium

- non-degree granting educational work completed

- ordination as a religious official

- honorably discharged veteran status

- proficiency on a musical instrument, as demonstrated by recitals or other performances

When responding to this question, it's best to present the information in the form of a list, providing dates and names as you would in listing your employment history:

> Lived in Aix-en-Provence, France, 1994–95, and developed proficiency in spoken and written French

Take a similar approach if the law school asks you to "comment on your application" or "describe any circumstances the knowledge of which would help the law school in judging your qualifications," or "identify any special circumstances that this law school should know about . . . that shed light on your academic record." These questions call for *explanations* and you can use them to try to minimize some shortcoming or weakness.

All the characteristics of a good explanation are in the following brief example:

> My grade point average would be a 3.65 if you leave out my uncharacteristically poor performance in the first semester of my sophomore year. I broke my leg in a job-related accident right before classes began. It's really hard to pay attention in class and study when you are on pain medication and crutches!

Notice that the student suggests a weakness—a low overall GPA number—but doesn't dwell on it. Instead, he stresses how much better his other semesters were. He identifies the reason for his single "uncharacteristically poor" performance (and incidentally demonstrates a strong vocabulary) in language that makes it clear that it wasn't his fault and is unlikely to be repeated.

If possible, you should suggest that the problem was a temporary one, or that it has been fixed. If you went through a messy divorce, note that the process has been completed. If you failed calculus because you couldn't see the blackboard, emphasize that your new glasses give you 20/20 vision. Note that you've moved out of the noisy fraternity house. Don't be afraid to admit that you sought professional help for your study problem, low self-esteem, or chronic depression. Law schools are used to hearing about adolescent problems, and they know that the ability to find and fix them is itself a characteristic of maturity. If you're a marginal applicant, most law schools will use your explanations when they evaluate your grades.

As a rule, you should emphasize the permanence of any improvement in your record:

> When I started college, my grades were poor. But if you look through my transcript, you'll see that each semester is better than the one before.
>
> *or*
>
> When I started college my grades were poor. But since I spent four years in the Marines they've improved dramatically.
>
> *or*
>
> I wasn't able to concentrate during my freshman year because my parents were divorcing. My grades improved when my home life became stable.
>
> *or*
>
> When I started college, I thought I had to seek a traditional woman's career. It took me a year to realize that I didn't want to be a schoolteacher and another year to realize that nursing is not for me. But since I decided to go to law school, my grades have improved.

In essence, the purpose of such an excuse is to convince the law school that it's not appropriate to use its usual predictor of success—the GPA—to predict the likelihood that you will succeed. Your case will be stronger if you can suggest some alternative evaluation criterion:

> I know that my GPA is a little below your median. I had a bad freshman year because I wasn't mature enough for college work. But in my junior year I had one 4.0 semester and one 3.8 semester. These grades show you what I'm capable of, not the overall GPA.

or

My GPA is deceptive. I've had weak semesters and strong semesters. The weak ones coincide with my working 30 hours or more a week and the strong ones coincide with when I didn't.

Here is the way one nontraditional student described his poor undergraduate showing:

When I went to college, many years ago, the curriculum was fixed. I had to take many required courses that didn't have much value to me, and consequently I didn't do very well. My grades in hard sciences were always higher than my grades in Latin, philosophy, and history.

You can use the same tactic with the LSAT:

My LSAT score is low. But I have a history of doing poorly on standardized tests and, as you can see from my grades, I have always done better than the tests predicted.

Some law schools suggest in their catalogs the kinds of compensating factors that they will view favorably. The University of Illinois notes that its admission committee may consider

. . . (1) physical handicap of the student, (2) maturity and experience achieved outside the undergraduate classroom, (3) presence of multiple LSAT scores with significantly differing scores or an undergraduate record marred by poor grades for only a brief period of time, (4) the student's success as an undergraduate in spite of the need to work significant hours outside the classroom, and (5) ethnic and cultural background of the applicant.

If you come across a list like this, you can phrase your explanations to fit into one of these categories.

You should also use the explanations paragraph to identify any special circumstances: write "Hold for fall grades," for example, if you want the law school to wait for an updated LSDAS report.

What to Enclose with the Applications

Depending on the school, you'll have to enclose supplementary forms and other materials. Here, in no particular order, are some common items:

- The required *application fee*. Three or four schools charge no application fee, and five schools charge fees as low as $10. The current high end is Northwestern's $75; the most common fee is $30 or $35. A few state schools have a discount for residents. Some will waive the application fee; if you're poor, consider requesting an informational interview for this purpose (see Chapter 12).

- One or more *preaddressed postcards*, if they are included in your application packet. The law school will use them to notify you of the status of your application. A typical school will ask you to return two or three. Some simply say, "We have received your application." Others may say "Your application is complete;" or "Your application is incomplete; we are missing _____." Address, stamp, and send back the preprinted postcards even if, as I recommend, you send your application certified mail. The law school will use the postcards anyway, as a matter of routine, and it may upset their record-keeping if they are omitted.

- One or more *essays* or *personal statements*: I'll discuss these in Chapter 10.

- *Letters of recommendation*, in sealed envelopes, if you are applying to one of the few schools that wants you to collect and forward these letters rather than having them sent directly to the law school. (See Chapter 11.)

- One or two *writing samples*. These may be publications, articles you've written for your student newspaper or literary magazine, essays that won prizes, or even very well-received school papers. (A good independent study paper is particularly impressive because you took the initiative to develop your own project, do the research, and then organize and write the report.) A writing sample doesn't need to be on a legal topic, and it's not necessary for you to mimic the heavily footnoted style you've seen in law reviews. But whatever you send should indicate that capable professionals— editors, awards committees, creative writing teachers—have judged you to possess strong writing skills.

Writing samples should be brief, either manuscripts of thirty pages or less, photocopies, or tear sheets. If you've written a book, you can submit a published copy. But avoid bulky typescripts. As a rule of thumb, whatever you send should fit, along with the application form itself, into a standard manila file folder. If you've written a graduate thesis, dissertation, or major essay, it's better to send an abstract or a research design rather than the entire volume. (But ask your dissertation adviser to write a letter of recommendation commenting on the scholarly importance of your project.)

One word of caution: The writing sample must be evidence that you can write clearly and well. Don't assume that your writing meets these standards just because it has been published. Some publications, and not just student-edited ones, are notoriously poorly edited. They regularly print articles filled with typographical errors and sloppy prose. If you send a law school an essay filled with howlers, you'll create the impression that you're a sloppy and careless writer. Proofread your sample carefully, or have a good writer proofread it for you.

Some law schools want you to fill out and return a *declaration of residence*, which will be used to determine your eligibility for the in-state resident tuition discount. If a residence form is included with your packet of application forms, read it carefully and follow the directions. You may have to have it notarized; you will have to sign it in front of a notary, who will ask you for identification and then affix a seal indicating that your identification matches the signature. Notaries are sometimes listed in the yellow pages and can commonly be found in the offices of lawyers and real estate agents. Your college controller or registrar may also have a notary available. Expect to pay a small fee for the service. Some residence forms ask you to supply evidence of your resident status; enclose photocopies of whatever is required.

- *Financial aid forms.* Each law school has its own rules for school-based financial aid. Most require you to apply for financial aid separately, after you apply for admission but before some deadline (see Appendix C). A few schools ask you to request financial aid when you apply for admission; others ask you to include a special form with your application indicating whether or not you intend to apply for financial aid. If you need support, you should follow these rules exactly.

What Not to Send

- A *cover letter* is unnecessary. This may disappoint you if you've learned to write a good cover letter in one of those courses that prepare you to apply for jobs in the business world. It won't hurt you to write a cover letter calling attention to some asset or advantage you possess: "I hope you'll look favorably on my good grades/good LSAT score/extensive work experience." But because the cover letter may not be read, be sure you repeat any information in it elsewhere in the application forms.

- You may still see forms or checklists that remind you to enclose the *LSDAS matching form* with your application. If you see such a statement, ignore it; it's only there because the law school hasn't revised its forms recently. Matching forms were little cards that the law school needed to get your report from the LSDAS. Law Services provided the forms, and you were supposed to enclose one with each law school application. Law Services moved to an electronic communications system in 1994 and discontinued the use of the matching forms.

- Omit *excuse notes* for things you've explained away on the application form. I once read an essay in which a student explained away his bad freshman year grades by noting that he had to take strong prescription medicine that made him drowsy and unable to study. This is fine: it's a one-time-only problem that had since been fixed. But the candidate also submitted a photocopy of his medical records, a section from the Physician's Desk Reference about the recorded side effects of the medication, and a note from his mother. This copious documentation only called repeated attention to his poor semester. Don't overdo the excuses. Focus attention on your good points.

- As a rule, avoid sending *bulky or oversized material*. I've had students submit bulky art works and even essays written on large chunks of wood. (I'll talk about "creative media" in Chapter 10.) They wanted to attract attention to themselves. They certainly succeeded in attracting the attention of the overworked secretary who had to keep track of material that doesn't fit into a standard manila folder. Such attention is rarely desirable. You're best advised to submit photos or slides of large art works or installations or videocassettes of performance art.

- But you shouldn't send *photos of yourself*. Portraits might seem innocuous, but they were traditionally used to enforce racial discrimination. A few schools still allow you to provide a photo on an optional basis, and Pepperdine allows you to file with your application the identification photo that you will need if you're accepted. But most law schools now refuse to accept photo portraits.

- There's no need to send *copies of award certificates or honors* either, unless they are so unusual that you weren't able to describe them fully on the application form.

- Older lawyers may have advised you to include copies of your *military discharge papers* with your law school applications. It certainly won't hurt to identify yourself as a veteran. But the papers are no longer needed, now that the draft is ended.

Mailing It Off

I suggest that you make a careful rough draft of the application form, any supplemental forms, and whatever personal statements (see Chapter 10) you intend to submit. Take the time to look up any phone numbers and addresses you are asked to supply. Make sure that the spelling and punctuation is correct.

Then type the final draft neatly. You probably won't be able to use your word processor, and many applications are on colored paper which makes neat erasures difficult if not impossible. So take your time.

If the form has such tiny lines and boxes that it can't be done neatly on a typewriter, it is acceptable to print. But do it neatly, in black or blue ink. At all costs, you want to avoid making it look like your application was dashed off at the last minute, perhaps while you were watching television and eating something greasy.

Make sure that your name appears on each page of the application, including any jump sheets and essays that you may attach to the main form. It's a good idea to number the pages. One system would be to type

Lermack application
1 of 9 pages

in the lower right-hand corner of each 8½" by 11" page. (Always begin with the main form that has your address and personal data on it.) Don't number the postcards, though.

Group all of the pages together with a paperclip. Don't staple them or use any other permanent fastener. Use your checklist—the checklist you made when you first went through the application packet—to make sure that you have all the forms. Then sign the main form and any other place that requires a signature. (Some law schools may ask you to sign or initial each page.) The law school will return an unsigned form, which will delay your application.

Application Checklist

Law School _____

____ Main application form
     ____ All questions answered
     ____ All pages present
     ____ Jump sheets clearly identified
     ____ Rough draft carefully proofread

____ Supplemental materials (cross out those not sent to this law school)
     ____ Application fee
     ____ Preaddressed postcard(s)
     ____ Essay(s)
     ____ Letters of recommendation in sealed envelopes
     ____ Writing sample(s) _____
     ____ Residency form
     ____ Financial aid form
     ____ Affirmative action eligibility form
     ____ (Other) _____
     ____ (Other) _____

____ Preparation for mailing
     ____ Final draft carefully proofread
     ____ Final draft signed and dated
     ____ All pages numbered
     ____ Pages assembled with paperclip, smaller forms on top
     ____ Photocopies made
     ____ Envelope addressed to correct law school
     ____ Envelope tightly sealed
     ____ Sufficient postage affixed

Mailed on _____
     (If certified, staple receipt to this page)

Certified mail receipt returned on _____
     (attach postcard)

Notification application received _____
     (attach postcard)

Notification application complete _____
     (attach postcard)

Make a photocopy of every page of every application, including the postcards and your check. If the law school loses some document, it may ask you to replace it. If you discuss your application with a law school official on the telephone or at an interview, your photocopy will remind you of what you told the school about yourself.

If you have numerous pages, you can use a manila file folder to keep them together and flat. But don't buy a fancy cover. When your application arrives at the law school, a clerk will place it in one of the law school's files and your cover will probably be discarded.

If a preaddressed mailing envelope came with the application, use it. That will maximize the likelihood that your application will land on the correct desk. (Some law schools even supply postage-paid envelopes.) If not, put everything unfolded into a manuscript-sized envelope. Make sure that the application to school A goes into the envelope addressed to A and the application to school B goes into the envelope addressed to B. Each year, one law school admissions official told me, eight or ten applications to other law schools turn up in her mail. Presumably, applications to her law school turn up in some other school's mail. Don't depend on law school officials to straighten out such messes. Some of them have a sense of humor about such things, but others don't.

Make sure that the envelope is sealed. You may need to use a strip or two of transparent tape.

I recommend that you mail your application by certified mail, requesting a return receipt. That way you won't be dependent on the law school for proof that the application was received. If you don't send it certified mail, be sure to affix sufficient postage. It will delay you if your application is returned for insufficient postage and embarrass you if it is delivered to the law school postage due.

Notification

Most law schools will mail back one of the preaddressed postcards to notify you that your application has arrived. Some law schools notify you when your application is complete—that is, when the LSDAS report and all the letters of recommendation have been received—by mailing off a second postcard. A few law schools send out notices only if your application is not complete by some fixed cutoff date shortly before the final application deadline. Some law schools send out no notices whatsoever.

It's your responsibility to make sure that your file is complete before the law school's formal deadline. A fairly common reason for rejection is the absence of some essential piece of information. In case of an appeal, you may have to document the submission of various items. Save your certified mail receipt and whatever communications you receive from the law school, even if they're just form letters. Write down the name of anyone at the law school you talk to on the telephone, and summarize your conversation. You may need evidence that you have at least begun the application process if something gets lost later on. Scrutinize your monthly LSDAS update reports. The LSDAS should send a copy of your file to a law school within two months of the date your application was received there. If it hasn't, call LSDAS to find out whether the law school requested the report. If the law school didn't, call to find out why not.

I tell my students to call the law school admission office six weeks after the application was mailed unless they are notified that the application is complete. Ask if you can find out the status of your application. The administrator should be able to tell you what documents have been received and what documents are missing. (Some officials won't give this information out on the phone, but will write you a letter if you request one.) You can then take steps to secure the missing documents. Most commonly, letters of recommendation are missing. You'll have to visit your recommenders and remind them to write. (See Chapter 11.)

The Early Application Advantage

Most law schools have only one entering class each year. Its studies begin in late August or September; the formal application deadline for that class may be as late as March 15 of the previous spring or as early as January 15. (Some local law schools still have no formal deadlines and accept applications until their first-year classes are filled.) But law school applications aren't like income tax returns. There's nothing to be gained by waiting until just before the deadline. If you apply earlier, in October and November— that is, 10 or 11 months before you will begin your legal studies—you may gain some small advantage over applicants who wait until the last minute.

Most law schools now use some variant of the rolling admissions system. Although these systems can be extremely complicated in practice, they are simple in principle. The law school doesn't wait until after its formal deadline to make its acceptance decisions. It doesn't collect all the applications, rank them, and then admit the top applicants based on that ranking. Rather, it makes a decision on each applicant as soon as his or her file is complete or, at some schools, as soon as a few complete files have accumulated. These decisions are based on a prediction of what the qualifications of the total applicant pool will look like.

At the beginning of the application year, the law school adopts a set of grade and LSAT score cutoffs. If an applicant's index number—the weighted combination of GPA and LSAT score, as determined by the school's LSDAS admission formula— is higher than the high cutoff point, the law school accepts the candidate automatically. By extending an offer of acceptance early in the placement year, the law school maximizes the likelihood that this desirable candidate will actually enroll.

There's a second cutoff point, with much lower GPA and LSAT scores, for rejections. If a candidate's index number falls below this second point, the law school will reject him or her out of hand. If a candidate's index number falls between the high "automatic accept" number and the low "automatic reject" number, he or she is put into a wait-and-see group.

Wait-and-see candidates are left until the end of the placement year, evaluated, compared one with another, and then ranked. Enough of them are then accepted to fill up whatever places are left unfilled by automatic admits. If you are in the wait-and-see group, letters of recommendation, essays, and other admission variables will be considered in detail. The law school may look behind the numbers with some care, to determine which candidates are most likely to succeed.

Being put in the wait-and-see group is the best marginal applicants can hope for. And it will give them the chance to display non-numerical qualifications to the admissions committee. But if you're a good candidate— that is, if you are applying to an insurance school or one for which you are highly competitive—then you want to be admitted automatically. You won't have to compete in a formal ranking against other applicants and you'll know the law school's decision early in the placement year. The automatic admit (or reject) decisions are based almost entirely on GPA and LSAT numbers.

Not entirely, of course. The law school will wait to make sure that your application packet is complete, and it may withhold admission if there's something wrong with one of the forms or if there is a question or omission. Some schools may informally give preference to applicants from known high-quality undergraduate schools, although in my experience most law schools consider this variable only for wait-and-see candidates. But except for this brief screening, all the other forms that you generate will be barely read. One reason for using a rolling admission system is that it's easier to accept or reject students based on numbers than it is to make the detailed evaluation necessary to rate candidates in the wait-and-see group.

This assumes that the cutoff points can be set at the appropriate level. The cutoff point must be high enough to capture only good prospects, but not so high that only a very few candidates are automatically accepted. Ideally, the cutoff point will be just high enough to capture exactly the number of candidates the law school wants to admit. If it wants, say, 300 admits—150 in the entering class plus 150 turndowns—the law school will look at the qualifications of its last several freshman classes and set the cutoff number to automatically admit candidates as qualified or more qualified than those admitted in previous years.

In the real world, however, prediction is never exact. No two application years are ever exactly alike; if a law school bases its cutoffs solely on previous years, it will always over- or underestimate the quality of the present applicants. If it underestimates, and sets the cutoff point too low, it will automatically admit more candidates than it has room for. If it overestimates, it runs the risk of automatically accepting too few and having a tough job late in the year filling up its entering class from its wait-and-see group. If it waits too long, it faces the nightmare prospect of having its wait-and-see applicants commit themselves elsewhere, leaving the law school with unfilled seats in its freshman class.

To prevent these dangers, the admissions committee monitors the automatic admissions through the year. If they seem to be running ahead of the previous year, the committee may raise the automatic admit line, consigning to the wait-and-see group some later applicants who would have been admitted automatically had they applied earlier. If admissions are running below anticipations, the admissions committee may lower the automatic admit line. Since computers can monitor the process with great precision, it is possible to raise or lower the line numerous times during the application year.

Now, how does this affect your application strategy? The admissions committee is afraid that it may wind up with too many first-year students. But it is much more afraid of having too few. Extra students can be accommodated with extra chairs in the aisles. But an empty seat in an entering class means that the school is short one student's tuition. Since transfer students are scarce, the shortage will likely continue for three years. And there will be one fewer alumnus to contribute to the annual fund. Rather than leave a seat unfilled, the law school will admit students from a wait-and-see group, from which the cream has been skimmed by other law schools, or from a waiting list that is even more poorly qualified. Setting the cutoff point too high, one law school official told me, is a "shortcut to a downward quality spiral."

As a result, law schools tend to allow a margin for error and begin the placement year with cutoff points lower than the predicted optimum. They expect the cutoff points to be raised later on. As a result, candidates who apply early have the benefit of a lower automatic admit point than candidates who apply later. Some candidates may be automatically admitted early who would be put in the wait-and-see group had they applied later in the year. The margin for error also affects the setting of the automatic reject point. Some applicants may be placed in the wait-and-see group—and thereby given a chance to display their subjective qualifications to the admissions committee—who would have been rejected automatically had they applied later in the placement year.

There may be, therefore, a small benefit in applying early. Underline the word *small*. Don't expect some magical bonus that makes otherwise uncompetitive applicants competitive. But the small advantage may help applicants who are just marginal for a given school. You should plan to apply early unless you have some specific reason for waiting.

It is, however, possible to apply *too* early. You shouldn't send an application before the first of October, because before that date law school staffs are still busy with the administrative chores relating to the previous application year, and there is a slight chance that your envelope could be put in the wrong pile. (Some law schools now formally refuse to receive applications before the first of October.)

Traditional students should mail their applications during late October, November, or December of their senior years. Nontraditionals should observe the same eight- to ten-month lead time.

About 20 schools allow first-year students to begin at mid-year, usually in January or February, and about 80 schools have evening divisions. The application timetables for these programs will be different. They may not use rolling admissions systems. But the same principle holds true: plan to apply early unless you have some reason for waiting.

10

Personal Statements

You should always submit an essay or "personal statement" with your application, even if the law school says it is optional.

In many respects, applying to law school is like putting together a court case—say, a criminal defense. The completed application form resembles a lawyer's brief or petition, studded with carefully arranged facts. The LSDAS report is the deposition of an expert witness who has reviewed your documents and specimens. Letters of recommendation are the statements of character witnesses. In this view, the personal statement resembles the moment when the defendant takes the witness stand, faces the jury, and tells his or her own story in his or her own words. The testimony doesn't just state facts. It also reveals character and personality; it discloses the presence or absence of traits like sensitivity and maturity. The jurors see the defendant as a person, not as a summary of other people's impressions.

In criminal cases, defendants have a constitutional right to remain silent. Some do not testify. But whenever this happens, there's a perceptible sense of disappointment in the courtroom. Jurors look forward to the moment of revelation; when it doesn't come, some of them feel cheated. They think that the defendant doesn't consider them important enough to talk to, and they conclude that the defendant isn't taking the process seriously.

At all costs, you want to avoid giving the law school the impression that you are a frivolous and casual applicant. You demonstrate your seriousness by submitting a carefully prepared personal statement. Law professors know that good essays are difficult and time-consuming to write. They expect to see the personal statement in your file and are put off if it is not there.

That doesn't mean that all of the essays that are submitted are read carefully. Just as the defendant's testimony won't sway the jury in an open-and-shut case, so a personal statement won't overcome poor numbers or add anything to very good ones. In such cases, essays are not evaluated in detail. A clerk places them in the appropriate applications files and an admissions official probably skims through them. They're rarely entirely ignored: "We try to at least read through all the essays," one law professor told me, "because of the potential for embarrassment if we admit someone who turns out really nasty."

If your numbers place you on the borderline between acceptance and rejection at a school that makes a point of considering subjective factors in its admission decisions, then your personal statement will be scrutinized with care for evidence that you can do law school work. It may be studied by several admissions officials and discussed in conference. It could make the difference between acceptance and rejection.

Your personal statement will also be of vital importance if you are applying to a Group I or Group II law school. Since all their serious candidates have superb numbers, these law schools have to rely on other criteria. Because the personal statement can reveal your character more clearly than any other part of the application process, it can provide evidence that you bring something unique to legal study: unusual abilities, or background traits, or experience, or just a distinctive way of looking at the world. You won't be admitted to a top law school unless you can distinguish yourself in this way.

But even at an insurance school, where your personal statement won't be read closely and can't help you that much, it *can* hurt. If it's unclear or filled with rhetorical errors, the law school may conclude that you lack the necessary communications skills. A glaring barbarism may catch even a skimmer's eye, and if your essay reveals you to be an offensive or insincere person the skimmer may flag your file. You may then be subjected to a more detailed evaluation instead of being automatically admitted under the rolling admissions program. You need to take care with your personal statement even when you're applying to a school that should be safe.

Length

Most law schools specify only a vague length limit, typically "one or two typed pages." A single sheet of double-spaced typescript will hold about 250 words; two single-spaced sheets contain about 1,000. I suggest that you aim for a personal statement between 500 and 1,000 words. Shorter essays are too sketchy to disclose a clearly developed and unique personal voice; longer ones may make the readers impatient. You needn't worry about running a few sentences over the length limit. As one law school official told me, "If a guy is telling a good story, I'm not going to stop reading it because I get to the end of the page."

Newspaper columns written by such clear and popular writers as Mike Royko, Mike Lupica, and George F. Will are about this length, and you can study them for indications of what you can accomplish. You can also review your own freshman English themes and school newspaper columns. There's space to describe an experience, or tell an anecdote, and draw a point. But there's no room for digressions or diversions. Your essay is too long when it stops resembling a newspaper column and starts looking like an anemic short story.

Choosing a Topic

Some years ago, one applicant told me that he was asked to "describe an embarrassing mistake and explain what you learned from it." But this was an unusual exception. Very few law schools follow the tradition of creative writing and MBA programs, which require applicants to write about very specific topics. Most law schools provide only the sketchiest of directions for their personal statements. These are among the more specific instructions:

> . . . The School of Law seeks to enroll a diverse student body to enhance its educational environment. If you believe that you could contribute to the School of Law's student diversity please briefly indicate your reasons. Personal characteristics that may be considered for diversity include age, geographic background, race, ethnicity, special educational experience, physical handicap, economic disadvantage, work experience, career goals, extracurricular achievements, and community service. [Santa Clara]

> In this personal statement you may wish to discuss . . . one or more of the following: 1) any social, economic or cultural obstacle you have overcome; 2) particular achievements or qualities not otherwise revealed by this

application; 3) your ethnic, cultural and/or linguistic heritage or any un-usual or interesting family or personal background; [or] 4) specific reasons you may have for choosing Boston University School of Law. A chronological listing of your experiences and achievements is better presented in the form of a résumé not in a personal statement. [Boston University]

These are vaguer and more typical instructions:

Please attach [an essay] describing an event or achievement that has been of personal significance to you. [Valparaiso]

. . . write a brief statement describing yourself and your qualifications. You may wish to explain or emphasize a particular part of your transcript or application. [Chicago-Kent]

On a separate sheet state why you wish to pursue the study of law and any factors concerning yourself that you think the admission committee should consider. [Northern Illinois]

On a sheet of $8\frac{1}{2} \times 11$" paper, please describe . . . any unique personal qualities, talents, and/or any activities in which you have been engaged which indicate significant achievement. State how these qualities relate to your aptitude for the study or practice of law. [Stetson]

Some schools provide no direction at all. Until very recently, Temple University's form said only that, "All applicants are encouraged to submit detailed personal statements." After noting that "applicants should make an effort to see that their application files contain evidence" of various background characteristics that make for a diverse student body, Washington University says only that

Personal statements are required and should be approximately 1–2 pages in length.

From the viewpoint of an applicant, there are both advantages and disadvantages in this vagueness. Because no specific topics are required, you can write about whatever will do you the most good or help present yourself in the most attractive way possible. Instead of having to write a separate essay tailored to the specific requirements of each school you are applying to, you will probably be able to make do with just a few essays, even if you apply to 15 law schools. If you face some detailed and specific requirement, like that of Santa Clara, you'll have to write an essay for that school alone. If you want to talk about a specific school in your essay—if, for example, you want to describe an incident that made you want to attend Hypothetical Law School—then clearly you won't be able to use that essay at any other law school on your application list. If you were raised in, say, Wyoming, you can emphasize your geographical uniqueness as a way of making yourself attractive to Eastern law schools. But such an essay won't help you when you apply to your home state university. With these exceptions, you're best advised to draft and polish one essay carefully, and to use essentially the same creation for all your schools.

The drawback of not having a precise topic is that you'll have to choose your own topic. Because you have your whole life to choose from, you'll probably find it hard to make a choice.

Here are some things to keep in mind:

Write about Yourself.   As Temple's new form says, "This is your opportunity to present yourself, your background, your experiences and your ideas to the Admissions Committee." Law schools are looking for information about you, as well as for evidence of your literary talents. They are looking for evidence that you will succeed in law school and as a lawyer. Some law schools find it necessary to remind you that you are not involved in an impersonal literary enterprise:

> We seek information about you; essays on the place of law or lawyers in our society typically will not be useful. [Case Western Reserve]

Don't confuse your application essay, which must be about yourself, with the term papers or publications you might submit as writing samples, which can be about anything.

Be Specific.   Write about events and activities. Describe something that happened or an incident in which you took part. Perhaps the best application essay topic is a description of some incident or activity which led you to the study of law.

Tell a Story.   One student wrote that he came to understand his character after he had been injured in a high school football game. His coach wanted him to use illegal steroid drugs to promote faster healing. He instinctively considered steroids a form of cheating, and he realized that unlike his coach he was not committed to winning at all costs. He wanted to win within the rules. He created an analogy between the rules of football and the civil and criminal laws, which are the rules of society, and concluded that he would be a good lawyer because his personality led him to compete zealously within the limits provided by a set of rules. His essay revealed a part of his character that couldn't be captured in numbers.

Others have discussed what they've learned from college jobs, from teaching, or from serving in the Peace Corps. Young women have written about the changes that came with childbirth. "I have to make the world safe for my children," one woman wrote. "Law is part of that."

Emphasize Your Own Uniqueness. Boykin Curry's *Essays That Worked—For Law School* (Memphis, Tenn.: Mustang Publishing Co., 1988) provides model essays, taken from successful applications to prestigious law schools, that you can study for inspiration. (You should also read whatever essays you can obtain from successful law students.) Curry emphasizes that an essay must be lively and gripping in order to stand out, and his sources suggest that you concentrate on revealing a coherent and interesting personality.

One caution: the essays in the Curry book are meant to stimulate your thought, not be models to be copied or imitated. I've avoided presenting sample essays here because I detect a tendency among otherwise capable applicants to imitate models too closely, or to worry if their essays do not resemble the models they've studied. Avoid the sin of imitation. Top law schools, which receive thousands of essays each year, tend to discount as uncreative those essays that seem to be nothing but copies of commonly available models. If you're going to convince the reader of your uniqueness and depth, you'll have to find a topic that reveals your own character. It's unlikely to be more than casually similar to the topic that another individual would choose.

You may not think of yourself as unusual in any way. Perhaps you've spent so much of your time on your grades that you haven't been involved in activities that add diversity to your personality. I recommend that you take some time to search for an incident or anecdote in your past that helped to shape your character, or contributed to your interest in law, or is simply interesting in its own right. Ask your parents or siblings if they remember anything. One successful applicant wrote about organizing a surprise birthday party for his brother. It wasn't an earthshaking accomplishment, but he was only four years old when he did it.

Law schools tend to seek tough-minded, logical problem-solvers, because studies show that people with these qualities are most likely to succeed there. A personal statement about how you solved some problem (like financing your undergraduate education) or overcame some obstacle is always appropriate. Or you can write about some unusual feature of your education. If your major is not a typical one for prelaw students, you can explain how you expect it to contribute to your legal education and career. One of Bradley's engineering majors, for example, first became aware of lawyers when he had to consult one about patenting a mechanical device he had invented. He found that he enjoyed solving the problems of patenting his device more than he had enjoyed inventing it.

Or you can find an interesting way to write about some feature of your personality. One successful applicant wrote about how his health improved when he became a vegetarian. Another wrote about the healthy sense of excitement that came over her whenever she finished her social sciences and humanities homework and was free to turn to the mathematics problems that she loved.

Now here are some things to avoid:

Don't Choose a Topic that Makes You Seem Immature or of Questionable Character. Law schools know that youth includes risk-taking and a certain amount of hedonism, and they're familiar with undergraduate excesses. But it's best not to dwell on things done only by the young and immature. You can write a very interesting essay about what you learned while you were supporting yourself through college by playing in a band without mentioning how many times you were ticketed for violating the local noise pollution laws. If you were social chairman of your fraternity, you can talk about your skill at organizing the homecoming weekend festivities without mentioning the award the fraternity council gave you for the most alcoholic beverages consumed within a 24-hour period. It's also not a good idea to talk about activities that raise ethical questions. Don't, for example, describe how you earned money for tuition by peddling a device you devised for cheating on exams.

Avoid Talking about Yourself in the Abstract. Law schools receive many essays which sound like the personals ads in magazines:

> Divorced man, tall, attractive, intelligent, hardworking, athletic. Likes legal concepts, debate, politics, long walks on beach. Can write well. Seeks compatible law school.

What can you infer if someone describes himself as, say, intelligent, without giving examples or details? And what kinds of things are covered by words like *athletic*? An English teacher would mark the ad as vague; it simply doesn't say very much. I find the same problem in many of the essays that undergraduates write. They often describe themselves as cheerful, or persistent, or likeable, without giving any evidence. They want to "work for world peace" or "bring about justice," but they don't describe any specific steps they would take to reach these ideals. Don't simply say you are a leader; describe some event or incident in which you exercised leadership skills. Don't say you are persistent. Show the reader persistence, by describing a success that followed several failures:

I knew it was going to be difficult to get my short story published. But I never imagined that I would accumulate 17 rejection slips before I found an editor who was interested in it. . . . :

Avoid Emphasizing Negatives. You may be tempted to use your essay to comment on shortcomings and to try to explain away poor grades or LSAT scores. But you can't display a positive and attractive personality while you are dwelling on negatives. Try to focus your essay on positives. Talk about what you've learned, not about how your grades were lower than those of other students. Keep the reader's attention on what is attractive in your personality, and avoid reminding him or her that you are not the ideal law school prospect.

If you need to explain away some shortcoming, you should do it on the application form itself, as I've suggested in Chapter 9. If there isn't a separate line on the body of the form for explanations or additional information, consider putting them on a jump sheet as an elaboration of an answer to an objective question. Or consider omitting them entirely. If you have no choice but to put an explanation in the essay, put it at the end, in as few lines as possible.

Allow Plenty of Time

Writing a clear and persuasive essay takes time. Even after you've chosen your topic, you'll need to organize and write several drafts, have the essay read and critiqued by others, and polish the grammar and rhetoric. In my experience, the chief reason that application essays are unpersuasive is that insufficient time is taken with them. Successful applicants sometimes put their essays through ten or more drafts.

Therefore, you need to start early and allow sufficient time. On the timetable checklist in Appendix A, I've recommended that you start working on your essays the summer before your senior year of college—in July or August, that is, for applications that will be mailed out in or after October. But you can start even earlier. You needn't wait for the most recent application form, for the personal statement requirement is unlikely to change from year to year.

Getting a Good Start

You've done this before. Writing the law school essay is no different than writing anything else, except that it may count more. A good piece of writing is a good piece of writing; it has unity, force, and coherence. It communicates clearly and persuasively. You can use whatever you've learned about writing in English composition courses.

There are different ways to organize a short written piece. You can present an anecdote or incident and then explain it, or you can describe two or three events and then explain what they all have in common. That is, you can begin with specific details and progress to a general conclusion. Alternatively, you can state some general principle or conclusion first, and then describe the pieces of evidence that support it.

Some essays fall more naturally into a deductive, or conclusion-first, mode of organization, while others are more effective if told inductively, or detail-first. I suggest that you practice by writing a few drafts, trying to make your point one way and then another. Don't worry if the drafts are much too long. Just try to set down all the information, tell your story as fully as possible, and get everything in, even if there's repetition and duplication.

Now, having made these sketches, look them over. What points or arguments seem particularly central or important? What detail seems effective? When you see them on paper, which details seem slick, sophomoric, or insincere?

At this stage you'll have to decide whether to use an inductive or a deductive model. After you've determined whether your main point will come at the end or the beginning, you can make an outline. Ask how each detail relates to the main point, and prune away anything that is irrelevant or repetitious.

If you want your essay to be read carefully, you'll have to catch the attention of a bored and exhausted admissions official. You do this by writing a forceful first sentence. You'll be judged on it, just as you make a first impression with your smile and your handshake.

This need to stimulate the reader's curiosity isn't unique to applications essays. Professional writers routinely spend large chunks of their working time writing and rewriting their opening sentences. Some of their efforts are memorable. Here is the first line of Camus's compelling novel, *The Stranger*:

Mother died today. Or, maybe yesterday; I can't be sure.

Can anyone who reads that line doubt that he is in the presence of a weird and fascinating character? Here is the opening line of Gabriel Garcia Marquez's *One Hundred Years Of Solitude:*

> Many years later, as he faced the firing squad, Colonel Aureliano Buendia was to remember that distant afternoon when his father took him to discover ice.

Garcia Marquez stimulates curiosity by juxtaposing inconsistent or contradictory images: military titles attached to a condemned man; military campaigns that are somehow linked in a character's mind to a child's sense of wonder; and a familiar object, ice, presented as a curiosity.

You can appropriate these techniques of fiction to make your essay more gripping. Remember the student who became interested in law after a football injury? Here is how he began his essay:

> I decided to pursue a legal career the morning after my knee was injured in a football game.

This sentence opens up a wealth of intriguing possibilities: is he going to say that he wants to study law so he can sue the linebacker who smashed his kneecap? Is he going to have the nerve to suggest that a legal career is a consolation prize for someone who is too frail to play football professionally? After tantalizing the reader with these intriguing possibilities, he developed the essay in a different direction, and talked about his discovery of his characteristic interest in rules.

You can use the same technique:

> You may wonder why a former professional dancer wants to go to law school . . .
>
> *or*
>
> You're probably wondering why someone from a big city wants to go to law school in Wyoming . . .
>
> *or*
>
> Although working on the _____ for President campaign was extremely time-consuming, I came to think of it as an essential part of my education.

In each case you've established at the very beginning of the essay that there's something unique about you as an individual, and you've presented that information in the form of a paradox or query to stimulate the reader's curiosity.

Writing It Out

Having begun well, you then have to provide exactly as much information or evidence as you need to support your point. Your essay has to be unified, in the sense that nothing in it is unnecessary. The classic shaggy dog story is difficult to listen to because of a lack of unity. The narrator begins well by describing the ghost that appeared to young Johnny, but then veers off on a tangent about how Johnny's father is the second cousin of that same Jed Snopes who was hanged for murder in 1930, or about how Johnny grew up to drive Packard cars exclusively, or about how he later married the sister of this very narrator . . . until you just want to scream, "Yes, yes, but what about the *ghost?*"

The trick is to keep your eye on the ghost. You need to prune away everything that isn't about the ghost, or that seems repetitious, or that doesn't advance the action. You can only do this if you start with a first draft longer than you need to end up with. You write a thousand-word essay by carving away at a five-thousand-word essay.

Having done that, it's time to type up the draft and ask people to read it. Lots of people. At least some of them should be strangers. Acquaintances have heard your stories before and can often guess what you're trying to say even if you haven't written it clearly. If you are a traditional college-age applicant, try to find at least one middle-aged reader who will be able to spot teenage slang or juvenile humor.

Some college professors are willing to critique essays. College placement offices often offer a reading service, but be sure the readers know it is a law school application essay and not an MBA or job application essay. You may be able to find a high school English teacher, a graduate student, a law student that you've met through the prelaw club's mentoring program, or even a professional editor whom you pay for an assessment. Your prelaw adviser may keep a list of qualified professionals, or you can look for ads for local editing services.

It's dishonest to let a professional—or anyone else, for that matter—write the essay for you. Law schools have a control mechanism for this kind of cheating: Law Services sends each of the law schools you apply to a photocopy of the essay you wrote as part of the LSAT. If a question arises about whether or not you actually wrote your application essay, this essay can be used for comparison. Though an extemporaneous essay written under time constraints will be different from a polished essay written at leisure, educators are experienced at allowing for such differences. "It's like Frank Sinatra singing on a record and singing in his living room," one English teacher told me. "The tone isn't as good in his living room and he may hit a flat note once in a while. But it's still Frank Sinatra."

So you can't let somebody else write your essay. It has to sound like you. The rule is that the essay must be "substantially your own work." But it's perfectly ethical to hire an editor to check the grammar and spelling. A good editor will suggest ways to improve the essay—for example, by re-working the organization to put the strongest parts in more visible places—but leave the final rewrite to you.

Tone

As your essay goes through draft after draft, its should be repeatedly critiqued. Always ask your readers to paraphrase the main point of the essay. Ask also if anything seemed confusing or unclear. Work on developing an earnest and sincere tone and rewrite or eliminate anything that strikes your readers as inappropriate, in bad taste, or offensive.

That last sentence requires some elaboration. The law professors and administrators who read your essay will be looking for information about you. They'll pick out specific details. But they'll also try to make an overall assessment of your personality. If your essay is carefully organized and unified, it's natural to assume that you are a neat and careful person. That's the kind of impression you want to create. But if your essay is brash and blaring—if, for example, you write a long essay about how you were able to squelch someone else with scathing wit—the readers may come to the conclusion that you're not a very attractive person. You *don't* want to create that impression.

Tone can best be assessed by a reader who doesn't know you at all or whose contact with you has been formal and detached. Always ask your readers how the essay makes you seem: would they hire such a person? Would they go out on a date with such a person? Does the essay make you seem too flippant? Is anything in it in poor taste?

If you tell a joke, make sure it is funny. Jokes depend on timing and delivery and often do not translate well from spoken to written English. They may also be generation-specific. Older and younger people find different things funny. Ask your detached readers whether they laughed while they were reading, and, if so, where. If younger readers laughed and older ones did not, eliminate the joke; grizzled old law professors may view it as evidence of immaturity.

If you're writing about why you want to become a lawyer, you are probably wondering whether you'll be viewed unfavorably if you admit you're in it for the money. This is a question of some delicacy. Even the most cynical lawyers seem to retain a degree of idealism about their profession and they don't like to emphasize its mercenary aspects. They prefer to focus on the intellectual challenge law presents and on the important role that lawyers play in society. They frown on applicants who seem to be interested only in money.

At the same time, however, they know that not all candidates will spend their careers working among the poor for little pay. They also know that research has indicated that a desire to make money is often part of a complex of personality characteristics that includes an interest in helping others and the ability to work without close supervision. Put bluntly, they know that an interest in making money isn't incompatible with the qualities needed to be a capable and ethical lawyer.

Your best bet is to express an intellectual interest in some legal topic and to explain how your career will be built around this interest. Try to convey the impression that you are mainly interested in the work, not the compensation. If you expect to work in a large firm or in some lucrative legal area, admit it. You're merely expressing a desire to do well as a by-product of doing good. That's the American dream.

You may also wonder whether admissions officials will read your essay with an eye to deducing your political views and, if so, if there's an orthodoxy of correct views you must subscribe to. The answer is no, in the sense that the readers won't care if you are a Democrat or a Republican, or if you did volunteer work for a soup kitchen for the poor or for a think tank whose goal is the lifting of environmental protection rules. They're lawyers. They recognize legitimate political differences.

But lawyers tend to be suspicious of views that seem far out of the mainstream. I'd hesitate to use my essay to describe the thrilling lessons I'd learned while studying marksmanship at a paramilitary summer camp run by neo-Nazis. Nor would I make ideological criticisms of law as a profession or of the admissions process itself.

Many law schools are pioneers in the ongoing effort to acknowledge and respect the differences between subgroups in our multicultural society. Being "politically correct" in this sense won't hurt you, and it may help. Use common sense. Don't write in such a way that you imply the inferiority of others. If you're a man, don't refer to young women as "babes" and don't reminisce about the good old days when women stayed home with the children. If you're a woman, don't write as though men are members of an alien oppressor class.

It's worth making an effort to avoid hurting the feelings of others. If you don't you may be accused of inadvertent insensitivity, like former U. S. Representative Robert Michel. While reminiscing about his youth, Michel once rhapsodized about the fun he'd had singing in minstrel shows, wearing blackface makeup. He expressed disappointment that that form of entertainment had vanished. It didn't occur to him that his nostalgia for what he remembered as an innocent amateur pastime could legitimately be taken as an expression of racial bigotry.

Inadvertent lapses of this kind can create an incorrect impression of you. They are easily caught by disinterested readers. Some computer editing programs will flag instances of politically insensitive rhetoric. They'll make such suggestions as "Use 'woman' for 'girl' " and "Try to find a gender-neutral equivalent of 'waitress.' " If the computer sends you a lot of these messages, seek the aid of an editor.

Making It Correct

Law professors may pore over your essay for evidence that you can communicate clearly in writing. You can best demonstrate the possession of a skill that eventually can be put to use writing legal memos and briefs by making sure that your essay uses the written English language properly according to the rules. You need to demonstrate that you can write mainstream English—that is, grownup—prose.

Many lawyers and law professors are dissatisfied with the quality of the prose that their colleagues turn out. Lawyers are said to write excessively wordy and lengthy sentences, and to rely unnecessarily on the passive voice and excessively on technical terms, vague words, and repetitive qualifying clauses. Because of this criticism, writing requirements have been stiffened at many law schools.

You can make yourself attractive by showing that your own prose does not suffer from the defects common in the profession. C. Edward Good's 1989 book, *Mightier Than The Sword: Powerful Writing In The Legal Profession* (Charlottesville, Va.: Blue Jeans Press, 1989), analyzes many of the rhetorical traps that legal prose commonly falls into, and gives suggestions for rewriting to avoid them. Try to avoid weak words like "perhaps," flabby constructions like "it may be thought that," and excessive use of the passive voice. It's a good idea to avoid footnotes.

Grammar and punctuation count. Word usage, proper paragraphing, and such sophisticated rhetorical techniques as parallelism, all count. If you have difficulty with such things, refer to any standard guide to English usage. *The Little, Brown Handbook* and similar manuals are commonly available on campus. Perhaps you've kept the copy you needed for freshman English composition.

Stick to standard English. If you're a nontraditional and you describe your work experience, make sure you define any unusual words and explain any technical processes. Unless you need it for some specific reason, it's best to avoid slang, especially teenage slang. The essay will be read by people substantially older than yourself, and it will not help you if they find it unintelligible. Avoid legal jargon unless you need it for some specific purpose and can handle it properly. Law professors will spot any errors; besides, legal rhetoric tends to make young people sound pompous and pedantic. Think of the law students you've met who speak in long, windy sentences full of big words and Latinisms.

A spelling mistake, even a minor one, stands out and makes you look like a clod. Having a spelling mistake on an otherwise neatly written paper is like having a spot of mustard on your face at a formal reception. The reader's eye goes right to it. Even people who can't spell themselves catch the spelling mistakes of others. If you're a poor speller, you should use one of the common word processing programs with a spelling checker and ask your readers to check for errors.

Once you've polished what you hope will be a final draft, you should seek out an English teacher for a final reading for grammatical and rhetorical correctness. (One student scheduled a creative writing course for the fall semester of his senior year, so he would have an academic reason for asking a professor to read his application essays.)

Format

Law schools have received essays scribed on birch bark and homemade parchment, drawn on watercolor paper with calligraphy pens, crayoned on manila paper, and even scrawled on cocktail napkins with bleeding fountain pens. Increasingly, they receive essays on videotape, either read aloud by the candidate or dramatized in some fashion. In response, most now instruct you to submit your work only on white $8^{1}/_{2}$" × 11" typing paper.

Even if you have a choice, don't use a bizarre format just to demonstrate "creativity" apart from the content of your essay. True, law schools keep insisting that they want creative students. But a lawyer's idea of creativity involves innovation within established forms. It's not the creativity of the sculptor who is free to choose steel, granite, or cream cheese, depending on his or her inspiration. It's the creativity of the cake decorator, who must decide how to make the cake look appetizing but whose choice of materials is limited by the overriding fact that the cake must remain safe to eat. A lawyer must express an idea clearly and persuasively. But he or she must do so in a brief written in very standardized language, typed on the kind of paper specified by the judge, and filed with a clerk by a certain deadline. Consider yourself bound by established forms. Use $8^{1}/_{2}$" × 11" paper unless some alternate medium contributes something to the message that can be added in no other way.

A few law schools want you to submit your essay in your own handwriting. This will enable officials to compare it with your LSAT essay and whatever other specimens of your handwriting are in your file to determine whether the essay is actually your own work. (Theoretically, it also permits detailed analysis by handwriting experts, but I don't know of any law schools actually doing graphology at the moment.) If no such requirement exists, your essay should be carefully typed. You need not buy extra-heavy bond paper or rent a laser printer.

As with anything you do, neatness counts. Typographical errors, and even blots and smudges, distract the attention of the reader from the content of the essay. The best way to avoid typographical errors is to type the essay yourself on word processing equipment, stopping frequently to proofread. Hired typists, and even friends, are less familiar with your own vocabulary and less well motivated to do a good job.

Before you send it off, make sure your name appears on each page of your essay. Number the pages, and use paper clips rather than staples. You want your final application to reflect attention to detail and thoroughness—the qualities admissions officers look for in potential future lawyers.

11

Letters of Recommendation

Recommenders, as I'll call them, are people who know you well and can objectively describe activities you have been involved in or comment on your character, talents, or intellect. They fill out forms or write letters. Although a few law schools discourage you from submitting letters of recommendation, most actively seek them, claiming that they provide valuable information about your potential for success in law school. Here, for example, is what the University of San Francisco hopes to obtain from recommenders:

> The Committee [on Admission] is interested in knowing how long, how well, and in what connection you have known the applicant. We are particularly concerned with your comments regarding the applicant's 1.) native intelligence and independence of thought; 2.) special interests, motivations, personal qualities, social and academic background or emotional makeup *which may distinguish the applicant from other applicants*; and 3.) overall promise, character and fitness to practice law. [Emphasis added]

Like personal statements, writing samples, and the other subjective parts of the application process, letters of recommendation are not central to the admit/reject decision. They will not outweigh poor numbers. They are counted and skimmed, and may be summarized by a secretary or clerk.

But at most law schools admissions officials do not scrutinize them carefully except in marginal cases or when a letter reveals some otherwise unreported blot on the applicant's character. Group I and II law schools, which must sort out large numbers of candidates with outstanding numbers, traditionally pay more attention to letters of recommendation.

Therefore, when you are applying to insurance schools, you should approach letters of recommendation defensively, making sure to obtain the required number of letters from well-chosen recommenders who are unlikely to write bad ones. In most cases, good letters are unlikely to make a critical difference (although they may help a little), but bad letters—or no letters—can hurt. By contrast, marginal applicants and applicants to top law schools must try to obtain the best possible letters.

How Many Recommenders?

Each law school determines how many letters of recommendation it wants you to submit. Most indicate, either in their catalogs or in the instructions that accompany the packet of blank application forms, that they require or "strongly recommend" two, three, or four. If you don't submit the required minimum, the law school may consider your file incomplete and take no action on it. Some law schools try to notify candidates if their files are incomplete. Others do not. Whether you are notified or not, you'll be rejected if your file remains incomplete when the school's application deadline has passed.

Some law schools have set maximums or ceilings. They state in their catalogs that they will read no more than four, or five, or six letters for any one applicant. They do so to protect themselves against uncontrollable increases in their workloads. The limits are also meant to discourage you from submitting barrages of letters from famous or politically influential people (perhaps friends of your parents) who know you only superficially. Law school representatives have reportedly received applications accompanied by as many as 30 superficial letters; they view these letters either as camouflage meant to disguise an otherwise poor record or as efforts to exert political influence. (One law school official described a blizzard of letters praising a poorly qualified applicant as an "epistolary snow job.")

Since they may not be read, there's usually little point in submitting more than the maximum number of letters. But there are exceptions. If you are a nontraditional applicant and you want to demonstrate a consistently distinguished, or at least interesting, business career, you should seek a letter of reference from each of the places you have worked. Warn the law school that a large number of letters will arrive by typing something like this on your application:

> In the oil business, salesmen tend to move around a great deal. I've had seven jobs in the last twenty years. To make sure you fully understand my employment history, I've asked each of these employers to write you a letter of reference. I hope you don't mind reading an extra letter or two. But I couldn't think of any other way to provide this necessary information.

You may also want to guard against the possibility that one of your recommenders will forget to send off his or her letter. This is not usually a problem. Most professionals and employers consider writing letters of recommendation to be part of their jobs and set time aside for that purpose. College professors, especially, tend to take pride in the professional placement of their former students. In a sense, it's what they have to sell. They're usually quite conscientious about writing useful letters and meeting the deadlines. However, there really are absent-minded professors out there. At some large schools the professors have so many students, and are so consistently overworked, that there is a very real possibility that a form will get misplaced or a deadline will be missed.

If you're worried that one of your recommenders may default, consider the strategy of seeking an extra recommendation. Arrange to submit three letters if two are required, or four if three are required. If all the letters arrive, you may have wasted time and effort. But if one of the recommenders defaults, you will have protected yourself against the risk of having your file set aside as incomplete.

Choosing Recommenders

You'll have to choose two to four recommenders, perhaps more. As a rule, you can use the same set of recommenders for all the schools on your application list. The best recommenders are people who know you well and have some special skills or experiences that make them good judges of the talents of young people. Examples include undergraduate teachers who have seen many former students go on to law school, employers who hire and supervise the work of young people, or counselors, psychologists and clergy who work with college students. Lawyers, who have personal experience of legal education, are also desirable recommenders. With certain exceptions, each law school will leave the choice of recommenders up to you.

Some law schools insist on at least one letter from a professor, because teachers are the best situated to comment on an individual candidate's intelligence, study-related skills, and academic accomplishments. Professors can often compare candidates with "known quantities": candidates from previous years, law students, and lawyers. Some professors write many letters; prelaw advisers and other teachers of BGE subjects often develop considerable experience in evaluating potential for legal study. As nearby law schools become familiar with a given professor's letters, they may give the letters greater weight. Some law schools divide letters of recommendation into two categories and give all letters from teachers greater weight than letters from other recommenders.

In his 1974 book, *How to Get into Law School*, Rennard Strickland quotes an admissions committee member as saying that letters from former teachers are "way yonder the most important." You should always submit at least one letter from a former teacher, even if it is not explicitly required. Your application will seem suspicious without it, as though you're trying to hide some disreputable aspect of your undergraduate career. You're unlikely to have difficulty finding at least one professor who will write a letter for you if your record is generally good.

A few law schools continue the old tradition of asking for a recommendation from a college dean. Years ago, when colleges were small enough for the deans to know all their students, deans would comment on an applicant's moral fitness, including such matters as whether or not the student was a regular churchgoer. Deans would also reveal any disciplinary infractions on an applicant's undergraduate record. But those days are long over. If you need a letter from a dean, ask your prelaw adviser what the policy is at your college. Most likely, you will be instructed to give the letter form to a certain dean—at Bradley, we use the dean of the college of liberal arts—and the dean will then ask you to suggest one or two teachers who can comment on your work. One of these teachers will be asked to draft a letter for the dean's signature. At other colleges the dean of students or some equivalent officer fills out the forms, notifying the law school of any disciplinary infractions in your file. If there are none, the dean will simply write that he or she doesn't know of any reason why the candidate should not be admitted. At still other colleges, the prelaw adviser fills out the forms over a dean's signature.

Employers who have been able to observe your job performance and who are in a position to comment on your motivation, enthusiasm, and ability to work consistently and well are also good recommenders. If you are a nontraditional applicant and want your work experience to be viewed as a qualification for legal study, good references from former employers are vital.

If you are a traditional student, all your co-workers have probably also been young people. Your immediate supervisor—the shift manager at the fast food place, the office manager or librarian at your college job—is in a good position to compare you with other students. You should choose a recommender who will make a favorable comparison.

If you have worked in a lawyer's office, your employers will probably consider a letter of recommendation to be part of your reward for a job well done. They have a tendency to exaggerate their influence. Don't overly rely on a lawyer's letter simply because she is a friend of the dean's, or has worked as an adjunct law professor, or donates lots of money to the school's fundraising efforts. Because many, many lawyer-alumni and lawyer-contributors write letters for various candidates, no one candidate can get any special benefits. Nevertheless, lawyers are desirable recommenders. They can testify about your work habits. Because they are familiar with legal education, they can comment authoritatively about your ability to perform necessary tasks like working regularly, writing clearly, or operating research computers. Like professors, lawyers can often compare you favorably with successful candidates of previous years.

Coaches and trainers often make surprisingly good recommenders. They know applicants well from direct daily contact, and are in a good position to comment on such qualities as drive, dedication, and persistence. They are often good judges of intelligence and communications skills. But never submit more than one letter from a coach. You don't want to give the impression that your undergraduate education was disproportionately focused on athletics.

As much as possible, you should seek recommenders who can comment on the important activities in your life. If you have been active in political campaign work, a letter from a party professional is appropriate. If you are a religious person who is active in church-affiliated youth groups, charity work, or religious study, your minister is a good person to choose to describe this work. But if your only contact with your minister is an occasional attendance at a church service, he or she is probably not a good person to evaluate your potential for law school success.

> Recommenders are most valuable if they are good judges of talent or character, have had a good opportunity to evaluate you, and perceive you favorably.

A letter from a lawyer, even a very respected one, will be of little value if it is clear that the lawyer doesn't know you very well and is writing only out of a sense of obligation to your parents. By contrast, one law school dean told me that he was moved by reading a letter from a construction contractor who described how hard, and how enthusiastically, the applicant worked at a tedious demolition job during a sweltering period of summer employment. Although the contractor was uneducated, he clearly knew and respected hard work. He had observed the applicant carefully over a period of time and the applicant had earned his respect.

Since a recommender should be able to comment objectively, he or she ought not to be a relative or a close friend with whom your contact has been mainly social or romantic. You ought not to seek letters from anyone who is indebted to or dependent on you, like an employee. As a rule, traditional applicants ought not to seek letters from people younger than themselves. Other students, even law students, are not good recommenders because they haven't had extensive experience judging youthful potential.

Format

Some law schools have no special forms for letters of recommendation. They tell you to ask your recommenders to write on their letterheads. Other law schools have elaborate "appraisal forms" or "referral forms"; some include detailed objective questions or scales that the recommenders are encouraged (but not required) to use to evaluate your intellectual skills and communications skills. Still other law schools provide only a half-page set of instructions which you are asked to give to each recommender. You should type your name and address on whatever forms the law school provides. Make photocopies if the law school didn't send enough for all your recommenders. Keep extra photocopies; if a recommender bungles the form, or loses it before it's mailed off, you'll have to supply a replacement.

Until 1974 law schools kept letters of recommendation confidential, on the theory that recommenders would be more candid if they knew that their comments would not be reported to the applicants whose qualifications they were discussing. But the federal Privacy Act of 1974 creates a right of access; a law school must show applicants the contents of their files if they ask to see them. Law schools responded to the Act of 1974 by asking applicants to accept confidentiality voluntarily. Most now include a section on their recommendation forms titled "Waiver of your right of access" which you are asked to fill out and sign. If you check the box marked "I waive my right of access," then you will never be permitted to see that letter of recommendation. The recommender will always know in advance whether or not you have waived your right of access.

Although you can't be forced to waive your right, I advise you to do so. Law school admissions committees naturally assume that confidential letters will be more candid and may give them greater weight. They may distrust even glowing letters if secrecy is not guaranteed. In any case, many professors refuse to write letters of recommendation unless access is waived.

Getting Good Letters

Beyond filling in your personal information and completing the waiver, you don't need to write anything on the appraisal forms. Your first chore will be to persuade each of your recommenders to fill them out.

At the outset, you should choose your recommenders carefully. Try to find people with whom you have worked closely. Professors with whom you have done independent study papers, or in whose seminars you participated in thoughtful discussions, or from whom you have taken several courses, are most likely to be familiar with your work. Choose them, rather than possibly more prestigious professors with whom you have had little contact. If a professor has frequently made approving comments about your work, or written warm compliments on your essays, he or she is more likely to write similar approbations in your letters. Professors who critique your written work carefully and write copious comments on your exams and term papers are more likely to write similarly copious letters.

You'll need to contact each recommender at least twice. Although you can communicate with them by letter or telephone, you'll get the best results if you visit personally. As soon as you've finalized your application list, visit the recommenders to ask whether they will be willing to serve as references. For traditional students, this initial contact will come very early in the senior year: late August or early September. Approach professors during their office hours and employers at some convenient time when they are not busy. If you don't have regular contact with a recommender, call for an appointment. At this initial stage, you need do little more than remind the recommenders of who you are and explain what they will have to do. Be modest and polite; the purpose of this first visit is to create a favorable impression and to remind them (in ways that I'll describe in the next section) that they think well of you.

Always indicate how many letters you will need. Don't hesitate to ask recommenders to write letters to five to fifteen law schools. In most cases, they won't write fifteen letters; they'll write one letter and copy it, with perhaps a personalizing end paragraph or two.

To make it as easy as possible for your recommenders, you should give them the forms for all the law schools you are applying to at the same time, during a second visit to each recommender's office. This second visit should occur before you mail your application forms to the law schools. For traditional students, it will come in late September, October, or early November—sooner if you will enclose the completed letters with your application and later if the recommenders will mail them directly to the law schools. (If you decide later in the year to apply to additional law schools, you can return to each recommender with more forms. Most professors will cooperate—at least once. Try to avoid repeated impositions.) At your second visit, you will also provide the information each recommender will need to write good letters for you.

Bad Letters and Good Letters

But what is a good letter? It's easy enough to imagine bad letters:

> Mr. ____ worked for me for two years, and he was such a consistent screwup that I hardly know where to begin. . .
>
> or
>
> Ms. ____ isn't the worst student I've had in my twenty years of teaching, but she came close. . .
>
> or
>
> I strongly suspected Mr. ____ of plagiarizing his term paper in my course in ____, but I didn't report it at the time because I couldn't prove it. Later on, I came across the proof I need, and I can say without fear of a libel judgment that Mr. ____ is a complete scoundrel.

In real life, it's rare for recommenders to try to discourage the law school from admitting you. Most people seem to subscribe to a code of chivalry; if they think you shouldn't be admitted to law school, they'll try to avoid having to write damning letters of recommendation by refusing to write any letters at all. If you ask someone for a reference and he begs off, perhaps with a lame excuse, don't try to change his mind. He may be signaling his unwillingness to hurt you.

This means that you can usually expect your letters to be good ones— in the sense that at least they won't be bad ones. But there are good letters and good letters. If I think an applicant is a poor prospect, I have the option of writing something like this:

> I have known ____ for three years, during which time (according to his transcript) he has been in three of my classes. I remember him as a quiet and diligent fellow who didn't speak much. He seemed pleasant and nice. And he must have some intelligence because he received two Bs and an A. I'm sure that his political science studies here will qualify him to do law school work.

This is not a bad letter. I haven't actually said that this student is a dud. But if that's all I write—and law schools receive hundreds of similar letters each year—then my letter is unlikely to help him. If a good letter should indicate, as Pepperdine requests, "as specifically as possible . . . what makes this applicant especially promising as a law student and, ultimately, as a member of the legal profession," then this one is too general and vague. It doesn't say anything that the law school can use as evidence of talent or achievement. Beyond counting it towards the required minimum number of letters, the law school will ignore it.

A helpful letter is detailed. It doesn't just say "John is intelligent" or "John is diligent and hardworking"; it provides evidence of these traits by describing some event, accomplishment, or incident. A good letter says

> John is an extremely hardworking student. He outlined each of the constitutional law cases that he was assigned so skillfully that I photocopied his outlines and distributed them to the weaker students.
>
> *or*
>
> John worked as one of my salesmen for three years, and each year he sold more than any other salesman in my district, and more than he had the year before.
>
> *or*
>
> John's M.A. thesis is a genuine contribution to the study of ____ because he went back to the original documents in the ____ library and corrected the errors of professor ____'s nineteenth-century book on the subject.

A detailed letter is useful; it supplies independent evidence that the candidate possesses some skill or character trait useful in law school. An admissions official can use this evidence to plug gaps in the candidate's record or gain an outside perspective on the information the candidate supplied in his application form. Richard Badger, an assistant dean at the University of Chicago Law School, identified a number of traits and accomplishments that are of special importance to success in law school, and which can often be inferred from good letters of recommendation. Among them were good language skills, analytical ability, diligence and good work habits, and the ability to handle complex questions to which there are no "correct" answers.

As a rule, useful letters are at least a full page long. Shorter letters are rarely detailed enough to describe a talent or accomplishment fully. Moreover, they may signal a lack of enthusiasm, as though the recommender doesn't care enough about the candidate to take more time. (Some law professors discourage letters over two pages long; if they ramble on and on, they can be tedious to read. But other admissions professionals perceive long and detailed letters as very strong recommendations, precisely because the recommender must feel very strongly about a candidate to take so much time.)

Experienced recommenders can also demonstrate that applicants can do law school work by comparing them to successful law students they knew in the past. Law schools encourage these comparisons. A comment that the applicant in question "is more intelligent than _____, who graduated from your law school last year" is extremely valuable. If professors and prelaw advisers are unable to compare applicants to other individuals with whom the law school is familiar, they are encouraged to compare them with their fellow graduating seniors. A prelaw adviser may say that so-and-so "is the best of the thirty or so seniors we have this year who want to go to law school." Many recommendation forms have spaces for academic recommenders to note the candidate's relative placement in his or her graduating class.

In summary, a good letter of recommendation is useful in the sense that it provides detailed evidence that the law school can use. This being the case, how do you get your recommenders to write the more detailed letters rather than the vaguer and less useful kind?

Visiting Your Recommenders

The first time you visit a recommender, you need to jog his or her memory by tactfully working in a reference to whatever distinguishes you from others:

> I thought you'd be a good person to ask because you liked the term paper I wrote on the Diet of Worms.

or

I figured you'd be a good person to comment on my work habits, considering that we worked night and day to get _____ elected last October.

or

Remember, you wrote a letter when I was put up for membership in the _____ honor society? I thought you could possibly write the same kind of letter to law schools.

or

Do you remember how when I was the president of the prelaw club you told me that working on program organizing was good practice for law school? Well, now I'm applying to law school. . .

In each case, you're tactfully signaling what you would like the recommender to write about.

After planting the seed of memory, tell each recommender that you will return on such-and-such a date with the necessary law school forms. Thank him or her in advance for agreeing to write letters for you, excuse yourself, and leave.

When you return for the second visit, bring with you the blank forms and envelopes. Also bring along a written summary of the accomplishments or incidents you mentioned on your first visit—the details you'd like included in your letter. The best technique is to put together an information packet for each of your recommenders. Always include a photocopy of your transcript. Recommenders will feel more confident discussing your academic record if they have the documentation at hand.

You should also enclose a résumé or partial résumé that includes the same details of your academic work, extracurricular activities, and job experience that you will list on your law school applications. But the recommendation résumé should be personalized; you should emphasize those details of your record that you want the recommender to mention in his or her letter. This is where you describe those thoughtful seminar discussions, or the outstanding term paper, or the hours of hard work you put in during the political campaign. If you want the recommender to reminisce about the time you organized all the political science majors to go down to the state capitol to protest budget cuts in higher education, make sure the incident is listed on the résumé.

Since you'll want each recommender to emphasize different aspects of your character and background, you may want to create a different résumé for each of them. Each résumé should be no more than a page or two in length. The experts at writing these "functional" résumés on your campus are in the placement center. Consult them if you have any questions about how to emphasize your good points.

Finally, include photocopies of anything you want specifically referred to. If you've chosen this recommender because she liked your term paper, provide a photocopy of the paper—preferably a graded copy, with her comments on it—and write at the top "this is the paper I mentioned when I was in your office last week." If you'd like the recommender to mention work you've done for an organization or awards you've won, include photocopies of letters of commendation or award certificates.

Put these documents in a folder with your name on it. Add the various appraisal forms that the law schools have provided. You should also provide preaddressed business-size envelopes, with stamps if you want the recommendations mailed directly to the law school, or without stamps if you'll collect them later. (Use the preprinted envelopes that the law schools have provided, if any were included with the application forms.) Leave the folder with the recommender at the end of your second visit. Thank your recommenders profusely for their time and trouble.

Timing

Expect your recommenders to take three weeks, or even a month, to write, type, and mail your letters. If the law school wants you to collect the letters and mail them along with your application (see the next section), during your second visit, schedule a third visit to pick them up.

If your application arrives before the law school's formal deadline, some law schools will wait for the letters to arrive before making an admit/ reject decision, even if the letters don't arrive until after the deadline. But read the catalog carefully; most law schools regard their deadlines as absolute and insist that all files be complete by the indicated cutoff date.

If you complete all the application steps in October and November, as I suggest, you won't need to worry about the formal deadlines. There isn't any need to send off your law school applications before arranging for letters of recommendation. Indeed, the reverse is true: you should arrange for the letters first. If your letters arrive at the law school before your application form, the law school will hold them. If you are asked to enclose your letters of recommendation along with your application, schedule your second visits at least one month before you expect to mail off the application form.

But if your advance planning doesn't work out and you have to apply at the last minute, be sure that your recommenders are aware of any deadlines they must meet. It's legitimate to tactfully mention that you need the letters by next Wednesday at the latest; most faculty members will try to expedite their letter writing in special circumstances. If your recommender is one of those people who are perennially late and always seem to be trying to catch up, consider telling a little white lie: if the letters must arrive before, say, the 15th of February, say that you need them by the first of that month.

How the Letters Will Be Mailed

There are three different systems in use for getting the letters from the recommenders to the law schools. Most law schools still want the recommenders to mail the letters directly to them. Professors are poorly paid and many colleges and universities are strapped for funds; consequently, many professors refuse to mail letters out unless you provide stamped preaddressed envelopes.

A few law schools prefer to have the letters sent all at once. In this system, you give each recommender an envelope addressed to yourself. The recommender puts the letter in it, seals it, writes his or her name across the flap (to discourage you from opening and reading it) and then either hands or mails it to you. You include the unopened envelopes from your recommenders along with your law school application. Or you mail the unopened envelopes to the law school, all together inside a bigger envelope shortly after you've sent off your application.

Law schools like this system because it minimizes their clerical work. But recommenders dislike it. Many believe that this system is not as secure as direct mail, and they are probably right. Indeed, the submission of fraudulent letters is one of the forms of cheating that worries Law Services. In 1992, the Midwest Association of Prelaw Advisers asserted that "[l]etters of recommendation should *never* be handed to the student for processing in the application process."

As a result, law schools won't insist on the all-at-once system and will always accept letters mailed directly from the recommenders. If you are applying to a law school that requests the all-at-once system, I suggest that you ask each of your recommenders how he or she prefers to respond. Indicate that you'll be happy to return to collect the completed letter. But if your recommenders indicate that they would prefer to mail them directly, give them all stamps and let them do so. Note on your application form that letters will arrive under separate cover.

More and more undergraduate schools have central clearinghouses for letters of recommendation. If there's a clearinghouse on your campus, your prelaw adviser will explain how it works. Usually, you request letters in person from the professors who will serve as recommenders. Each professor writes one letter for you and forwards it, along with your forms and envelopes, to the clearinghouse. There secretaries photocopy each letter and send a copy to each of the law schools on your application list. In general, letters sent out in this way are more impersonal than letters mailed directly from the professor's office. But the clearinghouse system reduces the cost of sending out thousands of letters each year. With this necessity in mind, law schools accept this way of doing business.

If the Letters Don't Arrive

At the end of the last chapter, I reminded you that it's your responsibility to make sure that your application file is complete. What if the letter that a certain professor was supposed to send never arrived? You'll have to jog his or her memory.

It's best to make a third personal visit to errant recommenders, rather than to telephone, so they can see how frightened and pathetic you look. If the recommender is a professor, visit during office hours. Bring along copies of the material you gave the professor when you asked him or her to write the letter. Also bring along evidence that your file is incomplete: the law school's postcard or the memo you made of your phone call to the law school admissions office. Say something like this:

> Professor _____ ? I don't want to bother you, but I got this notice. . . and I wanted to make sure that there hadn't been some mistake, and that the secretary didn't lose something. . .

Most likely, the professor will fumble through the forms on his or her desk and determine that your letter wasn't sent. Give the professor a chance to blame overwork, or a balky computer, or the centralized clearinghouse. Sympathize.

If the recommender still has the file you gave him, with the blank forms, envelopes, and résumé in it, ask him or her to note the law school's deadline on it. If your recommender has to write something down, he or she will be more likely to put the file in a place where it will be seen and remembered. If your file can't be found amid the clutter on the professor's desk, replace it. Always let the recommender decide what to do. In some cases, remorse-stricken recommenders have called law schools, acknowledged their forgetfulness, rambled on and on about how much poorer a law school entering class will be without you, and even asked for deadlines to be waived. (I've done this myself.)

If the recommender says that the letter was sent, tactfully suggest that it may be easier to send a photocopy than to argue with the law school about how and where it got lost. Offer to provide another stamped envelope. Try to dissuade the recommender from calling the law school and complaining about the incompetent file clerks who lost the letter and made him or her look bad; the recommender's anger distracts attention from your qualifications.

If you can't contact the recommender, or if he or she refuses to do anything more for you, your only option is to seek some other recommender. If the formal application deadline is coming close, and if your only problem is a single forgetful recommender, consider calling the law school and asking to have the deadline extended. In my experience, some law schools occasionally accept late applications for this reason.

12

Interviews

Format Interviews that Count

At one time, a formal interview was a very important part of the admissions process of many law schools. Each applicant would be required to appear in person at the office of a law professor, or perhaps of an alumnus, dressed to impress and trembling head to foot. The student would be allowed a half hour or so in the office or at a nearby restaurant or club, during which time he or she had to convince the interviewer that he or she would make a good law student and lawyer. The interviewer would then report to the admissions committee. The report would be given great weight.

Law schools rarely do it this way nowadays. When they began to study the admission process, they found that interviewers' reports were very poor predictors of law school success. Although a brief conversation might reveal whether or not the applicant was articulate and intelligent, it was almost impossible for an interviewer to determine whether or not an applicant possessed the necessary talent, drive, and work habits needed for success in law school.

Moreover, formal interviews lend themselves to prejudice and bigotry. They can be used as a tool for keeping the benefits of attending law school in the hands of white European males of the dominant social class.

Too often, interviewers were more interested in finding candidates like themselves—candidates who came from the right schools, or had the right family connections or the right manners—than they were in identifying the most talented. One older lawyer told me that his interviewer seemed more concerned with learning whether or not he could play contract bridge than with uncovering skills or interests that were relevant to legal work. Another recalled that his interview was conducted in a private businessmen's club. The alumni who served as interviewers were in the habit of using a quiet private room. When they had Jewish or African-American candidates to interview they moved to the bar, the only room in the club in which members were allowed to entertain "guests not themselves eligible for membership." The interviewers often interrupted the candidates to call out greetings and exchange pleasantries with passersby. Apparently, they'd never had to interview a woman applicant; women, even the wives of members, were never allowed in any part of the club.

Finally, as law schools expanded and began to attract applicants nationally, the work involved in scheduling all the interviews became prohibitive. As a result, no law school, to my knowledge, still requires an interview that counts as a routine part of its application procedure. Many law schools explicitly refuse to conduct formal interviews under any circumstances.

You may, however, be asked to undergo an interview if you apply to one of the top law schools. Its purpose will not be to determine whether you have the qualities needed to study law, for your superior numbers will have already identified you as a good prospect. Instead, the interviewer will try to find your particular strengths; he or she will look for whatever is unique in your background or character, so the law school can determine whether you will contribute diversity to the freshman class. A few other law schools have made formal interviews an optional part of their admissions procedures. You can request one if you are marginally competitive for a school that you particularly want to attend. You may also be asked to undergo a formal interview if you are applying for certain financial aid and scholarship programs.

The trick to doing well at a formal interview is to avoid doing badly. It's more important to create a general impression of competence and agreeableness than it is to hold forth at great length on your qualifications to study law. It's more important to avoid blurting out a single terrible howler than it is to give an unimpeachably correct answer to every question. At all costs, you must avoid insulting, alienating, or offending the interviewer. You want the interviewer to like you. If he or she likes you, minor errors will be overlooked.

Although this may seem obvious, I emphasize it because in my recent experience some students seem to think that the way to do well in an interview is to slouch into the interviewer's office late, sprawl in a chair, put their feet up on the interviewer's desk, light a cigar, and answer all the questions in a manner oscillating between indifference and calculated offensiveness. They have learned this technique from movies aimed at a teenaged audience. But take my word for it: it only works in the movies.

Any interviewer will be put off by an applicant who does not appear to be taking the process seriously. Older people may be more concerned with details of dress and appearance than younger people. Interviewers who are lawyers will be especially concerned with whether or not you possess good manners and are willing to follow the rules and make an effort to get along with others. Good manners and agreeableness are necessary in our legal system, for lawyers must work together as rivals and adversaries without becoming enemies.

Therefore, approach the interview defensively by avoiding the things that give offense. Dress neatly. Be punctual. Sit where you are told. Do not smoke. Avoid gum, candy, or other props unless the interview is conducted over food. (Many older people associate gum with immaturity.) If you are offered coffee, you have the choice of accepting and consuming it gracefully or (preferably) declining without making a fuss. But don't take the opportunity to launch into a diatribe against caffeine, the exploitation of Colombian peasants, or the pollution of the environment by styrofoam cups. Demonstrate that you've planned ahead for the interview by bringing along copies of whatever documents you've sent to the law school and anything you may want to refer to, perhaps collected neatly in a folder. But if possible avoid lugging bulky materials into the interview room.

When people who have done a lot of interviewing are asked what makes a favorable impression, they always say that they like applicants to convey an impression of energy and cheerfulness. You should practice an upbeat, positive manner. It's important to maintain eye contact. A firm but not bone-crushing handshake, a pleasant smile, and good posture—especially while sitting—are also frequently mentioned as assets. I quote here from a publication about job interviews circulated by Bradley's placement center:

> Applicants who fare best are eager, honest, directed, confident, poised and knowledgeable about the company and the position.

If you substitute "law school" or "scholarship program" for "company," you have advice that you can follow when you practice.

Preparation and practice will help you do well. Since formal interviews are commonly used by big companies when they hire entry-level professionals, your college placement center probably employs experts in the interview process. They train job applicants in interview technique by handing out literature and conducting workshops and practice interviews. If you expect to face formal interviews and you are uncertain about your ability to handle them, it's to your advantage to seek the help of these professionals. Attend a workshop or schedule a practice interview and critique.

Always attend any practice session dressed as you intend to dress for the real interview; the expert will critique your appearance, manner, and handouts as well as the answers you give to his or her questions. If the practice session is videotaped, scrutinize the tape carefully. You may detect unconscious yet annoying mannerisms. Once you are aware that you are doing it, you can consciously avoid drumming on the desktop with your fingers, twiddling with the clasp of your purse, or nervously licking your lips before you answer each question. If you have trouble giving clear answers, the coach may suggest practicing before a group of friends.

Decide in advance how you will answer easily anticipated questions. Expect to be asked about your interest in law and your career plans. As with your application essay (which the interviewer may have read), you should be candid and provide details. It's not necessary to pretend that your interest in law is wholly altruistic. But try to demonstrate an interest in legal processes, or in particular issues:

> I've always enjoyed reasoning through a problem.
>
> *or*
>
> I've enjoyed the time I've spent in debate in high school and college, and the best debates always seemed to involve court cases from the past. I'd find it fascinating to be involved in the debate on some ongoing court case.
>
> *or*
>
> I used to live in the Pacific Northwest, and I think the key problem there is to find some way for the environment to coexist with highly regulated industries like fishing and logging.

Expect to be asked why you've applied to this particular law school, or this particular scholarship program. Try to show that you've done some homework. Mention good old Hypothetical Law School's nationally known concentration in environmental law or its noteworthy scholarly tone. Name the friends or contacts who have attended and who encouraged you to apply. Best of all, describe your own information-gathering activities:

I visited Hypothetical last summer, and your Mr. _____ arranged for me to talk to some students who are also interested in environmental law. They were so positive and enthusiastic about the place that it seemed much more impressive than the other schools that are strong in environmental law, namely _____.

One technique is to prepare for the interview by choosing one aspect of your personality or background to emphasize: your consistently good grades, or your ability to succeed in a wide variety of tasks, or your work experience in a field related to law. Try to focus the answers you prepare for anticipated questions on this single point. If, for example, you decide to stress your strong knowledge about the realities of legal practice, you can answer a question about your career plans by summarizing the advantages and disadvantages of two or three legal specialties you are interested in. If you are asked why you want to be a lawyer, you can describe your work experience in a lawyer's office.

At the real interview, try to answer questions concisely and directly. The interviewer will deduct points if you seem to be waffling or dissembling, or if your answers are vague. And you'll lose more points if you manifest the kind of inconsistency that indicates that you are merely saying what you think the interviewer expects to hear. It's okay to politely disagree with the interviewer. But don't press the point. Try to avoid anything that could be described as a prolonged debate or an argument.

Don't be surprised if the interviewer is familiar with your law school application and your college transcript. Interviewers do their homework, too. Don't limit yourself to repeating what is already on the record. Amplify and expand. If the interviewer says, "I see you had a job in the office of my old friend so-and-so," don't say only, "Yes, I worked there in 1994." Instead, add, "Yes, she does mostly real estate law, and she taught me how to do a title search."

Interviewers sometimes use a set of stock questions that are supposed to reveal character, habits and intellect. These may include:

- What recent books have you read for pleasure? What impressed you about each?

- Describe a mistake you made that taught you a valuable lesson.

- Name two or three of your heroes.

- Which of your college courses did you find the most memorable? Which of your professors was the most impressive?

- Name a book or movie that played an important role in your education, and describe what you learned from it.

- Where do you see yourself five years from now?
- What's your worst flaw?

Expect to be asked to discuss your hobbies, your travels, or any note-worthy accomplishments you've listed on your application form.

Unlike job interviews, law school interviews are rarely stressful. Interviewers are unlikely to try to anger you or catch you off guard. But if they do so, try to remain calm. Stress techniques are designed to see how much abuse you can take before you lose your temper; they're often used in the business world to identify good candidates for unusually stressful management jobs. You win such a game by demonstrating grace under pressure. You lose when you become visibly rattled.

As the interview draws to a close, the interviewer may ask you if you want to ask any questions. Ask any questions raised by the conversation. If there are none, fall back on a prearranged question or two. If you've said that you were attracted to Hypothetical Law School because the author of a certain book teaches there, ask the interviewer if he or she has ever met the author, and, if so, what the author is like. Or ask the interviewer about his or her own specialty. Or, if you are applying to one of the numerous law schools currently expanding their physical plants, ask about the status of the new building project or the computer upgrade. This is your last opportunity to demonstrate that you've done some homework and have a sincere interest in the school.

Finally, it's a good idea to leave the interviewer with some non-bulky memento:

> Since I applied to Hypothetical, my boss promoted me from part-time clerk to part-time administrator. My duties are different. I've got an updated résumé. Would you put it in my file?
>
> *or*
>
> When I applied to Hypothetical I didn't have a writing sample to send you. But I've just got a term paper back, and the teacher said it was the best he'd seen this year. I've made a Xerox. Would you put it in my file?

Be sure that whatever you hand the interviewer has your name and address on it.

As soon as you leave the interview room, write down the name of the interviewer. In a day or two, write a brief thank-you note. A handwritten note on informal writing paper is best, although a typewritten note is acceptable. Express your appreciation for having had the chance to chat about such-and-such, and hope you'll have the chance to talk with the interviewer in the future. Mail it care of the law school.

Informational Interviews

You should seek an informational interview with law school officials if your status as an applicant is unusual, if you require some special consideration, or if you need to have the law school waive some part of its application procedure. I've identified a number of special circumstances the chapters above. Applicants who need special consideration include:

- older nontraditional applicants whose undergraduate work was done many years ago, and who want success in the business world to be considered a qualification for law school;

- applicants who were educated entirely or partly at foreign universities whose curriculums are different from those of American universities or whose records are difficult to understand or unobtainable;

- handicapped applicants who want some part of the application procedure waived and/or who will need some special accommodations in order to attend law school;

- impoverished applicants seeking a waiver of the application fee; and

- applicants with felony convictions or other black marks on their records, who need to determine whether or not they will be allowed to practice law.

These informational interviews aren't formally part of the application process. They don't count the way the old formal interviews did. You won't be compared with other "interviewees" or rated on your performance. But informational interviews can be extremely important in determining how the formal parts of your application will be viewed. Moreover, the interviewer's impression of you will always be recorded and it may carry great weight when the admissions committee decides whether or not to provide the special treatment you are requesting.

If you think you will need some modification of the application procedure, you should request an interview well before you apply. If you have a handicap such that the LSAT may not be a true test of your abilities, you should seek an informational interview before you register to take the LSAT. If you are not seeking special consideration but simply need to clarify how some aspect of your record will be viewed— for example, if you have a felony conviction on your record— you can wait until after you apply to seek the informational interview.

You can request an informational interview by explaining your circumstances to the law school representative you talk to when you visit, or simply by calling the law school admission office for an appointment. (Some law schools still have a box on their application forms that you can check for this purpose. An official will then call you to set up an appointment. However, you can't wait and use this route if you need the interview before you begin the application process.) It may take several phone calls before the informational interview can be scheduled, because the representative you speak to may have to arrange for the presence of a higher-ranking official.

In my experience, law schools are usually very sympathetic to applicants with special needs. They can be surprisingly flexible. (Remember, they *want* students with unusual backgrounds.) But they'll make special arrangements only for candidates whom they perceive as honest and sincere. For this reason, the impression you make is of vital importance. Approach the informational interview with the same careful preparation you would bring to a formal interview that counts. It is important for you to demonstrate that you've done your homework. And in all cases, it is important for you to appear energetic and cheerful.

You can expect to be asked some of the questions that I've discussed above, so you should plan for them. But to a large extent you yourself will set the agenda for an informational interview; it will focus on your handicap, problem, or special circumstance. You'll need to describe it fully. Be sure to bring with you whatever records you will need. Handicapped persons should submit appropriate medical documentation. If you can't obtain a transcript from the registrar of a foreign university, you should bring your own copy to show the interviewer, including a prepared translation if necessary.

Some law schools will ask you to put any request for special treatment in writing, in the form of a letter addressed to the dean. Even if a written petition isn't required, preparing one will help you clarify your thinking. Before the interview, make sure you know exactly what you are asking for and what you will settle for. Bring the petition to the interview. Also bring a notebook.

If you ask the law school to waive some part of the application process, you will have to convince the interviewer that this part—the LSAT, say— cannot dependably measure your qualifications for law school. Your argument will be much stronger if you can suggest some other way that your likelihood of success in law school can be predicted. "Alternative evaluation techniques" include statements of knowledgeable professionals, reports of success on standardized tests other than the LSAT, superb undergraduate grades, or successful dealings in the legal world. Each individual case is unique. Older nontraditionals should be prepared to document their business careers. Handicapped applicants are usually viewed favorably if they have been able to perform well in appropriate undergraduate programs; for them, grades are even more important.

Before you leave the interview room be sure you understand exactly what has been decided. Some law schools, for example, will offer only provisional or probationary admission to students for whom they have waived some aspect of the application procedure; others may offer admission only if you satisfy some additional condition. If you're asked to provide more information, write down what is needed and where it should be sent. If a decision on your request will be made at a later date, write down that date, the names of the authorities who will make the decision, the date by which you can expect to be notified, and the name of a person to contact if you have any questions. If a decision is made on the spot, write down exactly what has been decided. Ask the interviewer to write you a letter confirming that your admission fee—or LSAT, or foreign transcript—has been waived, and to put a copy of the letter in your file.

13

Minorities

After World War II, the top law schools abandoned their previous effort to maintain upperclass control of the legal system and devoted themselves to making the legal profession a meritocracy. They have consistently enlarged the pool from which they seek law students, first by recruiting aggressively among Jews and other established ethnic groups, then by developing affirmative action programs for protected categories, and later by throwing their doors open to women. Other law schools imitated these trendsetting institutions. Because of this history, there is a more idealistic commitment to diversity in legal education than there is in most other large American institutions. Since law is a channel of upward mobility, many legal educators attach a very high priority to efforts to bring more and more disadvantaged minorities into the system. In this chapter, I note some special considerations and programs of interest to members of some minority groups.

Protected Categories

Fewer than one American lawyer in ten is a member of a historically oppressed minority group. There are only 25,000 lawyers of Hispanic ethnicity, for example, and only about 30,000 African-American lawyers. Law schools want to recruit members of protected categories, and despite the recent political backlash against affirmative action programs they continue to devote resources to recruiting minority students.

However, the absolute numbers are still quite small. In 1994, only 14 of 178 accredited law schools had student populations that were 13 percent or more African-American. Of about 128,000 law students nationwide, only about 920, or 7 percent, were Native Americans. J.D. enrollment of members of other protected categories also lags. (Self-reported statistics are published in the Official Guide.)

If such an intense affirmative action effort is being made, why is there a lag? One theory is that law schools are having difficulty identifying minority prospects. They know only whatever information applicants reveal about themselves. Many individuals hesitate to admit that they are minority members because they fear that lingering bigotry that still plays such an important role in American life. They're making a mistake; in my experience, the benefits of affirmative action in the admissions process clearly outweigh the drawbacks of racial prejudice. If you are a member of a protected category, you should identify yourself as such whenever you have the opportunity to do so.

When you register for the LSDAS, sign up also for Law Services' Candidate Referral Service, or CRS. Law Services will put your name on the list of "candidates with affirmative action potential" that it makes available to law schools seeking such students. If you so authorize, Law Services will make your LSDAS file available to any law school that requests it for affirmative action admission consideration, whether or not you have applied to that law school. If your name is on the CRS list, don't be surprised if a law school you haven't applied to calls you on the phone and encourages you to apply. You register for the CRS by answering three additional questions on the LSAT/LSDAS registration form. There is no extra charge.

You should also request a copy of Law Services' free publication, *Thinking About Law School: A Minority Guide*. This extremely valuable little book contains information on financial aid and on researching and applying to law schools. Among other things, it identifies several critical pieces of information that minority applicants should obtain for any law schools they are considering: the graduation and attrition rates for minority students, the existence of support programs, and so on.

The *Minority Guide* also provides tips on how to collect this information. For example, some law schools hold minority-oriented open houses.

Their recruiters often attend minority-oriented job fairs and career fairs, even on quite small campuses. Some recruiters attend meetings of minority student organizations; they've also been known to solicit the names of promising students from minority faculty members, lawyers and law students, and ministers and other professionals. Try to get your name on as many minority-oriented mailing lists as possible.

Most larger law schools support an extensive roster of minority student groups. Hispanic, Native American, and African American groups, among others, are likely to be involved in recruiting new law students. Often, a law school contacts a minority prospect through a law student of the same ethnic background. Hispanic law students are especially valued because they can speak to prospects in Spanish. The president of one law school's Hispanic club has visited Bradley several times; she helped one graduating senior fill out his law school application, read over his essay and corrected the grammar, and then made follow-up phone calls to remind him of deadlines. It's worth your time to try to contact appropriate minority student groups at the law schools on your preferred list. If you visit, ask to speak to minority students. Or write to the addresses listed in the catalogs.

Some local law schools have also made special efforts to recruit African Americans who have had success in the business world or in community politics. If you are older, experience of this kind can partly compensate for poor undergraduate numbers. You can document the value of your experience by providing extensive letters of recommendation, by writing an essay discussing what you have learned, and by submitting newspaper clippings about your political or business activity that mention you by name.

To date, these aggressive recruitment efforts have been only partly successful. Because protected category members tend to do worse in college than the general population and are more likely to drop out before graduating, there is simply a shortage of well-qualified minority law school candidates. In the 1970s, some law schools lowered the numerical cutoff points in order to admit lesser-qualified affirmative action candidates. But two problems developed. Scandals erupted at some schools. For example, in 1991 the student newspaper at Georgetown University reported that African-American admittees posted an average LSAT score of 36 (on the old scale, out of a maximum possible score of 48), while white admittees posted an average score of 43. A score of 36 is at the 71st percentile; a 43 is at the 94.5th percentile. "Reverse discrimination" has become a potent issue. Courts have invalidated some affirmative action programs perceived to set "racial quotas." Law schools hesitate to upset constituents and vocal political leaders—especially public law schools, which depend on public support.

A second and more pressing problem, however, is that GPAs and LSAT scores still generally happen to be predictors of the ability to do law school work. Students admitted with poor numbers are more likely to drop out or flunk out. "It looks bad to make special admissions," one law school recruiter told me, "but it would *really* look bad to let black students in and then flunk them all out." Poor retention rates also damage law schools financially, for they depend on each student to pay a full three years' worth of tuition.

To improve the quality of the pool of affirmative action candidates, law schools, foundations, and state governments have begun to create enrichment programs. Though they differ in many ways, all have the same goals: to improve the educational backgrounds of minority students while they are undergraduates, to help them achieve good college grades, and to make it more likely that they will succeed in law school.

Most of these programs create minority equivalents of general student groups or activities. There are minority-oriented courses and internships; for example, the National Association of Latino Elected and Appointed Officials offers a summer internship program to undergraduates who are citizens of California, Florida, Illinois, New York, Arizona, Colorado, New Mexico, or Texas and who "possess a sense of commitment to the Latino community." You can contact NALEO at 3409 Garnet St., Los Angeles CA 90023. Since many of these programs are regional, or even local, you should seek them through your local prelaw adviser.

The Council on Legal Education Opportunity (CLEO) is an umbrella organization created to increase the number of minority law students. (You can discern the widespread support for this goal by studying the list of CLEO's sponsors: the American Bar Association, the Association of American Law Schools, the Law School Admission Council, the Hispanic National Bar Association, the National Asian Pacific Bar Association, and the National Bar Association.) CLEO now conducts six-week "institutes" designed to prepare undergraduates to attend law school. About 150 disadvantaged undergraduates each year are taught about legal method and law as a subject. The teaching is considered extremely rigorous. Law Services says that

> [s]atisfactory completion by the students gives them both a sense of accomplishment and a reason to hope that a law degree actually is attainable. It also provides admission officers with justification for issuing acceptances to persons with LSAT and UGPA credentials that, without more, could only raise doubts.

CLEO is also involved in providing financial aid for disadvantaged law students. You can contact CLEO at 1420 N St. N.W., Suite T-1, Washington DC 20005.

If you are a minority student, you should investigate these programs. Enrichment opportunities of this kind are extremely valuable, because they teach necessary skills and because they'll put you on an academic fast track, introduce you to helpful people, and mark you as a good prospect.

Because there is a shortage of well-qualified minority applicants, you are a scarce and desirable commodity if your numbers are strong. If your undergraduate grades are good, you can improve your law school prospects dramatically by doing well on the LSAT. To some extent, if you are a minority group member, you can compensate for poor grades with a high test score. Test preparation is especially important for this and a second reason: Law Services has determined that minority members are at high risk for making characteristic mistakes: "[i]t is especially important for minority test takers to practice pacing and to prepare by taking previously administered tests under timed conditions. . .minority test takers generally show a higher number of items not reached at the end of the test sections."

Unless you know that your test-taking skills are unusually good, you should seriously consider a test-prep course. But in one of those destructive American racial ironies, minority applicants, who can most benefit from test-prep courses, are least likely to know about and take them. If the problem is money, make inquiries. The Stanley Kaplan organization has some scholarship money for impoverished students, and your prelaw adviser may know of similar scholarships available from other test-preparation companies.

Disabled Applicants

There are lawyers in wheelchairs, lawyers with cerebral palsy, and even blind lawyers and deaf lawyers. There are lawyers with successful careers who have diabetes, multiple sclerosis or similar serious chronic illnesses. Law as a profession is diverse enough to provide career opportunities for people who cannot walk, cannot speak clearly, or cannot see. If you are handicapped, you are following in the path pioneered by capable and successful predecessors. You are protected from discrimination by the federal Rehabilitation Act of 1973, which forbids law schools to exclude you from any course of instruction for which you are otherwise qualified simply because you have a handicap. Moreover, law schools know that the struggle to cope with a handicap gives you a unique perspective. You can contribute a degree of educationally valuable diversity to a law school class.

For all these reasons, law schools seek and welcome handicapped applicants. Many publicize that fact extensively. Some maintain special resources, and even have special financial programs. For example, Stanford maintains the Folger and Levin endowed fund, used to pay for structural modifications to the law school, equipment such as computer-assisted learning devices, and salaries for note-takers, interpreters and research assistants.

Each handicap is different in kind and degree. Each handicapped candidate poses a unique problem to the admissions committee, because it isn't possible to gauge one person's potential for the study of law by comparing him or her with other handicapped persons. By definition, a handicapped person will require some special assistance, either during the application process or while enrolled in law school. But it isn't possible to determine with confidence what special assistance any one handicapped person will need by relying on the law school's previous experience with the handicapped generally.

Therefore, if you are handicapped, you will have to visit each of the law schools you intend to apply to and discuss your special needs. You'll have to schedule informational interviews, like those I described in Chapter 12, with responsible law school officials, before any problems arise. Bring with you whatever medical documentation you'll need to establish the nature of your handicap and the kinds of assistance that you require. If you expect to use a particular kind of wheelchair or other equipment as a law student, bring it with you to the interview. Especially bring any note-taking or communication devices you expect to use as a student.

If you think you will have problems with the LSAT, the interview should take place before you are required to register: in the winter, if you would normally take the LSAT in June, or in early summer if you're thinking about the October test. Depending on your needs, the law school may waive the LSAT and rely on other criteria when it evaluates your application for admission. Or it may advise you to seek special accommodations for taking the LSAT from Law Services. Depending on the nature of the disability, you may request

> . . . the use of a reader, an amanuensis [to take dictation], a reader, a wheelchair-accessible test center, additional rest time between sections, additional testing time, or a separate testing room. . . . The test is available in regular print; large, 18-point type print; in Braille; and on audiocassette.

The procedure for requesting special LSAT accommodation is described in the *Information Book*. Essentially, you'll need to request a special packet of materials "well before LSAT registration deadlines" from Law Services Test Administration, 661 Penn Street, Box 2000-T, Newtown PA 18940-0995. Or you can call (215) 968-1001 during business hours. Once you have the material, you need to file your request by the LSAT registration deadline for the test date you want. You may be required to document your handicap with appropriate medical information.

If you want some other part of the application procedure waived or modified, request informational interviews at the law schools on your application list after you take the LSAT but before you file your applications. Expect to suggest some alternate means of evaluating your ability to do law school work. If you simply need to determine whether the law school can satisfy your special needs for accessibility if you are admitted, you can visit the law school after you apply.

Although the interview is primarily a way for the law school to determine how the nature of the change it will have to make in its routine to accommodate you, it is also an opportunity for you to see for yourself what difficulties you will face if you decide to attend. Although the Americans with Disabilities Act of 1991 will make almost all public buildings handicapped-accessible over time, there are certain to be short-term problems. Most older buildings were not designed with the handicapped in mind. Even though a building is technically accessible, it may not be very user- friendly. The classroom building that I work in, for example, has curb cuts and handicapped parking, but only one elevator. During the ten-minute break between classes, the elevator is used by technicians, people hauling computers and audio-visual equipment, and many teachers; consequently, handicapped students frequently complain about being late for class. Such situations are best avoided, but are sometimes unavoidable.

At least in the short run, some schools may meet their legal obligation to make classes handicapped-accessible by moving or rescheduling them rather than by building new buildings or making expensive renovations of older ones. Not surprisingly, some schools are better at accommodating the handicapped than others. When you visit, ask to speak to some handicapped law students about their experiences. Find out if there are handicapped faculty members, a special counselor or advisor, and a support group.

Before you contact any law school, you may want to communicate with the HEATH Resource Center, which operates the National Clearinghouse on Postsecondary Education for Individuals with Disabilities, and which itself is a program of the American Council on Education. The Center can provide information about requesting disability-related accommodations, ascertaining the level of physical and programmatic access available at law schools, and thinking through disability issues surrounding the application process.

Being on the HEATH mailing list is a good way to collect specialized information. You can write to HEATH at One Dupont Circle, Suite 800, Washington DC 20036-1193, or telephone (202) 939-9320 (local) or (800) 544-3284 (outside DC).

You may also find it advantageous to communicate with the Association on Higher Education and Disability, or AHEAD, a "membership organization for individuals involved in the provision of quality support services to disabled students in higher education." Directly and (mostly) indirectly, AHEAD makes available information, technical assistance and advocacy to handicapped students. The organization can be reached at P.O. Box 21192, Columbus OH 43221-0192 or by calling (614) 488-4972. Their fax number is (614) 488-1174.

Women

Women still suffer from discrimination in legal employment and law school faculty hiring, but gender discrimination is no longer a problem in student admissions. At present, more than 40 percent of all law students are women. (Statistics are in *Barron's Guide*.)

Because they have large numbers of women students, law schools have been pioneers in addressing the problems that women complain about: day care for children, security, and sexual harassment. It's my impression that most law schools have done quite well with respect to day care and many, though by no means all, are highly security conscious. If you are concerned about either of these things, a school's situation can best be determined by a personal visit and by talking with women who are already enrolled.

Some schools continue to have problems with sexual harassment. The American Bar Association's Commission on Women in the Profession reported in January, 1996, that there are still complaints about professors who denigrate the class performance of women students. Perhaps this is a chronic danger in any institution in which the students are largely women but the faculty remains overwhelmingly male. More disturbing, according to the *New York Times*, are reports "that the performance of some women is suffering because of a resurgence of overt male hostility." It's best to avoid a school with this sort of reputation. There's some evidence that women find legal study more stressful than men do, even under the best of circumstances. You don't need to add to your burdens by attending a law school with an unfriendly gender-relations climate. Seek information from women law students or from one of the organized women's groups that operate on campus. Look also for the presence of female faculty members and administrators.

14

If You Don't Get In

If you've been able to apply under an accelerated admissions program, you should know the results within six weeks. Your other admissions and rejections will trickle in throughout the winter. The old high school guidance counselor's principle that a thin envelope indicates a rejection and a fat envelope indicates an acceptance remains generally true, but there are exceptions. Even acceptances sometimes come in thin envelopes nowadays; a packet of registration forms and leaflets may be sent separately. You should know the fate of all your applications by the first of April. If you've assessed your record correctly and followed the procedure I've sketched out in this book, you should have been accepted somewhere.

But what if you weren't?

It could happen. The future is never entirely controllable. Perhaps you ran into a bad placement year. When law schools receive an unexpectedly large number of applications, they raise their standards. Candidates who may have been admitted in other years are rejected. Or perhaps your record was not as good as you thought it was.

Waiting Lists, Conditional Admissions, and Appeals

Waiting Lists

Instead of being rejected outright, you may be notified that you've been placed on a waiting list. You will be offered admission only if other previously accepted candidates decide not to attend.

Being on a waiting list is a nightmare. You will be dangling, unable to make firm plans, well into the spring, and perhaps the summer. You'll hear stories about applicants admitted from waiting lists a few days before fall classes were to begin. At least some of these stories are true. But these late admittees are fortunate compared to wait-listed applicants who are never admitted and who wind up at the end of the summer without alternative employment.

For this reason, you should accept waiting list status only if you have no other options—only, that is, if all your other schools turned you down— or if the school you're wait-listed at is far superior in status to any school that has accepted you. Otherwise, write to the law school, announce that you will attend another law school, and politely ask to have your name taken off the waiting list.

If you must sweat it out, you should at least try to gauge your chances. Most law schools rank the candidates on their waiting lists and will give you some indication of where you stand if you call or visit. (Some law schools include your ranking in the letter they write to tell you that you have been wait-listed.) If you are ranked near the top of a waiting list at a Group IV or Group V school, you can feel fairly optimistic about your chance of eventual acceptance. Your prelaw adviser may have information about how wait-listed applicants at this school fared in previous years. If you're placed low on the waiting list, if the prelaw adviser gently discourages you, or if you are dealing with one of the law schools that explicitly refuses to disclose any information about the status of wait-listed applicants, you had best make other plans.

Conditional Acceptance

You should also ask about a conditional admission. In a sense, almost all law school admissions are conditional; they require you to complete your undergraduate work before you will be allowed to begin your legal studies. Some law schools occasionally offer admission with a more extensive set of conditions attached. In recent years, some foreign students have been admitted contingent on their ability to regularize their residency status.

A few law schools make admission, or a reconsideration of a rejection, contingent on completing some specific work. Widener University, for example, has a summer "Trial Admission Program" for students who were not admitted outright but "who show promise of success in law studies despite a relatively low score on one of the two principal measures used for admission." Some other law schools, especially those with evening or part-time divisions, have similar programs. (Some law schools, while rejecting your application for their day programs, may offer to consider you for their evening divisions.) If you've been rejected from such a school, you can call and ask to be put on the list for a probationary enrollment. The programs usually involve registering for and taking law school classes during the summer session. Alternatively, some allow you to attend regular semester classes on a probationary status for a limited period of time. If you do well, you've demonstrated that you are able to do law school work.

No summer program, to my knowledge, guarantees you admission to the degree-granting legal program. Instead, without making any commitments, the law school indicates its intent to admit the most successful candidates on a space- available basis. You can consider it to be the equivalent of earning a spot on the waiting list. Your fate will eventually depend as much on what previously admitted applicants decide to do as on your own satisfactory summer performance. But if you want to go to law school, it may be better than nothing.

Appeals

But don't give up just yet. If you've been rejected by your insurance schools—that is, schools at which your numbers should have been adequate to secure admission—or if friends and associates whose records are similar to your own seem to have done better, a mistake may have been made. Call the law school (or schools), explain the circumstances, and ask for an explanation.

In effect, you are demanding a recount. Each law school has a procedure for providing explanations. You may be able to ask for information on the telephone. More commonly, you will be required to put your request in writing, addressed to a dean or to the admissions committee. Be sure to include your GPA and LSAT numbers in your petition. Erroneous rejections are sometimes traced to some clerical or typographical error that attached the wrong numbers to the rejected candidate's application. The admissions committee will review your file; it may discover that a mistake has been made.

The admissions committee may decide that the mistake was yours, arguing that you were rejected because your file was not complete. In this case, ask what pieces of information were omitted. If the law school claims not to have received something beyond your control, like a letter of recommendation, you can then argue that the missing information was actually sent and lost by the law school, or you can protest that you weren't notified of the incompleteness in a timely fashion.

If you make a good case that you are being harmed because of something that is not your fault, the law school may offer to reconsider your application. Although it doesn't happen often, law schools sometimes offer admission to previously rejected candidates. Alternatively, they may offer conditional admission or waiting list status.

In most cases, however, an appeal does not result in a change of status. The admissions committee or dean may simply write back that your qualifications were not good enough. They may compare your numbers to the average numbers of the successful applicants. Or they may provide a more detailed explanation.

Trying Again

If you can't secure conditional or probationary admission and can't get in from a waiting list, you'll have to reevaluate your options. You'll need to determine if you have a chance to be admitted if you apply again or if your record is so poor that you are unlikely ever to be a serious candidate. Your prelaw adviser can evaluate your record and make suggestions. You should consider a second cycle of applications if your adviser determines that you

- ran into an unusually bad application year;

- might have been admitted if you hadn't committed one of the common applications blunders, like applying late; or

- overvalued your qualifications, and may stand a chance of acceptance if you apply to less selective schools.

You'll need to wait a year, make a new application list, and go through the whole procedure again. During the second cycle, you can avoid repeating any mistakes you made the first time.

You needn't fear that law schools will be prejudiced against you if you apply again. As I mentioned above, it's quite common for applicants to do other things before finally settling on law school. Many successful applicants have been out of school for some time before beginning their legal studies. Some have gone through three or four application cycles.

If you expect to go through a second cycle of applications within 12 months of your initial rejections, use the form in the *Information Book* for extending your LSDAS registration for one year. If you expect to wait more than a single year, you should let your LSDAS registration lapse. You will then need to return to Chapter 8 and reregister from scratch when you begin your second application cycle.

You should also ask your prelaw adviser whether you should retake the LSAT. I usually recommend retaking the test if the first score was merely marginal. If you decide to retake the test you should prepare carefully, as described in Chapter 4.

To maximize your chances of acceptance, you should use the eight months or more between your initial rejections and your second applications to make your record more attractive. You can increase the likelihood that a law school will perceive you as a uniquely valuable candidate by securing useful work experience. Spending a year working on a political campaign, at temporary government employment, on a hitch in the Peace Corps, or in political party or charity work are among the available options. Paralegal training followed by a period of employment at a law firm will allow you to claim greater familiarity with legal subject matter. In my experience, all have contributed to second-cycle success stories in previous years.

Perhaps the easiest way to improve your application status is to go to graduate school for a year or more. You'll have the opportunity to study some subject related to law (public administration, for example) and to improve your grades. In general, it's easier to make good grades in graduate school than it is in an undergraduate program. (The LSDAS does not include graduate work in its calculation of index numbers, but it forwards graduate transcripts to law schools along with undergraduate transcripts.) If you do well in a graduate program that is part of a joint-degree program with a law school, you may be able to convince the associated law school to offer you at least provisional admittance.

Unaccredited Law Schools

Most states allow only graduates of law schools approved by the American Bar Association to take their bar exams. But a few operate their own certification systems or open their bar exams to anyone who has graduated from a law school within their borders. In some of these states—including Alabama, California, the District of Columbia, Georgia (until 1998), and Tennessee—non-ABA accredited law schools still exist. In 1995, the *Official Guide* listed 33 such schools (excluding the Roger Williams Law School, which has since become provisionally accredited).

Students attending these law schools face considerable obstacles. Because the schools are not obligated to follow the national curriculum prescribed by the ABA, their courses of study may not be adequate for legal practice. Nor is there any consistent guarantee of quality. (Some states provide state supervision of unaccredited law schools but most do not. California has its own state system of accreditation, but not all of the non-ABA accredited schools in California have been state-accredited.) To keep costs low, unaccredited schools tend to rely more heavily on part-time instructors and may skimp on facilities and libraries. And since most students at such schools are there because they were unable to obtain admission to ABA-accredited schools, the learning environment may not be as fertile. Because of these educational handicaps, smaller proportions of graduates of unaccredited law schools pass the bar exam than graduates of ABA-accredited schools.

Unaccredited law schools qualify their graduates to take the bar exam only in the state in which they studied. It is virtually impossible for a graduate of such a school to establish a legal career in another state.

Still, if you don't get into an ABA-accredited school, where else can you go? Unlike young people interested in medical careers, you can't attend a foreign professional school. (Although North Carolina and a few other states treat graduates of certain Canadian, British, and Australian law schools like graduates of ABA-accredited law schools, the foreign schools are themselves highly selective.) An unaccredited school may offer you a chance at a legal career that would otherwise be unobtainable.

Moreover, unaccredited law schools are not without advantages. They are usually cheaper. Most recruit heavily among older nontraditional law students, conduct their classes in the evening, and may better accommodate themselves to the scheduling necessary to hold a full-time job while attending school. Being taught by local practitioners, their courses may better equip attentive and capable people to practice local law. Some argue that ABA-accredited schools overemphasize library law and claim that their own small classes and emphasis on clinical practice better prepare students for the real world.

If you consider an unaccredited school, make sure before you apply that you will be willing to spend the rest of your professional life in that state. Find out as much about the school itself as you can. (This may be difficult; most of the usual sources do not discuss unaccredited law schools.) Try to find out the attrition rate, the bar passage rate, and the turnover rate for faculty members. Ask about the kinds of jobs that graduates have been able to get. Be suspicious if the school is unable to provide lists of satisfied graduates in the local area, if it appears to be concealing statistics (like placement rates) that most law schools routinely make available, or if the bar passage rate is extremely low.

Some unaccredited schools are actively seeking ABA approval and advertise that they are gradually upgrading their standards to meet ABA requirements. If a school receives accreditation while you are a student, you will receive the benefits of attending an accredited law school at the cost of an unaccredited one. Some actually attain ABA-accredited status, most recently Roger Williams Law School and the District of Columbia Law School. But most of these successes are new schools that acquire ABA status fairly rapidly. It's best not to be too optimistic. Conversely, if an unaccredited law school folds while you are attending it, your credits cannot be transferred to another school. You'll just be out of luck.

Alternative Careers

If you want a career in law and can't attend law school, you can investigate the options available to paralegal professionals. Paralegals perform skilled legal services (some of which traditionally had been performed only by attorneys) under the supervision of lawyers. They interview clients, analyze documents, investigate, do legal research, prepare letters and other documents, and even negotiate with government agencies. Recent research has found paralegals employed in a wide variety of legal areas, including family law, immigration and naturalization, criminal process, landlord-tenant law, real estate, taxation, unemployment compensation law, welfare law, and workmen's compensation law. New specialties are constantly being created. In addition, paralegals are employed by government bodies, colleges and other large organizations.

According to the U. S. Department of Labor *Occupational Outlook Quarterly*, paralegals are employed in the fastest growing occupation "requiring some postsecondary training or extensive employer training," and the demand is expected to increase by 85 percent by the year 2005. Older paralegals may have only on-the-job training. Younger ones are increasingly likely to be college graduates who have received paralegal training after graduation at universities (including Roosevelt) or private specialized schools (Philadelphia Institute). The training programs run from a few weeks to 11 months, depending on the degree of specialization required. Many schools offer part-time and evening programs.

It's possible to have a good, challenging career as a paralegal. Moreover, there is always the possibility that if you work in the legal world for a while and acquire skills useful in legal practice, you will improve your attractiveness to law schools. In small but steady numbers, paralegals do go to law school.

I have mixed feelings about paralegals. It's quite true that you can have a professional career in the legal field in this way, and it's also true that there are many creative and independent jobs for paralegals. But not every paralegal has such a job. Many complain of repetitive and mindless work; others suffer the kind of burnout that comes with high stress coupled with lack of control of one's work situation. As in comparable "helper" professions like nursing, the pay tends to be low. According to one study, paralegals are paid about two-thirds the starting salary of a lawyer. Although it's true that some paralegals support themselves with office work while attending law school at night, others find their jobs too demanding for them to study part-time.

If you are interested in paralegal education, I suggest that you investigate your options carefully. Many programs recruit aggressively on college campuses, and information will be available from your placement center. Training programs vary in length and cost. You should understand exactly what kinds of jobs a program will prepare you for before you enroll. Some train you for nothing more demanding than clerical work. Ask what kinds of jobs alumni have gotten and, if possible, talk to some of them. Schools vary in quality as well. The American Bar Association accredits some paralegal programs. It's not necessary to attend an accredited program to qualify for a good job (at least not while there's a shortage of trained people), but accreditation provides a guarantee of at least minimal quality. If you consider a nonaccredited program, it's even more important to understand what you're paying for, and how well previous students have done, before you enroll.

There are other, less well known ways to remain in the legal field. Most require some graduate work. For example, there is a growing demand for judicial administrators who manage big-city court systems, large law offices, and similar businesses and bureaucracies. The University of Denver offers a Master of Science degree in judicial administration, a one-and-a-half- or two-year program that includes coursework in various aspects of legal management and a full-time internship. Its graduates have become court administrators, clerks of appellate courts, and administrators of the offices of prosecutors, arbitrators, and mediators. The University of Southern California has a similar program, and other graduate schools are also entering this growing field.

As prison systems expand, there are also growing opportunities in the field of criminal justice. Jobs in police administration, penal system management, and the like, are usually filled by college graduates who majored in criminal justice administration, sociology, social work, or other liberal arts subjects. But some schools, including Rutgers, Washington State, and Indiana, offer advanced degrees in criminal justice administration. Graduates become prison wardens, police administrators, and managers in bureaucracies oriented toward criminal justice.

Finally, you may want to investigate other career opportunities in government. Public administration is a growing field. Most careers require some graduate work, most commonly an M.P.A. or a similar degree. Ask your prelaw adviser to refer you to whomever on your campus does the career advising for these fields.

Appendix A

One Big Checklist of Virtually Everything You Have to Do

As promised here is one long list of pretty much everything I've suggested that you do in this book.

I've arranged the steps roughly chronologically, in the approximate order in which you should do each one. Some of the steps—preparing for the LSAT, drafting essays, filling out the rough drafts of the application forms—are tedious and time-consuming. I've indicated about when, during the sequence of events you should be working on each of them. The time frame is what we recommend for traditional students who will graduate in the spring and expect to attend law school the following autumn. Consider it a rough guide. It's more important to be working on the steps in the order indicated than it is to complete each step in the designated month. If you are a nontraditional applicant, you may be working on steps during different months, and in general you'll have more time and can spread out the application process. But you are still best advised to work through the steps in the order that I've described them.

Some of the steps have formal deadlines which change from year to year. I've included spaces for you to write in the deadlines for your year. Hopefully you'll be working well ahead of requirements.

I've assumed that you will take the LSAT in June at the end of your junior year. I've also repeated the LSAT steps on a timetable geared toward the October test. Cross out whichever does not apply. (When you see everything else that you'll have to do that October, you'll probably conclude that the June date is best.)

I've used parentheses to identify the steps that only a few applicants will need to complete. Cross out whatever doesn't apply to you.

JUNIOR YEAR

FEBRUARY
(____ Seek and have informational interviews at law schools you are considering applying to; handicapped students who want to have LSAT waived only)
(____ Request waiver of LSAT fees; disadvantaged applicants only)
(____ Request waiver of fees for LSAT prep course; disadvantaged applicants only)
____ Attend information sessions for LSAT prep courses

MARCH
____ Register for and begin LSAT prep course
____ Request law school catalogs by phone or mail
____ Develop criteria that you will use to make preferred list of law schools
____ Obtain Law Services *Information Book* from prelaw advisor

APRIL
____ Mail off registration form for LSAT and LSDAS
____ Use same form to order Official Guide
____ Use same form to order LSAT prep materials
June LSAT Deadline _____
____ Attend prep course or otherwise prepare for LSAT
____ Write away for law school catalogs

MAY
———— **LSAT admission ticket arrives** ————
____ Check LSAT admission ticket and inform Law Services of any errors

SUMMER BETWEEN JUNIOR AND SENIOR YEARS

JUNE

(____ Complete travel arrangements for LSAT and make dry run, students taking LSAT on unfamiliar campuses)
____ Take LSAT
____ Visit law school campuses
____ Develop preferred list of law schools

(____ Arrange for informational interviews at law schools on your pre-ferred list; applicants with unusual circumstances who want some modification of the application process only)

JULY
———— **LSAT score arrives** ————
____ Check LSAT score report for grading errors
____ Make any remaining visits to law schools
____ Prune preferred list and select application list from it

AUGUST
(____ Register for LSDAS, if you haven't already done so)
(____ Pay LSDAS for more schools, if you now plan to apply to more law schools than you paid the LSDAS to send reports to when you registered for the LSDAS)
____ Arrange for every college you have attended to send transcripts to LSDAS
List each college and date for making arrangements:

_____

_____

_____

_____

____ Write away for most recent application forms and catalog to any law school you intend to apply to for which you do not have a current catalog
____ Develop application strategy
____ Compile objective information for law school application forms: Make lists of all schools attended, previous addresses, jobs held. Look up zip codes, dates.
____ Begin rough drafts of application essays
(____ Register for October LSAT, if taking the LSAT over, or if you missed the June test)
October LSAT deadline _____

SENIOR YEAR

SEPTEMBER
———— **LSDAS master report arrives** ————
____ Proofread LSDAS master report and notify Law Services of any errors

_____ Decide whom you will ask to write letters of recommendation
_____ Inventory and photocopy all application forms for each law school you will apply to
_____ Develop file system to keep track of forms
_____ Make rough drafts of application forms
(_____ Secure proof of legal residence, if needed)
(_____ Secure proof of citizenship, if needed)
(_____ Secure proof of affirmative action status, if needed)
_____ First recommender appointments: ask recommenders if they'll write letters for you
_____ Work on essays
(_____ Arrange to have transcripts from foreign universities that you have attended sent directly to each law school you will apply to)
_____ Put together information packets you will give to recommenders
_____ Second appointments with recommenders; give each one
  _____ Law school recommendation forms
  _____ Stamped or unstamped envelopes
  _____ Information packets
(_____ Mail information packets and forms to recommenders who are too distant to visit)

OCTOBER
(_____ Take October LSAT)
_____ Prepare final drafts of law school applications
_____ Prepare final drafts of essays
(_____ Collect letters of recommendation in sealed envelopes from recommenders for inclusion with law school applications, but only if a law school requires you to use the all-at-once method; see ch. 11)
_____ Complete application checklists (ch. 9) and make sure each law school application is complete, with all necessary enclosures
_____ Mail law school applications (unless waiting for results of October LSAT or fall grades)

List chronologically the application deadlines for the schools on your application list:

_____

_____

_____

(_____ Request informational interviews, applicants with special problems who do not need some waiver of application process)

NOVEMBER
———— **Law schools acknowledge receipt of applications** ————
____ Secure financial aid forms; See Appendix C below
____ Call law schools that did not acknowledge receipt of applications

DECEMBER
(____ Third visit to recommenders, if necessary)
(____ Arrange for seventh semester transcript to be sent to LSDAS)
———— **October LSAT scores arrive** ————
(____ Mail law school applications, if waiting for results of October LSAT)

JANUARY
____ Complete and mail financial aid request forms; see Appendix C
Write in the financial aid deadlines for the schools on your application list:

_____

_____

_____

____ Complete and mail financial aid need assessment forms (see Appendix C)

Appendix B

Sources

Reference Books

American Bar Association Section on Legal Education and Admissions To the Bar. *A Review Of Legal Education In The United States*, [Date]. American Bar Association, 750 N. Lake Shore Drive, Chicago IL 60611.

Barron's Guide To Law Schools. 11th edition, 1995. Barron's Educational Press, 250 Wireless Blvd., Hauppage, NY 11788.

Curry, Boykin. *Essays That Worked—For Law School*. Memphis, Tennessee: Mustang Publishing Co., 1988.

Law School Admission Council/Law School Admission Services ("Law Services"). *Financial Aid for Law School*. Law Services Publications, Box 2400, 661 Penn St., Newtown PA 18940-0977; 215-968-1001.

——. *The Official Guide To U. S. Law Schools*.

——. *The Right Law School For You*.

——. *Thinking About Law School: A Minority Guide*

Marke, Julius J., and Edward J. Bander, eds. *Deans' List of Recommended Readings for Prelaw and Law Students*. 2nd edition, 1984. Oceana Publications, Inc., Dobbs Ferry NY 10522; 914-693-0402.

Useful Materials on Law School and Legal Practice

Bell, Susan J., ed. *Full Disclosure: Do You Really Want to Be a Lawyer?* Princeton, New Jersey: Peterson's Guides, 1989.

"The Best Graduate Schools." *U.S. News and World Report* (21 March 1994): 65–98. The most recent entry in this magazine's ongoing effort to rate law schools includes a list of "the top 25," relative rankings of other accredited law schools, and peer evaluations of top programs in certain categories. *U.S.News* puts out a new such report each year, typically in late March.

Childress, Steven Alan. "The Baby and the Bathwater: Salvaging a Positive Socratic Method." *Oklahoma City University Law Review* 7 (1982): 333–354. The Socratic Method is the technique of question-and-answer recitation used in freshman law classes. Though it has been widely criticized, Childress argues for reforming and retaining it.

Daniels, Edmund D., and Michael David Weiss. "Equality Over Quality," *Reason* 23 (July, 1991): 44–45. A report on allegations that admission, financial aid, and faculty hiring policies at the University of Texas Law School favor minorities.

Ellman, Ira Mark. "A Comparison of Law Faculty Production in Leading Law Reviews." *Journal Of Legal Education* 33 (1983): 681–692.

Epstein, Cynthia Fuchs. *Women In Law*. New York: Basic Books, 1981.

Getman, Julius G. "Colloquy: Human Voice in Legal Discourse." *Texas Law Review* 66 (1988): 577–588.

Goldfarb, Sally F. *Inside The Law Schools: A Guide By Students For Students*. 3rd ed.; New York: Dutton, 1984.

Good, C. Edward. *Mightier Than the Sword: Powerful Writing in the Legal Profession*. Charlottesville, Virginia: Blue Jeans Press Division of LEL Enterprises, 1989.

Gopen, George D. "The State of Legal Writing: *Res Ipsa Loquitur.*" *Michigan Law Review* 86 (1987): 333–365.

Kennedy, Duncan. *Legal Education and the Reproduction of Hierarchy: A Polemic Against the System*. Cambridge, Massachusetts: Afar Press, 1983. The classical statement of the early critical legal studies group's critique of legal education.

—— "The Political Significance of the Structure of the Law School Curriculum." *Seton Hall Law Review* 14 (1983): 1–16.

"Langdell, Chris" (pseud.). "Law School Curriculum: A Reply to Kennedy." *Seton Hall Law Review* 14 (1984): 1077–1081.

Lempert, Richard O. "Of Polls and Prestige: One Faculty Member's Candid Views." *Law Quadrangle Notes* (University of Michigan Law School) 34 (1990): 62–68. Lempert, himself a distinguished scholar in the field of law and society, not only debunks conventional schemes for ranking law schools but also says something original about how the quality of law schools should be measured.

McCleary, Roseanna, and Evan I. Zucker. "Higher Trait- and State-Anxiety in Female Law Students than Male Law Students." *Psychological Reports* 68 (part 2) (June, 1991): 1075–1078.

Mellinkoff, David. "The Myth of Precision and the Law Dictionary." *U.C.L.A. Law Review* 31 (1983): 423–442.

Moll, Richard W. *The Lure Of The Law*. New York: Penguin Books, 1990.

Schaffer, Thomas L. *On Being A Christian and a Lawyer: Law For The Innocent*. Provo, Utah: Brigham Young, 1981.

Strickland, Rennard. *How To Get Into Law School*. New York: Hawthorn Books, 1974. Though dated, this comprehensive guide to the law school admission process still contains many good stories, drawn from the author's experience as a law school faculty member and admissions committee member.

Swygert, Michael I. and Robert Batey, eds. *Maximizing the Law School Experience*. N.p., Stetson University College of Law, 1983.

Trillin, Calvin. "A Reporter At Large: Harvard Law." *The New Yorker* 26 March 1984, 53–83.

Turow, Scott. *One L: An Inside Account of Life in the First Year of Harvard Law School*. New York: Penguin Books, 1978. Turow's famous book is somewhat dated, but it's still the most perceptive dissection of student life around.

Van Alstyne, Scott. "Ranking the Law Schools: The Reality of Illusion?" *American Bar Foundation Research Journal* (1982) 649–684.

White, Thomas O. *Inside The LSAT*. Princeton, New Jersey: Peterson's Press, 1991.

Wice, Paul. *Judges and Lawyers: The Human Side of Justice*. New York: HarperCollins, 1991. The most up-to-date and thorough description we have of the demographic and organizational characteristics of legal practice.

Wilkinson, Michael, and Harry Wainmen. "Legal English: A Functional Course." *Journal Of Legal Education* 31 (1981): 664–672.

Appendix C

A Note on Financial Aid

Law schools are extremely expensive. Most students need some degree of support; according to Law Services, about 75 percent of them borrow at least some money. Fortunately, it's fairly easy to get financial assistance if you apply early and follow the rules. Law Services publishes a useful guide, *Financial Aid for Law School: A Preliminary Guide*, which you can request whenever you communicate with them about the LSAT or the LSDAS. Law Services also makes some financial aid information available on its Web site, http://www.LASC.org. I'll mention here only a few general considerations.

Most law schools now provide at least some need-based financial aid. They have financial aid offices, staffed by full-time professionals. Each law school has its own rules for qualifying for this financial aid, which are published in the catalog and also made available in literature and interviews by financial aid professionals. You can get answers to most specific questions about a law school by calling and asking to speak to a financial aid counselor. You should be able to qualify for an appropriate package of grants, loans, and (sometimes) part-time jobs, depending on your financial status.

A few law schools require you to apply for financial aid when you apply for admission. Most, however, will not accept your financial aid application at this time; they require you to mail it separately, to the financial aid office, *after* you apply for admission but *before* some deadline, typically the first of February. In some cases, the financial aid applications must be accompanied by photocopies of your income tax returns or other supporting documents. While you are filling out the application forms, you should also determine what financial aid forms will be required, and you should make sure that you have them all. There may be separate forms for loans and grants. There are often separate forms (and deadlines) for merit- based scholarships.

Most schools explicitly instruct you not to wait until you are admitted to file your financial aid forms. You should scrupulously observe any application deadlines. Law schools avoid charges of favoritism by rigidly and inflexibly applying the financial aid rules to everyone alike; they hesitate to make exceptions. I suggest that you tackle the financial aid forms as soon as you've mailed off your applications for admission and mail them as early as the law schools will accept them. There may be an advantage in applying early, and there's no reason to wait until the last minute.

In addition to conventional federal and private aid, you may be eligible for need-based state-administered aid if your state does not have a public law school of its own, or if the legislature has created a special state aid program. If your prelaw adviser doesn't know about the financial aid rules of your state of residence, check with the financial aid offices of the law schools you have applied to.

As you do your financial aid planning, you should be aware that some law schools now have loan forgiveness programs. These, like Cardozo's "Loan Repayment Assistance Program," generally provide at least partial repayment of your student loans if you later work at a low-paying legal job in the sphere of public interest. In this category, Cardozo counts jobs with legal aid societies, prosecutors' and public defenders' offices, governmental agencies, private foundations, and firms dedicated to public interest law and a variety of others. You may be comfortable with a larger burden of debt if you plan to work in one of these fields, because the forgiveness program will help you pay off your loans. But since the programs vary in scope, you should discuss your specific career plans with a financial aid counselor.

If you are a member of a protected category or come from an economically disadvantaged background, always ask to be considered for minority financial aid. Some law schools set aside considerable financial resources to support their affirmative action efforts. The Council on Legal Education Opportunity also makes some financial aid available; see Chapter 13.

If you apply for any form of need-based financial aid, you'll have to establish your degree of need. You do this by filing the Free Application for Federal Student Aid form, or FAFSA. This, to quote the *Official Guide*, is "a need analysis tool developed by the U.S. government. . . . [which] asks for information about your income, assets and other financial resources. The information you provide on the financial aid form will be used to compute how much you and your family should contribute toward your legal education." If you are a traditional candidate and still dependent on your parents, they may also have to fill out a disclosure form. You will probably have to provide other information, such as photocopies of tax returns and undergraduate financial aid documents.

You may still come across a law school which wants you to use a private need assessment service instead of the FAFSA. If so, the law school will provide an alternate form very much like the FAFSA, but more detailed. Make sure you know where to send this form, and what deadline you must observe. Whichever need assessment form you use, make sure that the financial data you provide is consistent with your income tax returns. Though the forms are routinely kept confidential, they can theoretically be subpoenaed by law enforcement agencies investigating allegations that laws have been violated.

In addition to need-based aid, many law schools have scholarship programs that base awards on merit. For example, Vanderbilt designates four John W. Wade Scholars in each law school class. The scholarship currently pays $17,000 for the first year, and can be renewed annually. Wake Forest provides a "substantial stipend in addition to all tuition and necessary books" to its A. J. Fletcher Scholars.

Merit-based scholarships are usually listed in the catalog and may also be advertised separately. At some law schools, all successful applicants are considered for whatever merit awards are open to freshmen. At many schools, however, you have to apply separately. If your undergraduate record is good and you are otherwise qualified for the program, it's worth taking the time to fill out yet another form and collect and submit yet another set of letters of recommendations and transcripts. Even when, as in most cases, the actual cash value of the award is small, a merit-based scholarship provides publicity, prestige, and valuable networking.

Aside from the law schools themselves, there are various other sources of grants and scholarships. Some awards are given on merit alone and some on need; some require you to satisfy various conditions. Some are listed in *Financial Aid for Law School: A Preliminary Guide*. Perhaps the single best source book in this area is Debra M. Kirby's *Scholarships, Fellowships And Loans* (10th ed.; Detroit: Gale Research, 1994). Also valuable are Daniel Cassidy's *The Graduate Scholarship Book: The Complete Guide to Scholarships, Fellowships, Grants and Loans for Graduate and Professional Study* (2d. Ed.; Englewood Cliffs, NJ: Prentice-Hall, 1990); and Keeslar's *Financial Aids for Higher Education* (14th ed.; Dubuque, IA: William C. Brown, 1992). The Reference Service Press of San Carlos, CA, publishes a series of specialized guides for minorities, women, handicapped persons, and veterans.

VGM CAREER BOOKS

BUSINESS PORTRAITS
Boeing
Coca-Cola
Ford
McDonald's

CAREER DIRECTORIES
Careers Encyclopedia
Dictionary of Occupational Titles
Occupational Outlook Handbook

CAREERS FOR
Animal Lovers; Bookworms; Caring
People; Computer Buffs; Crafty
People; Culture Lovers;
Environmental Types; Fashion Plates;
Film Buffs; Foreign Language
Aficionados; Good Samaritans;
Gourmets; Health Nuts; History
Buffs; Kids at Heart; Music Lovers;
Mystery Buffs; Nature Lovers; Night
Owls; Number Crunchers; Plant
Lovers; Shutterbugs; Sports Nuts;
Travel Buffs; Writers

CAREERS IN
Accounting; Advertising; Business;
Child Care; Communications;
Computers; Education; Engineering;
the Environment; Finance;
Government; Health Care; High
Tech; Horticulture & Botany;
International Business; Journalism;
Law; Marketing; Medicine; Science;
Social & Rehabilitation Services

CAREER PLANNING
Beating Job Burnout
Beginning Entrepreneur
Big Book of Jobs
Career Planning & Development for
College Students &
Recent Graduates
Career Change
Career Success for People with
Physical Disabilities
Careers Checklists
College and Career Success for Students
with Learning Disabilities
Complete Guide to Career Etiquette
Cover Letters They Don't Forget
Dr. Job's Complete Career Guide
Executive Job Search Strategies
Guide to Basic Cover Letter Writing
Guide to Basic Résumé Writing
Guide to Internet Job Searching
Guide to Temporary Employment
Job Interviewing for College Students
Joyce Lain Kennedy's Career Book

Out of Uniform
Parent's Crash Course in Career
Planning
Slame Dunk Résumés
Up Your Grades: Proven Strategies
for Academic Success

CAREER PORTRAITS
Animals; Cars; Computers;
Electronics; Fashion; Firefighting;
Music; Nature; Nursing; Science;
Sports; Teaching; Travel; Writing

GREAT JOBS FOR
Business Majors
Communications Majors
Engineering Majors
English Majors
Foreign Language Majors
History Majors
Psychology Majors
Sociology Majors

HOW TO
Apply to American Colleges and
Universities
Approach an Advertising Agency and
Walk Away with the Job You Want
Be a Super Sitter
Bounce Back Quickly After
Losing Your Job
Change Your Career
Choose the Right Career
Cómo escribir un currículum vitae en
inglés que tenga éxito
Find Your New Career Upon
Retirement
Get & Keep Your First Job
Get Hired Today
Get into the Right Business School
Get into the Right Law School
Get into the Right Medical School
Get People to Do Things Your Way
Have a Winning Job Interview
Hit the Ground Running in Your
New Job
Hold It All Together When You've
Lost Your Job
Improve Your Study Skills
Jumpstart a Stalled Career
Land a Better Job
Launch Your Career in TV News
Make the Right Career Moves
Market Your College Degree
Move from College into a
Secure Job
Negotiate the Raise You Deserve
Prepare Your Curriculum Vitae

Prepare for College
Run Your Own Home Business
Succeed in Advertising When all You
Succeed in College
Succeed in High School
Take Charge of Your Child's Early
Education
Write a Winning Résumé
Write Successful Cover Letters
Write Term Papers & Reports
Write Your College Application Essay

MADE EASY
College Applications
Cover Letters
Getting a Raise
Job Hunting
Job Interviews
Résumés

**ON THE JOB: REAL PEOPLE
WORKING IN...**
Communications
Health Care
Sales & Marketing
Service Businesses

OPPORTUNITIES IN
This extensive series provides detailed
information on more than 150
individual career fields.

RÉSUMÉS FOR
Advertising Careers
Architecture and Related Careers
Banking and Financial Careers
Business Management Careers
College Students &
Recent Graduates
Communications Careers
Computer Careers
Education Careers
Engineering Careers
Environmental Careers
Ex-Military Personnel
50+ Job Hunters
Government Careers
Health and Medical Careers
High School Graduates
High Tech Careers
Law Careers
Midcareer Job Changes
Nursing Careers
Re-Entering the Job Market
Sales and Marketing Careers
Scientific and Technical Careers
Social Service Careers
The First-Time Job Hunter

VGM Career Horizons
a division of *NTC Publishing Group*
4255 West Touhy Avenue
Lincolnwood, Illinois 60646–1975